A World of Others' Words

A World of Others' Words

Cross-Cultural Perspectives on Intertextuality

Richard Bauman

Blackwell
Publishing

© 2004 by Richard Bauman

BLACKWELL PUBLISHING
350 Main Street, Malden, MA 02148-5020, USA
108 Cowley Road, Oxford OX4 1JF, UK
550 Swanston Street, Carlton, Victoria 3053, Australia

First published 2004 by Blackwell Publishing Ltd

Library of Congress Cataloging-in-Publication Data

Bauman, Richard.
A world of others' words: cross-cultural perspectives on intertextuality /
Richard Bauman.
p.   cm.
Includes bibliographical references and index.
ISBN 1-4051-1604-8 (alk. paper) – ISBN 1-4051-1605-6 (alk. paper)
1. Communication in folklore.   2. Communication in anthropology.   3.
Intertextuality.   4. Oral tradition.   5. Cross-cultural orientation.   I. Title.

GR44.4.B38 2004
398′.01′4 – dc22

2004001155

A catalogue record for this title is available from the British Library.

Set in 10 on 12½ pt Minion
by SNP Best-set Typesetter Ltd., Hong Kong
Printed and bound in the United Kingdom
by MPG Books Ltd, Bodmin, Cornwall

The publisher's policy is to use permanent paper from mills that operate
a sustainable forestry policy, and which has been manufactured from
pulp processed using acid-free and elementary chlorine-free practices.
Furthermore, the publisher ensures that the text paper and cover board used
have met acceptable environmental accreditation standards.

For further information on
Blackwell Publishing, visit our website:
http://www.blackwellpublishing.com

Contents

Acknowledgments

This book, no less than the performers and texts it represents, lives in a world of others' words, and I want to acknowledge at least some of the dialogues that have had a formative influence on the making of the text now before you. I want first to offer my thanks to those patient, hospitable, and generous interlocutors in Nova Scotia, Texas, and Mexico who made a special effort to help me hear and understand the world of talk in which they live: Howard, Basil, and Isabel Bush, of Bush Island, Lunenburg County, Nova Scotia; Ed and Alma Bell, of Luling, Texas; and Pedro Muñoz and Refugio Ramírez, of Tierra Blanca, Guanajuato, Mexico. I am grateful also to a number of equally generous colleagues who shared with me some of their own field materials: Pat Mullen, Pat Jasper, Hallfreður Örn Eiríksson, and Hamish Henderson. For assistance with transcription and with the nuances of translation, I thank Birna Arnbjörnsdóttir, Ana Ochoa, Josefina Vasques, and Ramón Gódinez Estrada.

A number of institutions have supported and encouraged the research on which this work is based: the School of Scottish Studies, Edinburgh University, and the Stofnun Árna Magnússonar, Reykjavík, have granted permission to use materials from their collections; the Center for Transcultural Studies, Chicago, provided an intellectual environment for stimulating collegial dialogues that shaped my thinking about textuality and intertextuality; the National Endowment for the Humanities, the John Simon Guggenheim Foundation, and the Center for Advanced Study in the Behavioral Sciences at Stanford (with funds from the Mellon Foundation) offered fellowship support that gave me time to think and talk and write about the materials and ideas treated in the pages that follow. The American Council of Learned Societies, the University of Texas, and Indiana University also provided valuable financial support. I am grateful to all of these benefactors.

My work resonates with the voices of many colleagues, who have discussed ideas and work in progress with me and commented upon earlier versions of the chapters that make up this book. My thanks to Roger Abrahams, Donald Braid, Carsten Bregenhøj, Don Brenneis, Jesse Byock, Tim Choi, Jim Collins, Vincent Crapanzano, Sandro Duranti, Marcia Farr, Ruth Finnegan, Don Handelman, Galit Hasan-Rokem, John Haviland, Judy Irvine, Anniki Kaivola-Bregenhøj, Deborah Kapchan, Jeffrey Kittay, Ben Lee, John Lucy, Thomas Luckmann, Ronald Macaulay, Beth Mertz, Rick Parmentier, David Shulman, A. K. Ramanujan, Pamela Ritch, Michael Silverstein, and Greg Urban. Two colleagues deserve special thanks for the close, sustained intellectual and personal engagement that has shaped and energized my work on genre, performance, textuality, and intertextuality for the past decade and more. Bill Hanks has been a stimulating and generous interlocutor, always willing to exchange ideas and offer productive critical responses to my writings. And Charles Briggs, my closest colleague, has been scholarly partner, intellectual sounding board, tough critic, and dear friend throughout the process of producing this work. Many of the ideas presented here have been developed in collaboration with Charles, and what merits the work may have derive in no small measure from his contributions and support.

Finally, I offer deep thanks to Beverly Stoeltje, my partner in the richest dialogues of all.

The author and publishers wish to thank the following for permission to use copyright material:

Chapter 1 includes materials from the essay, "Genre," *Journal of Linguistic Anthropology* 9(1–2):81–84.

Chapter 2 is a revised version of "Contextualization, Tradition, and the Dialogue of Genres: Icelandic Legends of the Kraftaskáld." From *Rethinking Context*, edited by Alessandro Duranti and Charles Goodwin, copyright 1992 by Cambridge University Press. Reprinted with the permission of Cambridge University Press.

Chapter 3 is a revised version of "I'll Give You Three Guesses": The Dynamics of Genre in the Riddle-Tale. From *Untying the Knot: On Riddles and Other Enigmatic Modes*, edited by Galit Hasan-Rokem and David Shulman, copyright 1996 by Oxford University Press, Inc. Used by permission of Oxford University Press, Inc.

"The Miller and His Daughter," in the appendix to Chapter 3, is from *Till Doomsday in the Afternoon: The Folklore of a Family of Scots Travellers, The Stewarts of Blairgowrie*, edited by Ewan MacColl and Peggy Seeger, copyright 1986 by Manchester University Press. Reproduced with the kind permission of Peggy Seeger.

"The King and the Miller," in the appendix to Chapter 3, is from *The King of the Black Art*, edited and with an introduction by Sheila Douglas, copyright 1987 by Sheila Douglas, published 1987 by Aberdeen University Press. Reproduced with the kind permission of Sheila Douglas.

Chapter 4 is a revised version of "The Ethnography of Genre in a Mexican Market: Form, Function, Variation." From *Style and Sociolinguistic Variation*, edited by Penelope Eckert and John Rickford, copyright 2001 by Cambridge University Press. Reprinted with the permission of Cambridge University Press.

Chapter 5 is a revised version of "Ed Bell, Texas Storyteller: The Framing and Reframing of Life Experience," *Journal of Folklore Research* 24: 197–221. By permission of Indiana University Press.

Chapter 6 is a revised version of "Disclaimers of Performance." From *Responsibility and Evidence in Oral Discourse*, edited by Jane H. Hill and Judith T. Irvine, copyright 1993 by Cambridge University Press. Reprinted with the permission of Cambridge University Press. The chapter also includes sections drawn from "The La Have Island General Store: Sociability and Verbal Art in a Nova Scotia Community," *Journal of American Folklore* 85:330–343. By permission of the American Folklore Society.

Chapter 7 is a revised version of "Mediational Performance, Traditionalization, and the Authorization of Discourse." From *Verbal Art Across Cultures: The Aesthetics and Proto-Aesthetics of Communication*, edited by Helga Kotthoff and Hubert Knoblauch, copyright 2001 by Gunter Narr Verlag. By permission of Gunter Narr Verlag.

The poem "Neglected Merit" is from *Irish Bardic Poetry: Texts and Translations, Together with an Introductory Lecture*, by Osborn Bergin, compiled and edited by David Greene and Fergus Kelly, copyright 1970 by the Dublin Institute for Advanced Studies. Reproduced by kind permission of the Dublin Institute for Advanced Studies.

Every effort has been made to trace copyright holders and to obtain their permission for the use of copyright material. The authors and publishers will gladly receive any information enabling them to rectify any error or omission in subsequent editions.

Note on Transcription

I have employed various modes of transcription in rendering the oral texts presented in the chapters that follow, guided by heuristic and analytical considerations. In transcribing narratives, I have segmented the texts in terms of a combination of devices employed by the narrators, principally initial particles and other discourse markers, including prominently conjunctions that mark the paratactic structure of the narration; speaker change in the rendering of reported speech; and/or topic change. For the market language of Chapter 4, narrative excerpts in Chapter 6, and the oral poetry treated in Chapter 7, I have set out the transcriptions in lines marked by a combination of breath pauses and syntactic structures, or other devices of measure. New lines begin flush left. When presenting texts published by others, I have retained the transcriptional formats of the published versions, except where explicitly noted. The representations of non-standard phonology and syntax in Chapters 3, 5, and 7 do not pretend to strict linguistic accuracy. Rather, they are intended to foreground the vernacular oral style of the spoken originals.

I

Introduction: Genre, Performance, and the Production of Intertextuality

I live in a world of others' words.
Bakhtin (1986:143)

The relationship of texts to other texts has been an abiding concern of literary theorists since classical antiquity, certainly since Aristotle speculated on the potential shape of tragedies based on the *Iliad* and the *Odyssey* as against other relations of the fall of Troy and its aftermath (*Poetics* xviii.4, xxiii). Whether by the attribution of literary influence, or the identification of literary sources and analogues, or the ascription of traditionality, or the allegation of plagiarism or copyright violation – or, indeed, by any of a host of other ways of construing relationships among texts – the recognition that the creation of literary texts depends in significant part on the alignment of texts to prior texts and the anticipation of future texts has drawn critical – and ideological – attention to this reflexive dimension of discursive practice.

In the domain of oral poetics, intertextuality has been a defining focus since the latter part of the seventeenth century, when oral tradition became a key element in marking the juncture between premodern and modern epochs in the evolution of language and culture. In the late eighteenth century, Herder's celebration of the "sung again" quality of oral poetry, its circulation among the people, and its capacity to "spite the power of time," established the foundational orientations of the study of oral poetics toward the genetic relationships among "variants" and "versions" and the durability of the "oral tradition" constituted by the intertextual relationships that link these cognate texts. In this philological perspective, which had a formative influence on textual criticism more generally and which was inscribed into the scholarly tradition of folklore and anthropology by the Brothers Grimm and Franz Boas, the texts are conceived essentially as cultural objects: durable, repeatable, classifiable, linked to other texts by relationships of descent (both textual and national) and generic similarity (Bauman and Briggs 2003).

Moreover, one may find apparently corresponding – taken as corroborative – understandings among the "tradition bearers," those who carry and pass on the textual objects. When, for instance, Jón Norðmann, an elderly Icelandic storyteller, concludes a story about a nineteenth-century poet with magical powers – a narrative that figures centrally in a later chapter of this book – by remarking "Now Gudrun, his daughter, told my father this story," he would appear to be confirming the traditionality of the narrative, handed down from the past by repeated tellings, as well as identifying it by genre (*saga*: "story").

I would submit, however, that there is more going on here than simple folk confirmation, ancillary to the text, of what we have long known about folktales: that they are traditional and fall into generic categories. I would ask, rather, what might induce Jón Norðmann to follow up his narration with an account of the story's genealogy? What does he accomplish, in this instance, by explicitly linking his telling of the story to his father's telling to Gudrun's telling? Approached in these terms, the question is not about confirmation of the *a priori* traditionality of the story, but rather about Jón Norðmann's discursive practice. From this vantage point, his linkage of his performed text to other texts by filiation and genre is part of the discursive work by which he accomplishes his performance; the relationship of intertextuality that ties his story to an antecedent story is an interactional accomplishment, part of his management of the narrative performance.

The perspective that I am suggesting here is founded upon a conception of social life as discursively constituted, produced and reproduced in situated acts of speaking and other signifying practices that are simultaneously anchored in their situational contexts of use and transcendent of them, linked by interdiscursive ties to other situations, other acts, other utterances. The sociohistorical continuity and coherence manifested in these interdiscursive relationships rests upon cultural repertoires of concepts and practices that serve as conventionalized orienting frameworks for the production, reception, and circulation of discourse. Two such metadiscursive concepts that have proven especially productive in the domain of oral poetics and have provided a ground of convergence linking linguistic anthropology, literary theory, and the study of oral tradition are *genre* and *performance*. As a career-long denizen of that border territory, still devoted to charting its riches, I employ them again in this work as conceptual organizing principles. I have written a number of works on performance over the past several decades (see esp. Bauman 1977, 1986, 1992; Bauman and Briggs 1990); in this book, I foreground the concept of genre, against a background in which performance is never far from view. The focus on genre and performance, in turn, proves to illuminate still other metadiscursive concepts and practices that will provide further lines of connection among the chapters to follow.

Genre

The concept of genre has played a significant role in linguistic anthropology since the inception of the field, part of the philological foundation of the Boasian program.[1] The centrality of texts in the Boasian tradition demanded discrimination among orders of texts, and generic categories inherited from the European (especially German) study of folklore served this classificatory purpose. Genre received little critical or theoretical attention in the field, however, until the latter part of the 1960s, under the convergent impetus of ethnoscience, with its analytical focus on indigenous (emic) systems of classification, structuralism, in both its morphological and structural-symbolic guises, and the ethnography of speaking, in which genre served as a nexus of interrelationships among the constituents of the speech event and as a formal vantage point on speaking practice (Hymes 1989[1974]). More recently, the influence of Bakhtinian perspectives on genre as the compositional organizing principle that "guides us in the process of our speaking" under "definite conditions of performance and perception" (Bakhtin 1986:81; Medvedev and Bakhtin 1978[1928]:131) has given further prominence to the concept of genre in the work of linguistic anthropologists (Hanks 1987, 1996a, 1996b). The collective work of the Bakhtin Circle is especially productive, I believe, in its insistence on the radical integration of the formal and the ideological in the construction of genre (Bakhtin 1986; Medvedev and Bakhtin 1978[1928]; Voloshinov 1973[1930]). With Bakhtin (1986:63–67), I begin with style (as also Hymes 1989[1974]) as a point of entry, which will lead, ultimately, to ideology. In the chapters that follow, I foreground one or another aspect for analytical purposes, bearing always in mind, however, that they are inextricably interrelated.

I conceive of genre, then, as one order of speech style, a constellation of systemically related, co-occurrent formal features and structures that serves as a conventionalized orienting framework for the production and reception of discourse. More specifically, a genre is a speech style oriented to the production and reception of a particular kind of text. When an utterance is assimilated to a given genre, the process by which it is produced and interpreted is mediated through its intertextual relationship with prior texts. The invocation of generic framing devices such as "Once upon a time" or "*Voy a cantar estos versos*" or "Bunday!" carry with them sets of expectations concerning the further unfolding of the discourse, indexing other texts initiated by such opening formulae. "Once upon a time," of course, has come to signal the modern literary rendition of a fairy tale; "*Voy a cantar estos versos*" announces the singing of a *corrido*, the ballad form of Greater Mexico (Paredes 1976:83); "Bunday!" marks the beginning of a Bahamian "old-story" performance (Crowley 1966:19–22). These expectations constitute a framework for entextualization, the organization of a stretch of discourse into a text: bounded off to a degree from its discursive surround (its co-text), internally cohesive (tied together by various formal devices), and coherent (semantically intelligible).

The process of entextualization, by bounding off a stretch of discourse from its co-text, endowing it with cohesive formal properties, and (often, but not necessarily) rendering it internally coherent, serves to objectify it as a discrete textual unit that can be referred to, described, named, displayed, cited, and otherwise treated as an object (Barber 1999). Importantly, this process of objectification also serves to render a text extractable from its context of production. A text, then, from this vantage point, is discourse rendered decontextualizable: entextualization potentiates decontextualization. But decontextualization from one context must involve recontextualization in another, which is to recognize the potential for texts to circulate, to be spoken again in another context. The iterability of texts, then, constitutes one of the most powerful bases for the potentiation and production of intertextuality.

By *intertextuality* I mean the relational orientation of a text to other texts, what Genette calls "the textual transcendence of the text" (1997[1982]:1).[2] I take my primary inspiration in this exploration of intertextuality as discursive practice from Bakhtin. "The text," Bakhtin proposes,

> lives only by coming into contact with another text (with context). Only at this point of contact between texts does a light flash, illuminating both the posterior and anterior, joining a given text to a dialogue. We emphasize that this contact is a dialogic contact between texts . . . Behind this contact is a contact of personalities and not of things. (Bakhtin 1986:162)

What is of interest here, then, is the ways in which each act of textual production presupposes antecedent texts and anticipates prospective ones.

For Bakhtin, dialogue, the orientation of the now-said to the already-said and the to-be-said, is ubiquitous and foundational, comprehending all of the ways that utterances can resonate with other utterances and constitutive of consciousness, society, and culture. My concern in this book is considerably narrower: I focus in the chapters that follow on a range of relationships by which speakers may align their texts to other texts. But it is worth emphasizing again that my interest in intertextuality is not simply in the relational nexus between texts, but in how intertextuality is accomplished in communicative practice, including both production and reception, and to what ends. Generic intertextuality, as noted, is my primary concern, having to do with orienting frameworks for the production and reception of particular types of text. Reiteration, as I have suggested just above, is another: saying again what has been said before, in what may be construed as "the same" form. The reiterated text may be quoted or attributed to a prior speaker, that is, reported as having been said by another (or by generalized others: "The old people say . . ."), or it may simply be said again, without explicit attribution. Briggs (1986) and Barber (1999) demonstrate persuasively that within particular communities, genres may vary in the degree to which they are conceived as quotational, that is, framed as not-for-the-first-time reiterations of the already said. Parody, a third mode of intertextuality that figures in the chapters to follow, involves the ludic or inversive transformation of a prior text or genre.[3]

The formal relationship implied in the notion of generic intertextuality has pragmatic and thematic correlates as well. The situated production of generically informed discourse indexes prior situational contexts in which the same generic conventions have guided discursive production. The associational links might invoke any of the constituent elements of the situational context (e.g., settings, participant roles and structures, scenarios, goals and outcomes, etc.). Genre thus transcends the bounded, locally produced speech event. From this perspective, genre appears as a set of conventional guidelines or schemas for dealing with recurrent communicative exigencies – greetings, for example, as a means of establishing interactional access (Günthner and Knoblauch 1995; Luckmann 1995). It would be misleading, however, to assume – as some have done – that there is a one-to-one correlation between genres and speech events. While particular genres may be primarily identified with specific situational contexts of use – for example, curing chants with healing rituals – it is of the very nature of genre to be recognizable outside of such primary contexts. Thus a curing chant may be performed in another context for entertainment, for the pleasure afforded by the chanter's display of virtuosity, or recited in still another as pedagogical demonstration in the instruction of a novice curer (Sherzer

1983:118–120). Such recontextualization amounts to a rekeying of the text, a shift in its illocutionary force and perlocutionary effect – what it counts as and what it does.

Among the conventional expectations for textual production and reception that genre invokes are sets of roles and relationships by which participants are aligned to one other. Such participant structures must be approached in terms of local understandings of role eligibility, recruitment, and enactment (e.g., Maya shaman/patient/spirit (Hanks 1996b), or Akan chief/*okyeame* (spokesman)/petitioner (Yankah 1995); see also Chapter 7 of this book). But insofar as the texts emergent out of such generically regimented structures of participation are intertextually tied to antecedent texts and anticipate subsequent ones, so too do they presuppose and entail other participant structures. A shamanic performance of ritual exorcism, for example, presupposes a prior shaman–patient consultation and anticipates, perhaps, the patient's narrative account to her family of her healing experience (Hanks 1996b; cf. Irvine 1996).

The emergent configurations of such fields of discursive production and circulation are what motivated the functional-typological participant frameworks suggested by Goffman in his decomposition of traditional dyadic speaker-hearer models, discriminating, for example, the formulator of an utterance (the author) from the speaker who actually voices it (the animator) (Goffman 1981:167; see also Levinson 1988). We should be reminded here as well of Bakhtin's insistence that behind the contact between texts that establishes relationships of intertextuality "is a contact of personalities and not of things" (1986:162). That is to say, with regard to genre, that it is a primary means not only for dealing with recurrent social exigencies, but also for the expressive enactment of subjectivity; different genres implicate different subject positions and formations. Studies of gender and genre have taken the lead in exploring this line of inquiry (see, for example, Cox 1996; Gerhart 1992).

In addition to the pragmatic dimensions of genre just outlined, each genre will be distinguished in terms of thematic or referential capacities, as a routinized vehicle for encoding and expressing particular orders of knowledge and experience. Consider the *fairy tale*, for instance, set in an indeterminate time and place ("Once upon a time in a land far away . . .") in which the relationship between appearance and reality is characteristically ambiguous, often because of magical agents and transformations, as against the *myth*, set in a formative period in the development of the cosmos, when supernatural forces effected the transformations that shaped the world as we now know it. Such orientations to the world, implicated in Bakhtin's notion of chronotope, are part of the associational field implicated in relationships of generic intertextuality.

While generic intertextuality is a means of foregrounding the routinized, conventionalized formal, pragmatic, and thematic organization of discourse, the same relational nexus also suggests that generic convention alone is insufficient to account for the formal-pragmatic-thematic configuration of any given utterance. This is so because the fit between a particular text and the generic schema – or other instances of the generic class – is never exact. Emergent elements of here-and-now contextualization inevitably enter into the discursive process, forging links to the adjacent discourse, the ongoing social interaction, instrumental or strategic agendas, and other situational and extrasituational factors that interact with generic orienting frameworks in shaping the production and reception of the utterance. These in turn will influence the ways in which the constituent features of the generic framework are variably mobilized, opening the way to generic reconfiguration and change. Thus, generic intertextuality inevitably involves the production of what Charles Briggs and I have called an intertextual gap. The calibration of the gap – its relative restriction or amplification – has significant correlates and effects. Certain acts of entextualization may strive for generic orthodoxy by hewing as closely as possible to generic precedent and assimilating the utterance to conventional practices for the accomplishment of routine ends under ordinary circumstances. Think of the boilerplate fill-in-the-blank templates for the production of legal documents – wills, contracts, leases, and the like. By contrast, widening of the intertextual gap allows for the adaptation of generic frameworks to emergent circumstances and agendas, such as the hybrid forms of oratory developed by the first generation of Moroccan women to become vendors in the public markets (Kapchan 1996). Such adaptive calibration may involve manipulation of any of the formal, functional, and thematic elements by which an utterance may be linked to generic precedents (cf. Briggs 1993; Duranti 1994:87–100). It may also extend to the assimilation of a text to more than one generic framework, drawing upon and blending the formal and functional capacities of each of the genres thus invoked. Such generic mixing may yield what Bakhtin designates as "secondary genres," which "absorb and digest various primary (simple) genres" (1986:62), incorporating them into more encompassing generic structures. Oratory is a good case in point, as characteristically incorporating narratives, jokes, proverbs, and other genres. Or, mixing may yield various hybrid forms out of the merger of two primary genres – several of the chapters to follow deal with such blended genres, including riddle tale and cante-fable, which are themselves conventional genres. Likewise possible is a more ad hoc generic blending, produced in response to emergent circumstances, as in the market sales pitches discussed in Chapter 4.

The calibration of intertextual gaps offers a useful vantage point on the ideology and politics of genre (see, for example, Goodman 2002; Tuohy 1999). Within any speech community or historical period, genres will vary with regard to the relative tightness or looseness of generic regimentation, but certain genres may become the object of special ideological focus. Prescriptive insistence on strict generic regimentation works conservatively in the service of established authority and order, while the impulse toward the widening of intertextual gaps and generic innovation is more conducive to the exercise of creativity, resistance to hegemonic order, and openness to change. These factors will be closely tied as well to hierarchies of value and taste (which genres are evaluated as relatively higher, better, more beautiful, more moral) and to the social regimentation of access to particular generic forms (who can learn them, master them, own them, perform them, and to what effect). Ochs' classic analysis of the tactical struggles over the stricter versus looser regimentation of Malagasy wedding-request *kabary* – oratory in which spokesmen for the prospective bride and groom negotiate the terms of the marriage arrangements – provides a suggestive example, elucidating not only the contrasting genre ideologies, but the ways in which such ideologies are sited, interested, multiple, and contested (Keenan [Ochs] 1973).

Performance

The linked processes of decontextualizing and recontextualizing discourse – of extracting ready-made discourse from one context and fitting it to another – are ubiquitous in social life, essential mechanisms of social and cultural continuity. Clearly, however, these processes operate in different ways and with different degrees of salience across the various sectors of social life and the modes of discourse by which they are constituted. One measure of this variance, and a useful key to the nature and significance of the decontextualization and recontextualization of discourse in social life, is the mode of discursive practice we call performance. The performance forms of a society tend to be among the most markedly entextualized, generically regimented, memorable, and repeatable forms of discourse in its communicative economy. Likewise, performance forms tend to be among the most consciously traditionalized in a community's communicative repertoire, which is to say that they are understood and constructed as part of an extended succession of intertextually linked recontextualizations (Bauman and Briggs 1990). In one influential conception of performance, performance means "never for the first time" (Schechner 1985:36), which locates its essence in the decontextualization and recontextualization of discourse, with special emphasis on the latter. Lee Haring, in a suggestive essay convergent with the orientation that informs this book, offers the term "interperformance" to foreground the dynamics of performance in the production of intertextuality (Haring 1988).

Briefly stated, I understand performance as a mode of communicative display, in which the performer signals to an audience, in effect, "hey, look at me! I'm on! watch how skillfully and effectively I express myself." That is to say, performance rests on an assumption of responsibility to an audience for a display of communicative virtuosity, highlighting the way in which the act of discursive production is accomplished, above and beyond the additional multiple functions the communicative act may serve. In this sense of performance, then, the act of expression itself is framed as display: objectified, lifted out to a degree from its contextual surroundings, and opened up to interpretive and evaluative scrutiny by an audience both in terms of its intrinsic qualities and its associational resonances (Foley 1991, 1995). Where entextualization objectifies utterances, performance objectifies acts of expression. Both facilitate decontextualization and recontextualization.

The specific semiotic means by which the performer may key the performance frame (Goffman 1974) – that is, send the metacommunicative message "I'm on" – will vary from place to place and historical period to historical period, though some, such as special formulae ("Bunday!"), formal devices (e.g., parallelism, metrical patterning), figurative language (e.g., metaphor, simile), appeals to tradition as the standard of reference for the performer's accountability ("The old people say . . ."), and special registers (e.g., archaic language), recur with impressive frequency in the performance repertoires of the world's peoples.

The collaborative participation of an audience, it is important to emphasize, is an integral component of performance as an interactional accomplishment (Barber 1997; Duranti and Brenneis 1986). From the point of view of the audience, the act of expression on the part of the performer is laid open to evaluation for the way it is done, for the relative skill, effectiveness, appropriateness, or correctness of the performer's display. The interpretive process of evaluation invokes an intertextual field in its own right, constituted by the past performances that provide a standard for the comparative assessment of the performance now on view. A performer is thus accountable to past performances, however the standards and measures of accountability may be construed in particular cultural and historical milieux. As with genre, the alignment of performance to past performances demands calibration of the intertextual relationship between them. Taking responsibility for correct doing may impel a performer to close replication of past performance in an enactment of traditional authority, while distancing of a performance from established precedent may foreground the distinctiveness of present exigencies. Indeed, ideologies of performance – and of genre – characteristically foreground and valorize particular regimens of calibration, that is, expectations and values bearing on the degree to which individual performances should conform with or depart from what is taken to be normative for the genre. The distinction between classicism and romanticism, for example, by which Western historians of the arts characterize entire eras as well as contrastive performance styles, turns on just such ideological opposition that incorporates standards of evaluation.

Insofar as evaluation opens the way to engagement with and appreciation of the intrinsic qualities of the act of expression and the performer's virtuosity, performance is an invitation to the enhancement of experience. Performance is affecting; one of its central qualities lies in its capacity to "move" an audience through the arousal and fulfillment of formal expectations – getting the audience into the "groove" – as well as through the evocative power of resonant associations (Armstrong 1971; Burke 1968[1931]:123–24; Kirshenblatt-Gimblett 1990).

Performance, like any other metacommunicative frame, is labile, and it will be a central task of some of the chapters that follow to explore how texts may be rekeyed from performance to another interpretive frame, or how performance may be variably calibrated vis-à-vis the other multiple functions – referential, rhetorical, phatic, or any other – that a given utterance may serve, either within the course of a single utterance or across successive iterations. Understandably, our analyses of oral poetics have tended to center on forms and instances of apparent or assumed full performance. We tend to seek out and record the star performers and favor the most fully artful texts. But we lose something by this privileging of full performance just as we do by taking any rendition of an artfully organized text as performance. Approaching performance in terms of the dynamics of recontextualization opens the way to a recognition of alternative and shifting frames available for the recontextualization of texts. Successive reiterations, even of texts for which performance is the expected, preferred, or publicly foregrounded mode of presentation, may be variously rekeyed. A performed text may be subsequently – or, to be sure, antecedently – reported, rehearsed, translated, relayed, quoted, summarized, or parodied, to suggest but a few of the intertextual possibilities. Here again, a focus on the calibration of the intertextual gaps between successive reiterations of a text in the dialogic history of performance illuminates the discursive foundations of sociohistorical continuity.

Plan of the Book

The first three chapters to follow all treat the formation of what Bakhtin terms secondary genres, that is, "complex genres composed of various transformed primary genres" in "a single integrated real utterance" (1986:98–99), which "absorb and digest various primary (simple) genres that have taken form in unmediated speech communication. These primary genres are altered and assume a specific character when they enter into complex ones" (1986:62). While Bakhtin identifies secondary genres as arising "in more complex and comparatively highly developed and organized cultural communication (primarily written) that is artistic, scientific, sociopolitical, and so on" (1986:62), ethnographers of speaking know better: Chapters 2–4 present and analyze a series of complex, secondary *oral* genres. The central question addressed in these analyses is *how* the constituent genres are brought together in the formation of complex generic hybrids. How is the dialogue of genres effected in formal terms, and what are the functional and thematic correlates of this hybridization process?

Chapter 2 centers around the performance with which I opened this introduction: a narrative performance about a poetic performance by a nineteenth-century Icelandic *kraftaskáld*, or "magical poet." In larger scope, the chapter explores a poetic device that is very widespread in the world's cultures – especially salient in Icelandic folklore and literature – and that has intrigued theorists of genre for millennia: the integration of prose and verse within a text. As Harris and Reichl observe in a volume surveying a range of examples of what they term "prosimetrum," "the blending and mixing of verse and prose," this device demands attention not only to genre, but to mode of delivery as well, insofar as the contrast between verse and prose characteristically implicates contrastive modes of presentation (1997:1–6). In analyzing how the verse and prose are brought into articulation in Jón Norðmann's performance, I consider also the additional dimensions of intertextual work that frame his performance: his linking of his own current performance to prior performances and his manipulation of the intertextual tension between replication and the purposeful construction of an intertextual gap.

Chapter 3 takes up a similar problem in the dialogue of genres, examining another venerable form of generic hybrid, the riddle tale. The texts that serve as examples consist of two related tales, told in succession by Andrew Stewart, a Scottish Traveler. Here, the analysis centers on what it is, in formal and functional terms, that allows for the efficacious blending of riddle and tale. What are the formal and functional capacities of the two constituent genres that allow riddles to be narrativized and narratives to be riddle-ized? At issue is not only form–function interrelationships in the blending of two primary genres, but also the emergent configuration of Stewart's performance and his management of the intertextual relation between the two texts in terms of the conventions of the riddle tale as a secondary genre.

In Chapter 4 the focus turns from hybridized forms of narrative to the generic organization of vendors' calls in a Mexican market. The oral advertising of market vendors takes two characteristic generic shapes: a condensed and pithy simple form, here labeled "call," and a complex, extended form, the "spiel" (after Lindenfeld 1990), which absorbs and digests calls, sayings, narratives, media commercials, and other forms. The analysis of the relationship between form and function in the call and spiel opens the way to a consideration of an emergent form that combines the features of both and identification of the exigent conditions that render this hybrid form potentially efficacious.

The latter three chapters of the book explore a range of modes by which the establishment and calibration of intertextual links and gaps may bring texts into alignment with each other in discursive practice. My concern in these chapters is to elucidate in terms of form–function–meaning interrelationships how genre and performance may be keyed and rekeyed, contextualized and recontextualized, and turned to the fulfillment of social ends.

Chapter 5, "Bell, You Get the Spotted Pup," examines the generic resources employed by Ed Bell, a virtuoso Texas storyteller, in the expressive performance of self. One of the striking features of Bell's repertoire and mode of performance is the extent to which he casts his stories – both true and fictional – in the first person, as narratives of personal experience. This characteristic tendency on Bell's part, coupled with his marked inclination toward expressive self-fashioning, suggest the possibility of intergeneric coherence across the forms of first-person self-representation in his repertoire. The elucidation of the dialogue of genres by which Ed Bell performs his life offers a critical corrective to those approaches to life stories that take account only of narratives framed as "true."

If Ed Bell was the consummate performer, always "on," Howard Bush, the subject of Chapter 6, was a hesitant performer at best, notably reluctant to assume the kind of responsibility to an audience that performance represents. In this chapter, which reports on an ethnographic encounter with Bush in the La Have Islands, Nova Scotia, I examine the negotiation that attended my efforts to elicit from him stories from the local repertoire of traditional narratives. I was asking Bush to perform, by the traditional standards of performance within his community, and he was – for reasons discussed at length within the chapter – reluctant or unwilling to do so. The elucidation of the emergent alignments by which Bush related his tellings to traditional performances offers a further critical corrective to our tendency, as students of oral poetics and performance, to concentrate our efforts on virtuoso performers and full, authoritative performance. The examination of hedged, negotiated, disclaimed performance expands and sharpens our view of how participants engage with texts, align them to prior texts in webs of intertextuality, and assume different subject positions in discursive interaction. Likewise, the close analysis of an ethnographic encounter provides a critical vantage point on the dialogic co-creation of anthropological knowledge.

Chapter 7, "'Go, My Reciter, Recite My Words': Mediation, Tradition, Authority," draws together many of the threads traced in the earlier ones, including the organization of participation, the keying and rekeying of performance, and traditionalization and authorization as intertextual practice. The chapter turns on two related problems: generic finalization and the organization of participation. The general understanding of genre in terms of discursive practice is that genre represents a way of packaging unitary, bounded utterances, that is, genre is instantiated in individual utterances. Bakhtin makes this explicit: "Each separate utterance is individual, of course, but each sphere in which language is used develops its own *relatively stable types* of these utterances. These we may call *speech genres*" (1986:60; italics in the original). And again, "The idea of the form of the whole utterance, that is, of a particular speech genre, guides us in the process of our speaking" (1986:81). In Bakhtin's framework, the generic organization of the utterance endows it with formal, compositional wholeness, one aspect of "the finalized wholeness of the utterance" (1986:76–7). This picture is too simple, however, In this chapter, I examine genres the full realization of which transcends the single bounded utterance. These are metapragmatically regimented in such a way as to require a mediating relay, a pass-it-on reiteration of a source utterance. The relay process in turn renders the participant structure of the mediational routines more complex than elementary, dyadic speaker-hearer or sender-receiver models can accommodate. My examination proceeds from a formal analysis of mediational performances to a consideration of what such routines might accomplish in functional terms, including traditionalization, authorization, and the socialization of discourse. The Epilogue turns the findings of this analysis once again to a critical consideration of ethnographic practice, bringing to reflexive awareness the ways that ethnography positions us in a world of others' words.

2

"And the Verse is Thus": Icelandic Stories About Magical Poems

Spieglein, Spieglein an der Wand
wer ist die Schönste im ganzen Land?

Mirror, mirror, on the wall,
who in this realm is the fairest of all?[1]

Introduction: The Blending of Prose and Verse

This narcissistic query, addressed by Snow White's Wicked Stepmother to her magical mirror, is perhaps the most familiar instance in the European repertoire of a widespread poetic device, the incorporation of verse within prose narrative to mark points of magical transition or the margins between natural and supernatural domains. As a recent survey amply demonstrates, there are myriad ways of accomplishing this formal and epistemological contrast, one class of which involves the blending of genres, that is, drawing into juxtaposition genres characterized respectively by prose and verse (Harris and Reichl 1997). It is that order of generic juxtaposition that I wish to explore in this chapter by examining Icelandic legends concerning magical verses produced by "power poets."

The blending or alternation of prose and verse within a text is a widely exploited stylistic resource in the repertoire of many poetic traditions (Harris and Reichl 1997). To be sure, the discoveries of ethnopoetics over the past several decades have rendered the distinction between prose and verse more problematic in the domain of oral poetics, revealing patterns of measured verse in oral narratives formerly assumed to be prose (Hymes 1977). Nevertheless, the orientation to performance that underpins

ethnopoetic analysis allows us to recognize even more clearly in certain performed texts contrastive modes of formal regimentation and presentational
style that sustain at least an operational or perceptual distinction between
prose and verse. This warrant is stronger still when such stylistic contrasts
are the basis of local genre distinctions. In these cases, the blending of prose
and verse within a text represents a species of intertextuality productively
considered as a dialogue of genres, which in turn invites investigation of
how this generic blending is achieved, that is, how the mutual contextualization of the genres is performatively accomplished. That is my initial
concern in this chapter. Analysis of the contextualizing interplay of genres
in dialogue, however, alerts us to other dimensions of intertextuality in the
performance at hand and their relationship to generic intertextuality. Ultimately, then, my purpose in this chapter is to suggest some of the ways in
which the performative management of generic intertextuality and other
modes of contextualization may be seen as parts of a unified expressive
accomplishment in a specific oral performance.

Legends of the *Kraftaskáld*

Many of the world's cultures attribute magical power to poets and magical
efficacy to poetry. The theme is especially resonant in Nordic tradition: the
poetic skill of the skaldic poets, for example, was seen as a divine gift
(Almqvist 1965:209); continuities have been suggested between skaldic
poetry and shamanism (Kabell 1980); and the damaging effects of the
shaming *nið* verses, best known from the famous episodes in *Egils Saga*,
appear in at least some instances to have been attributed to their magical
qualities (Almqvist 1974:185–186). In Iceland, one of the expressive foci of
this theme is the figure of the *kraftaskáld* or *ákvæðaskáld*. Kraftaskáld, the
more commonly used term, is perhaps most literally translated as "power
poet." but commentators also use the term "magical poet" to render
kraftaskáld in English (Sigurðsson 1983:437). *Ákvæði*, meaning "uttered
opinion" (Cleasby, Vigfusson, and Craigie 1957:42), "decision, verdict"
(Zoëga 1910:33), is also used in popular tales and superstitions in the more
marked sense of "spell," or "charm." An ákvæðaskáld is thus a spell-poet,
whose verse has magical power. The two terms are often cited as synonyms
(Cleasby, Vigfusson, and Craigie 1957:42; Almqvist 1961:73), though
ákvæðaskáld may suggest the use of magical verse for more negative ends.

    The kraftaskáld is an individual – most are men, but some are women
– who has the capacity in problem situations to improvise verses which

have magical efficacy: they may turn inclement weather, drive away preda-
tors, procure food and other provisions in time of need, or vanquish adver-
saries. It is important to emphasize that the verses of the kraftaskáld are
not traditional, ready-made incantations, charms, magical formulae, or the
like, but are composed spontaneously for a single occasion only. All of
the approximately two hundred kraftaskálds[2] documented by Bo Almqvist
in his historical searches (1961) were known to compose other poetry
as well and for the most part they appear to be people of uncommon
character and ability, strong-minded, passionate, and quick to anger
(1961:77).

Three factors are worth noting with regard to the source of the magical
power of the kraftaskálds and their verses. First, many of the kraftaskálds
were ministers, with special spiritual powers. In addition, it appears that
the artistic excellence of the kraftaskáld's verses was independent of their
magical efficacy: it is said of one Þorsteinn from Varmavatnsholar that
"Although Þorsteinn was a bad poet, he seemed to have in him a trace of
the kraftaskáld" (Almqvist 1961:76). Finally, the verses of the kraftaskáld
are characteristically composed in moments of strong feeling. Taken
together, these factors indicate that the magical power of the kraftaskáld's
verses is the combined product of poetic formalization of the utterance
and the charismatic power of the kraftaskáld's character – both seem
necessary.

There are numerous legends about kraftaskálds in the classic Icelandic
folktale literature, with the oldest documentary records stemming from
around 1600, though the earliest mention of the terms kraftaskáld and
ákvæðaskáld occurs only around 1830 (Almqvist 1961:73–74). But this
legend tradition is now moribund, if not fully dead, in contemporary
Icelandic oral tradition. I am fortunate, though, to have a number of
recorded texts, made available to me by Hallfreður Örn Eiríksson, Icelandic
folklorist, from his own collection. These stories were recorded in the late
1960s from quite elderly informants in old age homes. I will base this
preliminary discussion on one of these narratives, a story about a
well-known kraftaskáld of the 19th century, the Reverend Páll Jonsson
(1779–1846) of the Westman Islands, widely called Páll skáldi, Páll the Poet.
Páll was a difficult and quick-tempered man, who drank heavily and lived
the last ten years or so of his life without a position in the church. Nevertheless, he was known to be a man of intelligence and a talented poet
(Sigfússon 1946:60). The story was recorded by Eiríksson from the telling
of Jón Norðmann, in Reykjavik, November 10, 1968. A transcription and
translation of the text are given below. Line breaks mark breath pauses,
though not all breath pauses in the delivery of the text mark the beginning

of new lines; I have also taken account of syntactic structures in rendering the printed text.

Pall skáldi/Páll the Poet

HÖE 1   Voru nokkrir fleiri . . . voru fleiri kraftaskáld talin þarna í Skagafirði?
Were any others . . . were others reputed to be kraftaskálds in Skagafjord?

JN 2   Ég man að nú ekki núna í augnabliki,
I don't remember that now, just now at the moment,

3   en eitt ég nú sagt þér ef . . . ef þu kærir þig um.
but I can tell you now if . . . if you care (to hear it).

4   það er nú ekki beint úr Skagafirði,
It is, now, not exactly from Skagafjord

5   og þó, það er í sambandi við Gudrúnu,
although it is connected with Gudrún,

6   dóttur séra Páls skálda í Vestmannaeyjum.
daughter of Reverend Páll the Poet in the Westman Islands.

7   Páll skáldi þótti nú kraftaskáld,
Páll the Poet was thought, now, to be a kraftaskáld

8   og það þótti nú ganga eftir einu sinni, honum lenti eitthavð saman við
and that was thought, now, to prove true one time he had something of a conflict with

9   einhvern vertíðarmann þarna í Vestmannaeyjum,
some seasonal fishermen there in the Westman Islands,

10 og . . . og hann . . . þessi vertíðarmaþur, hann kvað einhverja vísu um . . . um Pál
and . . . and he . . . this seasonal fisherman, he spoke some verse about . . . about Páll

11 þar sem hann spáir honum því að hann muni drukkna
where he prophesies about him that he will drown.

12 Og Páll reiddist og gerir vísu.
And Páll got angry and makes a verse.

13 Þetta var á vertíðinni.
This was in the fishing season.

14 Og sú vísa er svona:
And the verse is thus:

15 Fari það svo að fyrir lok   Should it turn out that in the end
16 fáirðu að rata í sandinn,   you get to fall into the sand,
17 ætti að skerast ofan í kok,   may it cut itself down in your
                                       throat,
18 úr þér tungufjandinn.   out of you, the tongue-devil.

19 En ðaþ fór nú svo að þessi maður
    And it turned out, now, such that this man

20 þegar hann var að fara í land,
    as soon as he was going to the mainland,

21 þá drukknaði hann við Landeyjasandur
    that he drowned by Land-Isles Sand

22 og þegar hann fannst, hafði marfló étið úr honum tunguna.
    and when he was found, a shrimp had eaten his
    tongue out.[3]

23 Og . . . ja (laugh) . . . etta gat nú vel allt hafa skeð án ess að
    visan hefði komið,
    And . . . well (laugh) . . . that could, now, all well have
    happened without the verse having occurred,

24 en þetta hittist nú svona á.
    but that is how it turned out, now.

25 Nú Gudrún dottir hans sagði föður minum þessa sögu.
    Now Gudrún, his daughter, told my father this story.

Kraftaskáld legends, as I suggested earlier, recount an instance in which the poet, confronting a situation of adversity, gains mastery by means of a magical verse, composed on the moment. In other words, what we have here are stories about poems, or better, narrating about versifying. One of the things going on in them, then, is the creation of a narrative context for reporting a poem, a problem in the interaction of genres. In addition to contextualizing the verse, the narrator also contextualizes the narrative itself, weaving a complex web of verbal anchorings for his discourse that link it to a range of other situations and other discourses, endowing it with traditional authority in the process. What I want to do is trace the strands of this web through the text before us to illuminate the ways in which con-textualization in its various dimensions may be accomplished in the act of recounting these legends.

The story of Páll and the seasonal fisherman illustrates clearly the general structure of kraftaskáld legends. While the narrative may open and close with framing matter, as this one does (of which more later), the plots characteristically begin with the situation of adversity confronting the poet, here the prophetic verse attack on Páll the Poet by the fisherman. The poet then composes a verse to counteract the problem situation, which is recited by the narrator as part of the narration. The third structural plot element, following the verse, recounts the overturning or reversal of the adverse circumstance – from the poet's point of view – a transformation of state brought about by the magical verse. In the story before us, the seasonal fisherman drowns and, to make Páll's victory still more complete, his adversary's villainous tongue is eaten out by a shrimp.

The Dialogue of Genres

Let us look first at the problem of contextualization in terms of genres, that is, the interplay of the two genres, verse and story, in the text. This is an instance, par excellence, of a Bakhtinian dialogue of genres, resting not primarily on dialogue in the turn-taking social interactional sense, as in riddles or knock-knock jokes, for example, but on the interplay of two (or more) primary genres, each with its own formal and functional characteristics (Bakhtin 1986:60–102). That we are dealing here with the juxtaposition of two locally recognized primary genres within a more complex text is evidenced by the actual naming of the two generic forms within the text itself: *vísa*, or verse (lines 12, 14, 23), and *saga*, or story (line 25). Even a preliminary reading – or hearing – of the text reveals that the verse is contained by the story. Accordingly, we have at least a preliminary warrant to approach the interplay of genres in terms of the contextualization of the verse by the surrounding narrative. And indeed, the formal analysis of the text sustains this procedure.

Lines 1–6 in the transcript are metanarrational framing matter, and I will return to them later. The actual recounting of the narrated event – the conflict between Páll the Poet and the fisherman and its resolution – begins with line 8, marked by the adverbial formula *einu sinni* "one time" that marks the onset of the narrative action in so many Icelandic folktales. However, line 7 – "Páll the Poet was thought, now, to be a kraftaskáld" – is the opening step in the process that moves toward the presentation of the verse, by anticipating what is most reportable about a kraftaskáld, that is, the poetic exercise of his magical powers. This process is further advanced by line 8 – "and that was thought, now, to prove true one time . . ." – which reinforces the expectation set up in line 7 that we will hear an account of an actual incident confirming Páll's status as a kraftaskáld. The mention of

the conflict in line 8 establishes the situation of adversity that Páll will over-
come with his magical verse.

In lines 10 and 11, the seasonal fisherman, also a poet, attacks Páll with
a verse, identified as a prophecy, which means, importantly, that it is merely
a prediction of the future, lacking the performative power actually to bring
about the happening it foretells. Knowing already that Pall is a kraftaskáld
and that this represents an incident in which his magical power was used,
we begin to recognize a nascent parallel being set up by the narrator: the
fisherman spoke a verse predicting Páll's drowning, but without the power
to bring it about, while Páll will produce a verse about the fisherman's fate
that will actually cause it to happen. Note too that the fisherman's verse is
merely reported in the narrator's voice, not quoted.

In immediate response to the fisherman's challenge, "Páll got angry and
makes a verse" of his own (line 12), thus beginning the fulfillment of the
anticipated parallel. It is worth observing that while the fisherman *spoke*
his verse, Páll *makes* his, suggesting more agency, power, and immediacy in
regard to the latter. Páll's anger represents the motivational impetus for him
to employ the full force of his magical power; the magical verses of the
kraftaskáld are commonly called forth by strong emotion.

Finally, line 14, culminating in the demonstrative adverb *svona* "thus," is
the quotative frame that directly offers up the verse itself as direct discourse.
Note the shift of tense here. To this point, the recounting of the narrated
event leading up to the verse has been in the past tense or the historical
present (line 11: "prophesies," line 12: "makes"), but in line 14 the narrator
shifts to the present tense: "And the verse is thus." That is, the verb forms in
lines 7–13 index the narrated event, the event told about, while the verb
form in line 14 indexes the narrative event, the event in which the story is
told. Line 14, then, accomplishes that merger of narrated event and narrative event that is characteristic of quoted speech, which does not merely
recount, but re-presents the quoted discourse. The two instances of historical present tense mediate the transition. In this first part of the legend, then,
we may observe that much of the narrative work in the text is in the service
of the verse to follow, building a structure of anticipation for its presentation and ultimately (in line 14) pointing directly to it.

We arrive, then, at the verse itself, which is heavily set off from the surrounding discourse by formal contrasts, including the following:

- meter, with alternating 4 and 3 stress lines;
- rhyme, in an *abab* pattern;
- loudness, with the poem delivered more loudly than the surrounding narrative;

- figurative language, in the personification of the "tongue-devil";
- mode, marked by the subjunctive verb forms at the head of the first three lines, contrasting with the indicative mood of the surrounding narrative;
- temporal dynamic, shifting from the linear progression that moves from the more distant to the more proximal past in lines 7–12, to the future orientation of the verse;
- syntax, marked by the unconventional form of lines 17–18, which would more normally be "*ætti að tungufjandinn ur þér skerast ofan í kok.*"

In general, with the advent of the verse the narrator takes on the voice of the poet, serving as a kind of surrogate for him. While the verse is performed as Páll ostensibly performed it, with Páll at the deictic center of the utterance (note the second person pronouns in the verse which index the fisherman, not the folklorist), the narrator is not making the verse but representing it and the verse is shorn of its performative power; it will not cause the person to whom it is directed in the narrative event to drown and lose his tongue.

When the verse is completed, the style shifts back to that of the preceding narrative, in the past tense, less heavily marked in formal terms, and so on. Stylistic contrast notwithstanding, however, there is marked cohesion established between lines 19–22, which follow the verse, and the verse itself. There is, first of all, a parallelism of action sequence, in which the drowning of the fisherman and the cutting out of his tongue, recounted in the narrative past tense, correspond to the anticipation of these events in the verse, delivered in the subjunctive mood. We may also observe the use of lexical cohesion through the use in lines 19, 21, and 22 of grammatical variants of the words used in the verse:

- *Fari það* (15) vs. *það fór* (19) = "Should it turn out" (subjunctive) vs. "it turned out" (preterite);
- *sandinn,* (16) vs. *-sandur* (21) = sand- + definite article suffix vs. *-sand* + accusative case marker;
- *tungu-* (18) vs. *tunguna* (22) = *tung-* + genitive case marker vs. *tung-* + accusative case marker.

We can see clearly, then, in lines 19–22, that the verse has a strong formative influence on the narrative discourse that follows it; it has the capacity to shape and permeate the narrative beyond its own formal boundaries.

If we examine the verse in functional as well as formal terms, we can see why this should be so. In his analysis of magical discourse, Tzvetan Todorov has suggested that "the magical formula is a micro-narrative" (1973:44, my translation), resting his contention on the essential presence in such formulae of a verb form that signifies a change of state, a necessary condition for the existence of a narrative. He goes on to point out, however, that the narrative of the magical formula is different from other narratives insofar as it designates a virtual action, not an actual one, an action that is not yet accomplished but must be. While I would reserve the term "narrative" for accounts of action reported as accomplished, I believe Todorov's observation of the structural relationship between magical discourse and narrative is very acute, holding the key to the relationship between the verse and the ensuing narrative in our legend text. The magical verse sets forth virtual action – the drowning of the seasonal fisherman and the cutting out of his tongue in the subjunctive mood – while the subsequent narrative portion of the text recounts the realization of that virtual action in the past tense. Hence the power of the verse over the narrative, its formative effect on the narrative discourse that follows it. The verse itself, however, is formally impenetrable, as we have seen. The preceding narrative stops short at the initial boundary of the verse, and the subsequent narrative picks up again immediately after it, but the narrative exercises no shaping influence at all in formal terms on the verse. Performative efficacy resides in the form of the verse; the narrative merely describes the external circumstances of the verse and reports on the realization of the change of state that it effects.

In this generic dialogue, then, the narrative is formally and functionally subordinate to the verse. While in one general functional sense we might perhaps say that there is a mutual process of contextualization going on, since there are ties of cohesion linking the story and the verse together, the point I want to emphasize is that it is through the framing narrative that all the work of contextualization is accomplished. The narrative is accommodated to the verse at the end, while the verse retains its unitary integrity, if not its performative power. Note, however, that this is not a necessary consequence of merging narrative and verse. That narrative can take over and subordinate verse is clearly evidenced by line 11, in which the fisherman's verse is merely reported, preserving only a reference to its general poetic form and illocutionary force. It is Páll's verse, with its magical efficacy, that is the point of the story, hence its dominant position in the interplay of genres.

For comparative purposes, and to demonstrate that the organization we have discovered in Jón Norðmann's story is not unique to his performance, we may examine a second text, one of the legends surrounding Þormóð (d. 1747), a kraftaskáld who lived for a time in Vaðstakks Island in Breiðafjord (Almqvist 1961:82, 87). After a brief reminder of a Þormóð story she had recounted to Eiríksson on an earlier occasion, Ólöf Jónsdottir narrated the following (April 10, 1968):

Um þormóð /On þormóð

1   Og svo var það önnur visa
    And then there was another verse

2   sem að líka að hann hefði kveðið
    that I also heard that he had recited.

3   það var . . . það var líka að hann var í eyjum eða í þessari ey
    That was . . . that was also when he was on the islands, or on this
    island

4   og . . . og þurfti endilega að komast til lands
    and . . . and needed to come to the mainland

5   en ég man ekki hvrenig . . . hvernig það var,
    but I don't remember how . . . how it was,

6   en það var alveg kvikófart veður og ekki nokkur leið að komast
    but it was completely impassable weather and no way to get there

7   og þá hefði hann ort vísu þessa:
    and then he composed this verse:

8   Kristur minn fyrir kraftinn sinn   My Christ, for his power
9   kóngurinn himna dáða,   King of heavenly deeds,
10 gefi þann vind að græðist lind   may there be wind to calm the
                                        water
11 að gott sé við að ráða.   so that it may be well for us.

12 Og þá hafði lyngt svo að hann komst til lands.
    And then it had calmed so that he came to the mainland.[4]

13 Hann var kallaður kraftaskáld, hann Þormóður þessi.
    He was called kraftaskáld, this Þormóð.

This narrative, much leaner than Jón Norðman's story of Páll the Poet,
nevertheless displays the essential features of that earlier text. Following a
metanarrational introduction that aligns the narrative to other recitations
by Þormóð that Mrs. Jónsdóttir has heard (lines 1–2), she sets up the
adverse conditions that elicit the focal verse (lines 3–6) and the demon-
strative-quotative frame that points to the verse itself (line 7): "and then he
composed this verse." As before, the verse is presented as direct discourse,

set off stylistically from the discourse that surrounds it by markedly increased formal regimentation and presentational contrast: meter, rhyme, loudness, a shift of tense and mood, and so on. And again, notwithstanding the formal contrast, there is clear cohesion between the virtual action of the verse – "may there be wind to calm the water" (line 10) – and the actualization of that action in the narrative passage that follows (line 12), as the verse, itself impenetrable by its cotext, exerts a formative influence on the subsequent prose. Thus, as in the story of Páll the Poet, the narrative is formally and functionally subordinate to the verse, so much so that Mrs. Jónsdóttir's professed inability to recall in detail the circumstances surrounding the narrated event beyond the inclement weather that kept the poet from reaching the mainland – "but I don't remember how . . . how it was" (line 5) – does not derail the narration.

I have already noted in Mrs. Jónsdóttir's narration the intertextual link she establishes with other kraftaskáld verses and stories about them and with antecedent tellings in which she heard about these reportable recitations, summed up in her framing statement, "And then there was another verse that I also heard that he had recited" (lines 1–2). This aspect of Mrs. Jónsdóttir's performance invites attention to an important aspect of intertextuality in practice beyond the dialogue of genres that has thus far been our primary focus of attention; for a fuller consideration of which we may turn back to Jón Norðmann's story of Páll the Poet.

Traditionalization

Returning now to Páll the Poet, thus far in the analysis I have focused my discussion on lines 7–22 of the text, which constitute the narrative portion of Jón Norðmann's discourse in the formal and functional senses I indicated earlier. Let me turn now to the other portions of the text to examine the dynamics of contextualization at work within them. There are, in fact, several kinds of contextualizing work evidenced in these opening and closing sections, including a small negotiation by which Mr. Norðmann shifts the discussion from kraftaskálds in Skagafjord, his own region in the very north of Iceland, to Páll the Poet, a kraftaskáld from the Westman Islands off the south coast, a little job of contextualizing this story vis-à-vis the preceding discourse between himself and the folklorist. For present purposes, however, I am more concerned with a different order of business accomplished in the lines at the beginning and end of the transcript, in particular lines 5–8 and 23–5. First, lines 5, 6, and 25: "although it is connected with Gudrún, daughter of the Reverend Páll the Poet in the Westman Islands," and "Now Gudrún, his daughter, told my father this story." What I want to suggest is that this linking of his story to the antecedent tellings of his father and Gudrún represents the work of traditionalization, traditionalization in practice.

Now, in conventional folkloric terms, the story would be reckoned to be traditional by several interconnected measures. The tale can be documented in what is recognizably the same plot, though with some variation, in texts in the folktale collections, all gathered from "oral tradition," so called, meaning the oral storytelling of narrators who heard them aurally from other narrators. In one of the more interesting of these, for example (Sigfússon 1946:59–60), Páll's adversary is not a seasonal fisherman, but one Jón Torfabróður, a rival poet with whom Pall engaged in heated verse battles. Pall's magical verse is given as follows, clearly a variant of the verse in our text:

> það færi betur fyrir þin sprok
> þu fengir að rata í sandinn.
> það ætti að skerast uppvið kok
> úe þér tungu-fjandinn!

> It would be better for (all) your talk
> (if) you got to fall into the sand.
> That may it cut itself up (out of) your throat
> out of you, the tongue-devil!

Interestingly, in this version both verses are successful: Jón drowns and his body is found with its tongue missing, but Páll drowns also. Thus, this story would be considered a traditional item on two standard grounds: it is handed down orally from generation to generation and it exists in different versions in the social group within which it is current. This is a kind of objective and analytical conception of tradition, in the sense that it views folklore items essentially as persistent objects, rooted in the past and passed on from person to person through time and space. And, indeed, Mr. Norðmann's testimony may be viewed from this vantage point as corroborative recognition by the folk of this handing down of the story from Gudrún, Páll's daughter, to Mr. Norðmann's father, to Mr. Norðmann, and ultimately to the folklorist.

From an agent-centered point of view, however, looking at Mr. Norðmann's storytelling as social practice, other questions must arise. What we have in this text is Mr. Norðmann directly and explicitly engaged in an act of symbolic construction, drawing the links of continuity by which he may tie his story to past discourses as part of his own recounting of it. This is the act of traditionalization, and it is part of the process of endowing the story with situated meaning. "The traditional begins with the personal" (Hymes 1975a:354) and the immediate here, not with some objective quality of pastness that inheres in a cultural object but with the active construction of connections that link the present with a meaningful past. When examined, this process of traditionalization in the text before us manifests itself as a species of contextualization. Mr. Norðmann locates his discourse in relation to a sequential series of other discourses, starting in fact with Páll's own and proceeding through those of Gudrún and his father, so that his story, in effect, contains them all. That Gudrún told the story to his father, who told it to him, constitutes one dimension of the story's social meaning and value in the situational context of Mr. Norðmann's telling of it to Eiríksson. Specifically, traditionalization here is an act of authentication, akin to the art or antique dealer's authentication of an object by tracing its provenience. Mr. Norðmann establishes both the genuineness of his story as a reliable account and the legitimacy and strength of his claim to it by locating himself in a direct line of transmission, including lines of descent through kinship, that reaches back to Páll himself, the original speaker of those reportable words that constitute the point of the narrative. By orienting his talk to his father's talk, to Gudrún's talk, to Páll's talk, Norðmann endows his discourse with a dimension of traditional authority in a Weberian sense. If the original event is reportable, Mr. Norðmann's direct connection with it through the links with his father and Páll's daughter establishes and enhances the legitimacy of his claim to report it himself.

It is important to establish, though, that Norðmann's claims about the authenticity of the story, his argument for it as the real thing truly told about Páll by people with a strong claim to reliable knowledge, is not also an argument for the validity of others' interpretations of the story. In fact, Mr. Norðmann leaves open the possibility of calling into question certain aspects of others' tellings of the story. Observe, for example, his statements in lines 7–8 that Páll was "thought" to be a kraftaskáld, and that this was "thought" to prove true in the events narrated in the story, picking up on the framing of Eiríksson's question about those who were "reputed to be" (*talin*) kraftaskálds. This does not question the external events recounted in the narrative, but it certainly leaves open the question of whether Páll's verse actually did have the magical efficacy attributed to it. Even stronger is Mr. Norðmann's metanarrational comment in line 23: "that could, now, all well have happened without the verse having occurred." This raises the question of alternative explanations quite directly; others may interpret the fisherman's drowning and loss of his tongue as brought about by Páll's verse, but Mr. Norðmann acknowledges that it might have happened anyway. Thus, his traditionalization of the narrative by contextualizing it vis-á-vis others' discourse has a dual thrust: it authenticates the story as a significant piece of discourse, strengthening its claim – and his own – on our attention, but it questions the authority of others' expressed interpretations of the story. In the process, then, he reframes the story by taking a different line toward its meaning, though one at least partially set up by the framing of the folklorist's question to him. The plot is accepted – even valorized – in terms of its connection with certain talk that preceded it, but the meaning of the story, as also given expression in earlier talk, is subjected to question in the assertion of an intertextual gap. This represents an active engagement with tradition, the use of traditionalization to endow the story with dimensions of personal and social meaning; it is not simply a recognition of an inherent quality of traditionality in a particular cultural object.

Contextualization, Genre, and Tradition

This recounting of the legend of Páll the Poet, then, emerges from our examination as a structure of multiply embedded acts of contextualization in which talk is oriented to other talk: Páll's verse, Gudrún's story, Mr. Norðmann's father's story, the interpretive talk of those who commented on the story, and Mr. Norðmann's own recounting of it to the folklorist. I have intended in my examination of the text to suggest how an analysis of the management of these contextualizations may illuminate certain other foundational concepts beyond context itself, specifically genre and tradition.

Genre is a classificatory concept, a way of sorting out conventionalized discourse forms on the basis of form, function, content, or some other factor or set of factors. Scholarly thinking about verbal genres, both in folklore and linguistic anthropology, has been much influenced by canons of scientific taxonomy, whether from an etic or an emic point of view: genre classifications must be based on the application of consistent sorting principles throughout, they must be exhaustive, the categories must be mutually exclusive, and so on. But even in the enthusiasms of ethnoscience, there were constant reminders from the data that human expression doesn't fit so neatly into taxonomic categories. Gary Gossen (1974), in the most elegant of the elucidations of verbal genres in native terms, noted that he could only get agreement – more or less – from his Chamula sources down to five taxonomic levels, below which agreement on what went in which category was not to be achieved. And, in folklore scholarship, there has always been some unease about those anomalous, blended forms that do not fit neatly into systems of genre classification, such as neck riddle, riddle ballad, cante fable, and the like, that serve as nagging reminders that genres leak. These are themselves conventional forms of folkloric expression in which what are analytically considered as primary genres are brought into dialogue with each other.

Kraftaskáld legends represent another instance of such dialogic genres in Bakhtin's sense of the term, not necessarily involving two or more inter-locutors but rather the interpenetration of multiple voices and forms of utterance. My use of Bakhtinian terminology here indicates the potential usefulness of Bakhtin's ideas in the elucidation of such compound forms, and, indeed, I have been much stimulated by his dialogic perspective (especially Bakhtin 1981, 1986; Medvedev and Bakhtin 1978[1928]; Voloshinov 1973). As suggestive as they are, however, Bakhtin's writings engender a certain amount of frustration in the analysis of dialogic forms; his per-spective seems to demand a dimension of formal analysis, but he never pro-vides it. *How* are genres brought into dialogue? *How* is dialogization actually accomplished? What I have tried to suggest in this chapter is the pro-ductiveness of such formal analysis, framed as a problem in the mutual contextualization of primary genres. In order to accomplish a telling of a kraftaskáld legend, the narrator must accomplish the management of con-textualization, determined to a significant degree by the formal and func-tional capacities of the genres brought into dialogue, here saga and vísa, story and verse. My analysis has been meant to show for this one dialogic form how that generic contextualization gets done. For other mergers, it would have to be accomplished differently. One value of the kind of formal and functional analysis I have attempted, I believe, is its potential for estab-lishing a basis for the comparative investigation of such hitherto poorly understood dialogic genres as a key to a significant dimension of generic creativity. Let me suggest some of the possibilities in a very preliminary way by reference to a few examples.

Consider, for instance, the class of epics known as shamanic epics (Oinas 1978:293), such as the Finnish *Kalevala* (Lönnröt 1963), which deal in significant part with deeds that are accomplished by magical means. Throughout the *Kalevala* narrative, we find the heroes and heroines employing magical charms. Not surprisingly, in light of our examination of kraftaskáld legends, the virtual transformations given expression in the charms are subsequently reported as having been realized, with the charms pointing ahead and giving shape to these narrative reports. In the *Kalevala*, however, all is in verse. Thus, by contrast with the parallelism of action sequence and occasional lexical cohesion that we observed between the magical verse and the ensuing narrative prose in the story of Páll the Poet, we find a far tighter line-by-line parallelism allowed for in the *Kalevala* between the magical charm and the account of its working:

> Make a cloud spring up in the east, raise up a cloudbank in the northwest,
> send others from the west, drive others from the south.
> Shed rain gently from the heavens, sprinkle honey from the clouds
> on the sprouting shoots, on the murmuring crops.
> He made a cloud spring up in the east, raised a cloudbank in the
>   northwest,
> sent another from the west, drove one from the south.
> He pushed them right together, hanged them against one another.
> He shed rain gently from the heavens, sprinkled honey from the clouds,
> on the sprouting shoots, on the murmuring crops.
> (Lönnröt 1963:12–13)

Or take the tale often cited as the prototype of the cante fable, "The Singing Bone" (Grimm no. 28, AT 780), summarized thus by Thompson: "The brother kills his brother (sister) and buries him in the earth. From the bones a shepherd makes a flute which brings the secret to light" (1961:269). The secret is brought to light by means of a verse sung by the bone flute (hence *cante fable*, singing tale). Here, once again, we have the merger of story and verse, but in this case it is the preceding narrative that has at least a partial determinative effect on the embedded verse, as the verse recapitulates the preceding action. In "The Singing Bone" the verse, far from being impenetrable as it is in our legend text, is shaped into a narrative sequence of its own by the prose that precedes it.

A similar process is at work in the dialogic form known as the neck riddle, blending narrative and riddle (Abrahams 1980, 1985; Dorst 1983). The term "neck riddle" derives from the common framing of such narratives in terms of a man who saves his neck by propounding a riddle that his executioner cannot answer, but the form also includes the strategic use of unanswerable riddles as a kind of test or wager. According to Abrahams and Dundes (1972:133): "The essential characteristic of this type is that the riddle must be based on some experience that only the riddler has undergone or witnessed." Perhaps the most widely known example is Samson's riddle (Judges 14:14): "Out of the eater came forth meat, and out of the strong came forth sweetness," referring to a lion he had earlier killed by rending it apart and in whose carcass a swarm of bees later nested and produced honey. As in "The Singing Bone," the antecedent narrative gives shape to the inset form, here the riddle, but while the bone flute's verse is meant to reveal what has transpired, the riddle is meant to obscure it, hence the opaque language of the riddle. I will analyze these dynamics in greater detail in the next chapter.

These three brief examples represent the merest scratching of the surface of the possibilities suggested by an exploration of dialogic genres. Nor is this process confined to conventional blending alone; there is always the potential of bringing genres into dialogue in more spontaneous and emergent ways (e.g., Sherzer 1979). Ultimately, the exploration of how such generic blendings are accomplished in performance will highlight a creative dimension of human verbal expression that has tended to be obscured by established notions of genre, revealing more closely how people use verbal art in the conduct of their social lives.

Now this illumination of the problem of genre is but one of the outcomes of an examination of this text in terms of the contextualization of discourse by other discourse. Beyond the contextualization of the verse by the story, the other task accomplished by the narrator is the outward contextualization of his story by situating it in a lineage of other tellings or commentaries. This act of contextualization, I have suggested, represents traditionalization in practice. What is accomplished thereby is the authentication of his discourse, the endowing of it and himself with a species of authority, a claim on our attention and interest. Tradition here is a rhetorical resource, not an inherent quality of a story. To be sure, tradition is always such a resource, but in folklore and anthropology traditionalization has overwhelmingly been a resource of intellectual outsiders, a means of selectively and analytically valorizing and legitimizing – or denying the value and legitimacy of – aspects of culture frequently not their own by locating them within lineages of descent and structures of authority for scholarly rhetorical and analytical purposes (Bauman and Briggs 2003). Examination of this text highlights the significance of a complementary strategy at the folk level, the active construction of links tying the present to the past. Oral tradition, in these active and local terms, is a particular strategic form of the contextualization of speech vis-à-vis other speech, a way that those who use spoken art forms as equipment for living invest what they say with social meaning, efficacy, and value.

There are many implications here for written literature as well, but that would carry me far beyond the scope of this chapter. I will confine myself to one especially relevant example. Devices that establish a linkage between current discourse and earlier discourses have been a prominent focus of discussion in the scholarship devoted to the classic Icelandic sagas, with special reference to saga origins (see, for example, Andersson 1966; Bell 1976; Liestøl 1974[1930]:33–34). Proponents of the "freeprose" argument that the sagas are deeply rooted in oral narrative tradition point to the frequent use of such oral "source references" as *svá er sagt* (so is said), *frá því er sagt* (it is related), *þat segja menn* (so men say), or *er þat flestra mann sǫgn* (it is the report of most men) as evidence of an active oral tradition antecedent to the written sagas, while adherents of the more literary "bookprose" position tend to dismiss such devices as mere stylistic convention.

While the written sagas as we have them unquestionably represent a literary genre, no one familiar with the dynamics of an oral tradition can doubt that the sagas are strongly tied to such a tradition in Commonwealth Iceland. Debates over origins aside, however, I would maintain that the findings of this chapter concerning the dynamics of traditionalization offer a useful vantage point from which to consider the "source references" of the classic sagas. Like the intertextual linkages forged by the narrator of our kraftaskáld legend, the establishment of ties to other discourses by the writers of the sagas represents traditionalization in action, the active process of contextualizing the saga narratives in a socially constituted field of verbal production that endows them with traditional authority in a society that relied centrally on such authority in the conduct of social life. The source references are stylistic devices in the service of rendering the saga accounts in which they are employed socially authoritative. Whether or not they point to what someone really said in every instance is to this extent beside the point. The rhetorical effect of traditionalization through the weaving of interdiscursive ties is what is significant; this process endows the sagas, like our kraftaskáld legend, with a distinctive element of social groundedness and force.

Context to Contextualization

The analysis of oral performance in context directs attention to the anchoring of verbal art in the social and cultural worlds of its users, to the complex, multidimensional web of interrelationships that link performed texts to culturally defined systems of meaning and interpretation and to socially organized systems of social relations. In the general usage of folklorists and anthropologists, however, the notion of context invokes three principal dimensions of such interrelationships: (1) the context of cultural meaning, that is, what it is one needs to know about a culture to make sense of its verbal art; (2) the functional context, social or psychological, that is, how verbal art forms operate to validate social institutions, maintain social solidarity, socialize children, alleviate psychological conflict, and the like; and (3) the situational context, focusing on the social use of verbal art in the conduct of social life, within culturally defined scenes and events. If I may venture a generalized, but still, I think, accurate, characterization of these three contextual perspectives, they tend largely to approach oral texts from the outside in, constructing a kind of contextual surround for the folklore forms and texts under examination which is seen to have a formative influence upon them. I have endeavored in this chapter, by pursuing a more practice-centered line of analysis, to explore a perspective on context from the inside, as it were, using textual performance itself as a point of departure, and allowing it to index dimensions of context as the narrator himself forges links of contextualization to give shape and meaning to his expression. The aim is not to dismiss the more collective, institutional, conventional dimensions of context, but ultimately to provide an analytical counterweight to them in the service of moving us closer to a balanced understanding of that most fundamental of all tensions constitutive of the social condition, the dynamic interplay of the collective and the individual, the ready-made and the emergent, in human life.

3

"I'll Give You Three Guesses": The Dynamics of Genre in the Riddle Tale

And they said unto him, Put forth thy riddle,
that we may hear it.
And he said unto them, Out of the eater came
forth meat, and out of the strong came forth
sweetness. And they could not in three days
expound the riddle.
    Judges 14.13–14

Sphinx: What walks on four legs in the morning, on two at noon, and on
   three in the evening?
Oedipus: Man.
   Sophocles, *Oedipus Rex*

Turandot: What is like ice, but burns?
Calàf: Turandot!
   Puccini, *Turandot*

The Problem of the Riddle Tale

These brief excerpts, taken from some of the most familiar and symboli-
cally resonant narratives in our cultural canon, afford us a vivid reminder
of the productiveness of riddle as a narrative and dramatic device. Samson's
riddle, based upon his experience of bees swarming in the skull of a lion,
leads ultimately, we recall, to his massive slaughter of the Philistines.
Oedipus' correct answer to the riddle of the Sphinx opens the way for his
marriage to Jocasta, the foundation of the tragic events and relationships

that have become for us the name of a deeply conflictual psychological state. And Princess Turandot's riddles are the life-or-death tests that she poses to her suitors in Puccini's passionate opera of loyalty, death, and the redemptive power of love. But these three works represent the merest sampling of a much more extensive corpus. Folklorist Christine Goldberg has inventoried a broad range of folk and literary narratives about riddling that extend geographically from Iceland to India and historically from classical antiquity to the present (Goldberg 1993; see also Dundas 2002). Critics have propounded a variety of theories concerning the narrative and dramatic efficacy of riddles in structural and functional terms: riddles as symbolic means of bringing unrelated terms into relation, or, conversely, as a means of highlighting ambiguity; riddles as useful devices for framing the agonistic dynamics of contests or tasks; and so on. Here, as in the preceding exploration of Icelandic stories about magical verses, I want to approach the interrelationship of narratives and riddles as a problem in generic intertextuality. How do riddles lend themselves to narration? How is the generic interaction of narrative and riddle performatively accomplished?

Riddles and related enigmatic genres turn, characteristically, on ambiguity and multiplicity of meaning. Hence, it is scarcely surprising that these enigmatic forms are themselves generically ambiguous. Certainly, the definition and classification of such genres is notoriously problematic, as observed by Laurits Bødker in offering the rationale for his dictionary of riddle terms in the Nordic languages:

> The riddle is so short and concise that, unlike e.g., the ballad and the folktale, it is easy to handle. But as regards content, and very often form as well, it is at the same time so richly faceted and ambiguous that it easily lends itself to classification in any of several groups, a fact which is well known to everybody who has tried to find a certain riddle in the published collections. (Bødker 1964:7)

Sorting out the elementary forms of the riddle is difficult enough, but the capacity of the riddle and related enigmatic forms to blend with other genres makes the problem still more complex.[1] The blending of riddle and narrative is especially slippery, making for expressive complexes that are marked by a high degree of generic variability.[2] In this chapter, I will explore some of the factors that give shape to this generic dialogue between narrative and riddle. Specifically, I will examine riddle tales in terms of formal features, the functional loads and interrelationships of these constituent features, and the implications of this generic blending for the field of meaning that the resultant hybrid forms invite us to enter.

My primary data consist of two riddle-narrative texts recorded by Hamish Henderson of the School of Scottish Studies from Andrew Stewart, a Scottish Traveler from Perthshire,[3] in the 1950s. The tales are versions of AT 922 The Shepherd Substituting for the Priest Answers the King's Questions (The King and the Abbot) (Thompson 1961:320–321) and AT 927 Out-riddling the Judge (Thompson 1961:324–325), the classic neck riddle tale type. They were recorded one right after the other in that order, and Henderson and Stewart link the latter tale to the former. Thus, the two tales were interrelated in performance and I will treat them as a package. I should note explicitly that by identifying these texts as riddle tales, or neck riddles, or tale types 922 and 927, I do not mean to subscribe to the assumptions and classificatory principles that underlie the standard terms and the Type Index, only to identify the material under study for preliminary and heuristic purposes in terms recognizable to readers. I have transcribed the texts from a copy of Henderson's field tape; both texts are also in Katharine Briggs' *Dictionary of British Folktales*, volume 2, but my transcription differs somewhat from hers in format and in closer fidelity to the original (see Briggs 1970:485–487, 501).

Andrew Stewart is a member of one of the most renowned and well-documented families of traditional storytellers, singers, and musicians known to folklorists.[4] Two of his older brothers, Alec and John, also recorded versions of type 922, and I have included their texts in an appendix for further comparison. I will not discuss their versions in close detail, but will draw upon them to expand upon specific points that emerge in the analysis of Andrew Stewart's riddle tales. Here are Andrew's tellings.

Text 1: The King and the Miller
There was once upon a time a miller. He had a meal mill in this country place. And in those days the kings was very strict with them, they would take the land off them, and their premises, you see, for some reason.

So the miller (it was a Sunday), and the miller was walkin' down the lade-side, the river-side, and he saw the King and his army comin' on horseback, you see?

So the King stopped and he says, "Hello," he says, "are you the miller along here?"

And the miller says, "Yes," he says. He knew he was a nobleman of some kind.

So he says, "Well," he says, "I've come," he says, "to collect your mill and take everything, your land off ye," he says, "and your meal and that," he says, "for every year that you're makin' it," he says. He says, "But I'm a sportin' man. I always give a man a chance." He says, "I'll give you three guesses," he says, "and if you can guess the three guesses within a year and a day," he says, "you can keep your mill."

So the guess he was given, it was impossible for to get them. That was the sort. They just gave the men a chance, to keep them in agony, you know, and thinkin' aboot the thing.

So anyway, he says, "What is the guesses?"

"Well," he says, "First," he says, "I want to know the weight of the moon." You see?

And what was the next one? How many stars was in the sky?

And the next one, "Could you tell me what," the king, he says, "Can you tell me what I'm thinkin' on? And I'll give you a year and a day to find that out."

So the miller says, "Now," he says, "wait a minute," he says. "That's the weight of the moon," he says, "and all the stars that's in the sky, and what you're thinkin' on," he says, "your Highness."

And the King says, "Yes."

"Well," he says, "all right," he says, "a year and a day."

So of course the army and the King rode away.

But as the years . . . as the weeks was goin' by and the months was goin' by the girl asked him – he'd a lovely daughter – and he [sic] asked him, she says, "Father, what's wrong with you?" she says. "You look awful worried," she says, "this last two or three weeks."

"Och," he says, "nothing." He wouldnae tell her, to keep the girl frae worryin', you see?

But at the finish up, he coaxed her [sic] to tell, and he told her, "Well," he says, told her about the King giving the guesses. And he says, "How I'm gonna do it," he says, "I don't know."

But here, this is where Jack comes in. There was a man, Silly Jack, wasn't there? So Jack . . . She goes and she tells Jack. He was a workin' hand aboot the place, but he was a kinda daft fella, this, and she goes and tells him what happened, his [sic] father was goin' tae . . . Anyway.

So Jack made a bargain wi' her. He says, "If I can get your father's life saved," he says, "and save his property," he says, "will you marry me?"

And the girl says "Yes," she says, "Jack, I'll do anything that you want if you can save my father's life and save the mill and a' thing." You see?

So anyway, the father's goin' aboot worried, he cannae think. He takes tae his bed at the finish-up, no well, you see?

And Jack, so he's workin' aboot the mill as usual, and when the year and the day come up, at the time he had tae meet the King, Jack goes and dresses hissel' as this old miller. He puts a gray wig on his heid, a beard, a long white beard, and his white moustache, and a stick, and the miller's old claes, and a pair o' white boots (meal that was on his boots, you see?), and he goes along the mill-lade, just marching along as usual as what the miller does. But here the old man's lyin' in the bed no well. That was Jack that was goin' along, you see?

So he meets the King, and he stops as usual.

And he says, "Are you the old miller?" he says. "You look very old."

"Aye," he says, says the miller, he says, "I am gettin' old."

He says, "Did you find out," he says, "the guesses?" he says. "I want ye," he says, "to know," he says, "what I'm thinkin' on," he says. "Have you got the riddles yet?" You see?

So he says, "No," he says, "but," he says, "it didnae give me no thought," he says, "but," he says, "I'll try my best," says the miller, he says, "and guess them." See?

So the King says to him . . .

"Well," he says, "what is the first one?" He says, "What is the first one again?" he says to the King.

The King says, "The first one is," he says, "Jack," he says, "is the weight of the moon."

So Jack says, "Oh, that's easy."

But he thought it was the old miller. He thought it was the miller, you see. The old miller says, "Oh, that's easy."

"Is it?" said the King. He says, "What is it?"

"Well," he says, "there are four quarters in the moon," and he says "four quarters in a ton," he says. "That must make the moon a ton." You see? A ton. Four quarters in the moon, there's four quarters of a ton, the moon must weigh a ton.

So he says, "If you don't believe me," he says, "you can go weigh it," he says, "or do somethin' like that to prove it."

So the King says, "Well," he says, "it might be so," he says. "I don't know," he says. "I believe," he says, "you're right there."

"But," he says, "the second one," he says, "will puzzle you," he says. "How many stars are in the sky?"

So of course Jack looked at him and blundered oot a big figure, you know, that the King couldn't hardly follow, you see?

And the King looked at him, scratched his head, looks at him and says, "Well . . ."

And says Jack, "If you don't believe me," he says, "just start and coont them."

So the King couldnae coont all the stars, you see, and he says, "Well," he says, "it could be right," he says, "but the last one'll beat you," says the King. He says, "You cannae tell me," he says, "what I'm thinkin' on."

"Oh yes," says Jack. He says, "You're thinkin'," he says, "you're speakin' to the old miller," he says, "but you'll find it's his goodson you're speakin' tae," and he pulls off the wig and the beard off his face, and straightens hissel' up.

And it was very clever, wasn't it?[5]

Text 2: Under the Earth I Go

HH: Do you know a story, the same sort of story, // with a rhyme . . . ?
AS: //It's something the same. And the joke in this one was, "Under the earth . . ."

The boy had to give this King a joke that the King's men and his knights and that couldnae guess, and the King himself couldnae guess, so he got a year and a day for to do the same thing in this other place, you see?

So it was the opposite way aboot, like: the boy had to give the King the riddles.

So here when the boy gave the riddles, he'd a year and a day. He hadnae to tell the riddles, he had to give the riddles when he landed in the place. And he got a year and a day to think what riddles he was gonna give the King, you understand?

So here he mounted his horse, Jack, and he went to the King's palace, and all the army was there, you see, and the King's guards, so the riddle had tae be read oot, so Jack . . . one o' the men read the riddle out, and the riddle was:

> Under the earth I go,
> On the oak leaf I stand,
> I ride on the filly that never was foaled,
> And I carry the dead in my hand.

So they tried to guess and guess, and everybody tried to guess, but they couldnae make out what it was.

And what the thing was, Jack, his father had an old mare, a horse, you know, a mare – she was in foal. He knocked the mare down, killed her, cuts up the mare, which was near foalin', takes the foal out, out of her stomach, you see, takes the foal out, rears it up, gets on its back, he fills his hat up with earth, puts oak leafs in his shoes, and that's where the riddle goes. He made a whip o' the mother's hide, skin, and that was what the riddle was, and they couldnae guess it.

And he told them, "Under the earth I go": he takes his hat off – it was full of sand.

He takes his boots off. He says, "On the oak leaf I stand": there was oak leafs in his boots.

He says, "I ride on this filly," he says, "that never was foaled," he says: he told them how he'd done it.

And he says, "I carry the dead in my hand": it was the mother's dead skin that he had in the hand for the whip.

It's quite good, isn't it?[6]

"Impossible for to get" to "Oh, that's easy"

Taking nothing for granted, let us begin by establishing in general and pre-liminary terms the basis for treating these texts as generic hybrids of folk-tale and riddle. The first text, we may observe right away, opens with the classic generic marker of traditional folktales: "There was once upon a time a miller," and both additional versions, second in the appendix, begin with variants of this formula. Alec's version, second in the appendix, also ends with a conventional Scots folktale closing formula that brings the narra-tion back from the tale-world to the storytelling event and that explicitly identifies the text as a "story": "The last time I was past the hoose I got a cup o' tea and some breid, and that's the end o' my story." Moreover, all our texts are clearly narratives in formal terms, reporting events in terms of a temporal sequence of actions in which the relationship of sequentiality also implies consequentiality. Again, all are crafted in such a way as to move from a state of tension, conflict, and imbalance to a resolution of the dis-equilibrium, a criterial attribute of the folktale (and, some would say, of all narrative) (see Toolan 1988 and the references therein). Still further, the central protagonist in both of Andrew's texts is Silly Jack, the generic hero in the traditional folktale repertoire of the Scots Travelers, the humble, unpromising youth who prevails at the end of the story (see Douglas 1987:9). In overall compass, then, these are clearly folktales.

Within the tales, however, are enigmatic dialogic routines consisting of two parts, organized around the elicitation of a verbal response; these rou-tines are most often called "guesses," but are also referred to in the text as "riddles." In John Stewart's text, they are called "questions." By using the term "riddle," Andrew gives us at least a preliminary warrant to examine the text in terms of the interactive combination of folktale and riddle, though the alternative terms alert us to the possibility that the dialogic rou-tines are generically ambiguous. In eliciting the second text, Henderson asks for a "story with a rhyme," using two generic terms, and receives this narrative with a rhyme in it. Stewart, however, refers to the rhyme once as a "joke" and three times as a "riddle." As Kenneth Goldstein (1963) informs us, "joke" is an alternative term for riddle in the northeast of Scotland, and a good riddle in that region has to be rhymed, as this one is. While "joke" and "rhyme" open up other intergeneric dimensions, I want to stick for the moment to interaction between riddle and folktale, warranted by the narrator himself. Finally, we may observe that Stewart closes both tales with his own evaluations of the riddling: "And it was very clever, wasn't it?" and "It's quite good, isn't it?" This too is a common feature of riddling in the northeast of Scotland (Goldstein 1963).

Now, although Andrew Stewart's calling the enigmatic questions "riddles" opens the way for us to examine what relation they actually bear to riddles as conventionally defined, we must not simply take the term as transparent, but look closely at what they are and how they work. Clearly, the King's questions are not of the classic "true riddle" type, that is, "enigmatic questions in the form of descriptions whose referent must be guessed" (Abrahams and Dundes 1972:130). Rather, they are what folktale scholars call "wisdom questions," that is, questions that test the knowledge or wisdom of the person to whom they are posed. To be sure, they do have certain riddle elements. They are enigmatic, which is to say they require special interpretive work, and the first two guesses, concerning the weight of the moon and how many stars are in the sky, employ common riddle terms: a glance at Archer Taylor's *English Riddles from Oral Tradition* (1951) reveals that the moon is a richly productive riddle image and referent and the uncountability of the stars is also a traditional riddle figure.

A bit of clarification may be useful here concerning the characterization of the dialogic routines as "questions." Clearly, the three questions in our texts do not all take the surface form of interrogatives. Scholars have long observed that riddles may take a variety of surface forms: questions, descriptions, commands, and so on (see, for example, Pepicello and Green 1984). Nevertheless, however the first part of the routine may be realized, it *functions* as a question. In more precise terms, drawing on Austin's theory of speech acts, it has the illocutionary force of – that is, it counts discursively as – a question, insofar as it is meant to elicit a verbal, informational response. Some of the questions in our texts, to be sure, are combined with other illocutionary speech acts. "[Y]e must tell me, hoo many stars is in the heavens," for example, couples a requirement (Bach and Harnish 1979:47) to a question, but the question–response pairing remains central throughout. Nevertheless, these enigmatic questions differ fundamentally from riddles in being unanswerable; riddles, as generally defined, must be answerable, though with difficulty, and must contain within themselves a basis for arriving at the answer, however disguised (Pepicello and Green 1984:88). To this point, then, we have some riddle-like non-riddles, in formal and functional terms. How do they work in the tale?

The narrative opens with an assertion of the King's power, expressed as an intention to take away the mill from the miller. This is institutional power, the right of the King to confiscate his subjects' property. The King does offer a way out, however, though not a very promising one: if the miller can guess the answers to the questions the King will pose to him, he can keep his mill. In effect, the King makes his institutional power subject to a kind of contest of interactional power, pitting the difficulty of his questions against the miller's ability to come up with the right answers. There is an intellectual element here as well, of course, insofar as figuring out acceptable answers requires cleverness and wit, but I emphasize the interactional dimension because it is the speaking of the questions and answers by which the contest is played out and this is governed by interactional abilities and conventions. We are dealing, then, with two different spheres of power, institutional versus interactional, which, while they are frequently related, are potentially separable from one another; a person who is structurally subordinate in institutional terms may nevertheless dominate a structurally superordinate person in a given interaction by force of wit, rhetorical skill, or some other interactional means. This is, in fact, a common theme in folktales, as witness the large number of motifs in the Motif-Index of Folk Literature, sections J1250–J1499 Clever verbal retorts and J1500–J1649 Clever practical retorts, that turn on this dynamic. Riddles and related enigmatic forms serve well, we might say, as narrative resources for expressive deployment as "weapons of the weak" (Scott 1985; cf. Goldberg 1993:171; Wells 1950:162–163).[7] In our tale, then, Jack's transformation of the King's enigmatic questions serves as the means to a basic folktale end.

Now, because of the King's institutional power, he is in a position to load the scales to his own interactional advantage. First, and most obviously, he is the one who sets the terms of the contest: the miller must answer his questions or lose the mill. Second, the King claims an advantage by setting up the interactional contest in terms of questions and answers: interrogation vests significant control in the hands of the interrogator. The compulsive power of questions has been illuminated by the sociolinguistic explorations of Emanuel Schegloff and Harvey Sacks (1973), J. Sinclair and R. Coulthard (1975), Esther Goody (1978), and others. Questions and answers belong to a class of conversational utterance sequences that Schegloff and Sacks have labelled "adjacency pairs"; these consist of a pair of utterances, spoken by two different interlocutors in the conversation, the second utterance elicited by and following directly on the first. The speaking of the first pair part of an adjacency pair exerts a strong compulsive force on the addressee to produce the second pair part; when a question is asked, the expectation is that the next utterance will be a relevant answer. As summarized by Goody, "The most general thing we can say about a question is that it compels, requires, may even demand, a response" (1978:23). The King's questions are, in Goody's terms, strong "control" questions: expressing the presumption that the King's wish to have the information he elicits has the compulsive force of a requirement ("I want to know," "you must tell me," etc.), not mitigated by deference or politeness markers (as in "Excuse me, could you please tell me what time it is?"), backed by the King's institutional power, deeply consequential for the addressee, and so on. Finally, the King's questions are intended to be – and are framed in the story as – unanswerable. They are especially enigmatic questions which nevertheless demand an answer.

As if the King's advantage in the interactional contest were not enough, the situation is made still worse as the story proceeds. The miller, so overburdened by the difficulty in which the King has placed him, takes to his bed. When his daughter is finally able to draw out of him the reason for his distress, to whom does she turn but Silly Jack, "a kinda daft fella" in her father's employ. How can a silly, daft hired hand (or the humble youths in the other two texts) answer the terribly enigmatic questions on which the fate of the miller and his daughter rests? The story now hangs on whether – and how – Jack can render the King's unanswerable questions answerable. Note here that Jack's bargain with the miller's daughter gives him a special stake in answering the King's questions; the questions now function for him as a suitor test. How does Jack beat the King at his interactional game? What he does, by a variety of fascinating stratagems, is to reframe the King's questions, transforming them from unanswerable control questions to something else, from "impossible for to get" to "Oh, that's easy." Let us examine the transformations one by one. These elements of the tales remain remarkably consistent across all three tellings in our corpus. Accordingly, the transformational strategies that the two youths employ in Alec and John Stewart's versions are the same as those that Jack employs in the version recounted by Andrew.

For the first question, "What is the weight of the moon?," Jack's strategy is to transform it from an unanswerable control question into something more nearly akin to a riddle he can answer. He accomplishes this by resorting to one of the basic formative principles of riddles, namely, analogy (Maranda 1971), etymologically "equality of proportions" (from the Greek *ana*- "according to" + *logos* "proportion"). Thus, a ton (or a hundredweight in John's version) – a unit of weight and therefore an appropriate basis for analogy – is conventionally divided into "quarters," so that the word "quarter" can refer to a quarter of a ton. The moon too has quarters, in this instance a unit of time. By analogy, then, the moon weighs a ton. Rendered fully as a riddle, Jack's transformation would yield:

> Why does the moon weigh a ton?
> – Because it has four quarters.

In addition, Jack exploits a basic vulnerability of the King's question, namely, that the King does not know the answer himself, which deprives him of full interactional power. Jack's answer is unverifiable, so he is able to seize the interactional advantage by challenging the King to weigh it himself.

This latter strategy, exploiting the King's lack of knowledge of the "true" answer to his own question and challenging him to verify the answer Jack gives him, is used by itself to neutralize the power of the King's second question, "How many stars are in the sky?" Any large number will do as an answer, and the King is bested once again.

Jack's neutralization of the third question is the most interesting of all. Here too, as in question 1, Jack resorts to a riddling strategy, but at a deeper structural level. The enigma represented by the third question, "What I'm thinkin' on," rests on the fact that the King's private thoughts are unknowable to others – the King himself is the enigma. This time, however, the King does know the answer, or so he believes. Accordingly, the question should have full power. In order to neutralize this power, Jack transforms himself, makes himself into an enigma. More specifically, he makes himself into a kind of metaphor by predicating another sign image – the miller – upon himself and so formulating a deception, the manipulation of features of the situation in such a way as to induce the King to have a false or misleading sense of what is going on and so to behave to his own disadvantage (cf. Goffman 1974:89; Bauman 1986:36). The block element in the situation, as it were, is the metaphor "The miller is Jack." The narrator foreshadows Jack's answer between the first and second exchanges by telling us, "But he thought it was the old miller. He thought it was the miller, you see." Now, because Jack has manipulated the basis of the King's knowledge, his thoughts, he has the means of turning the tables. For at least one aspect of the King's thoughts, Jack has knowledge that the King does not, but thinks he does. He is able to tell the King what he is thinking, but even further, and more powerfully, he is able to falsify that knowledge, thus gaining a still greater measure of interactional power. In John Stewart's version, the impact of the young man's transformational ploy is enhanced still further by withholding it from the audience, unlike Andrew's and Alec's versions, revealing it only at the end, at the same moment that he removes his disguise before the King.

Thus, by the use of his wits and his interactional skills at reframing the interrogation, Jack wins the day. By reframing the interrogational routines, Jack renders the questions answerable, neutralizes and overcomes the King's advantage, and reverses the power relation of their interaction. And just as the King's perceptions are overturned, so too are our own, as Jack transforms himself from the daft Silly Jack, the miller's hired hand, to clever Jack, the miller's son-in-law ("goodson").

The transformation of the enigmatic forms in the course of the tale represents one significant element of the narrativization of these forms, the narrative, in fact, turning on the process of transformation and its outcome. This returns us, then, to the problem with which we began, that is, the interaction of the so-called "riddles" and the "story," in the constitution of the hybrid generic form in which they are blended together. One further point worth making in this regard is that the transformational process just mentioned is not the only means exploited in the text of narrativizing the enigmatic forms. A second device for creating sequence is the trebling of the interrogational routines. Threefold repetition, of course, in compliance with Olrik's Law of Three (1965 [1909]), represents yet another characteristic structural feature of the European folktale. In this text, the questions are not only trebled, but the sequence of three is rendered three times: once when the King first poses them to the miller, again when the miller reviews the questions after they have been posed, and yet again when the King returns after a year and a day and poses them to Jack, now disguised as the miller. In the other two versions, the sequence of three questions is also trebled: the first posing of the questions by the King or laird, the relating of the questions to the young substitute, and the climactic posing of the questions at the end, when they are answered. The replays, we may observe, may take a variety of forms, cast as reiterations, reports, questions, abbreviated reminders, and so on. And earlier in the chapter, in discussing the compulsive power of questions, I appealed to Schegloff and Sacks' notion of adjacency pairs, in which the utterance of the first pair part calls for a response. The speech acts that constitute adjacency pairs thus have a temporal, sequential order. Contrary to Dorst's (1983) contention, then, that riddles are atemporal, riddles and analogous interrogational routines like the ones in this story are inherently sequential. Accordingly, the question–response sequence lends itself to narrativization; the reporting of a question–response sequence can itself constitute a minimal narrative.

In this text, as in the other two, the crucial narrated events are built on this basic interactional structure. The first key event centers on the posing of the questions by the King. The completion of the adjacency pairs, however, is suspended, as the King gives the miller a year and a day to come up with the answers. The resultant lack of closure, in turn, provides the dynamic tension of the narrative. This tension can only be resolved by the provision of the second pair parts, the answers to the questions. When these are provided by Jack, narrative closure is achieved. But the narrator – in Jack's voice – goes still further, elaborating upon the sequentiality of riddling interactions by adding other optional elements to the account, namely, explication and elaboration of the answers and acceptance of them by the King. Jack explains the reasoning that has led him to his answers and challenges the King to refute them. The King cannot do so, and is thus constrained to acknowledge that Jack's answers are "right." The "riddles," then, have a formative – indeed, a constitutive – effect on the structure of the narrative, at the same time that they are contained by it, as reported speech.

One last point. In the climactic narrated event of the story, the first two question–answer sequences are rendered as reported speech. The speech acts that make up these sequences constitute the narrative action. In the third exchange, however, there is an important additional element. Here we have not only the speech acts of the King and Jack, represented as direct discourse in which the King poses his enigmatic question and Jack answers, but also the enactment or embodiment of the ultimate enigma: the miller is Jack. That is to say, the final interaction consists of two kinds of action, speaking and metaphorical enactment. Jack simultaneously speaks the answer and is the answer. Moreover, he goes on, as before, to explicate his answer by removing his disguise. Thus, the third enigmatic exchange is narrativized both mimetically, in the quoted speech, and diegetically, as the description of action.

Ultimately, then, the text reveals its hybrid generic makeup as the interpenetration and mutual adaptation of a transformational sequence of enigmatic interrogational forms, themselves formally and functionally related to riddles, and the narrative folktale. The structure of question and answer adjacency pairs and the riddle dynamic of enigma and transformation give form and texture to the narrative, while the narrative in turn encompasses the interrogational routines and folktale conventions contribute additional elements of structure (e.g., the opening formula, the Law of Three) and content (e.g., Silly Jack, the marriage of the unpromising hero) to the textual mix. The resultant text is a complex generic hybrid that blends riddle-like interrogational routines with the folktale in the construction of an emergent generic blend with its own structures of form, function, and meaning.

"The Opposite Way Aboot"

When we turn our attention to the second of Andrew Stewart's texts, we encounter again the playing out of the tension between institutional power and interactional power. In this version of the classic neck-riddle tale, the King exercises his royal power by setting Jack the task of posing a riddle that he and his knights cannot answer, with the implication that the task will be difficult. Accordingly, Jack is given the formulaic year and a day to accomplish it. In this text, the consequences of failure are not specified, but again the implication is that Jack will pay a penalty if he is unsuccessful; this is a generic convention of the folktale.

By contrast with the first text, then, as the narrator himself observes, the interactional roles of the riddling exchange are reversed: "So it was the opposite way aboot, like – the boy had to give the King the riddles." From a functional point of view, however, either role – riddler or riddlee – may serve as a basis for achieving interactional dominance. Riddling is contestive: if the riddlee cannot answer the riddle successfully, the poser wins, while if the riddlee does come up with the answer, he wins. Thus, when the King and his knights are stymied by Jack's riddle, he has bested them, overturning by his interactional skill the power that allowed the King to set him the riddling task at the outset. In terms of narrative structure, the disequilibrium established by the difficult task is resolved by Jack's successful posing of a riddle that the King cannot solve.

The factor that makes Jack's riddle insoluble is that, like the King's third enigmatic question in the first text ("Can you tell me what I'm thinkin' on?"), it is based on private experience. Jack formulates his riddle on the basis of his own unusual actions, inaccessible to the King and his retainers. Again, as before, Jack's success turns on his ability to create a disjunction between appearance and reality by means of concealment. As he prevails by means of disguise in the first text, he succeeds in the second text – at least in part – by concealment, hiding the dirt under his hat and the oak leaves in his shoes. Extending the comparison still further, we may observe that both routines turn on Jack's transformation of himself into the embodiment of the enigma. By disguising himself as the miller in text 1 and by concealing the dirt and leaves on his person in text 2, Jack turns the verbal interrogational routines into narrative action. The enigma is both spoken and enacted.

When we examine the workings of the riddle in formal terms, several interesting factors come to light. First, note that this riddle takes the form of a rhyme, a valued feature of riddles in the northeast of Scotland; the first and third lines display half rhyme, while the second and fourth lines exhibit full rhyme. Thus, while the enigmatic questions of the first text can be invaded by the surrounding narrative discourse, as witness the indirect discourse in which the King's second question is rendered ("How many stars was in the sky?"), the form of this riddle makes it impenetrable. As read out by the King's men, it is quoted speech, retaining the first person singular "I" of the personified riddle referent. This mode of personification is a common riddle device (see, for example, Taylor 1951, nos. 35, 38, 89, 92, 97, 100, etc.), so at the point when Jack's riddle is posed, it is not necessarily clear that the first-person voice of the riddle is his own. The revelation that Jack embodies and enacts the riddle only occurs with the ensuing explications.

In this text, as in the first one, the dialogic structure of the riddle, consisting of a question–answer adjacency pair, again shapes the structure of the narrative, though in a different way than before. In the earlier tale, the King's questions establish the central disequilbrium, resolved when Jack supplies the answers after the year and a day have elapsed. Here, though, the disequilibrium is produced by the King's setting of the riddling task; resolution is thus achieved when Jack produces the riddle and it does prove unanswerable. To stop here, however, would still make for a lack of closure. It is a convention of riddling that if the riddlee cannot guess the answer, the poser will provide it, as Jack does in the tale (Burns 1976); moreover, the narrative audience will want to know the answer as well. Accordingly, the end of the tale is shaped by the structure of riddling events. And, as before, the structure includes an explication of the riddle.

Closer examination of the narrativization of the riddle, however, reveals additional degrees of complexity. Note, to begin with, that the first explication of the riddle is directed at the storytelling audience, outside the narrated event ("And what the thing was . . ."). When the riddle is posed in the story, both the King and his retainers in the narrated event and the audience in the narrative event share the same information state: ignorance of the answer. This first explication establishes a differential; now the audience knows more than the King and his knights. Specifically, the hearers of the tale learn how Jack has enabled the riddle by his private actions: "and that was what the riddle was and they couldnae guess it." In many neck-riddle tales, this enabling action is part of the plot, preceding and leading up to the making of the riddle and its presentation to the riddlee. In this text, however, the basis of the riddle is given after the riddle is posed, which represents a temporal displacement. Note too that this first explication, for the audience, follows the chronology of Jack's enabling actions, not the sequence of descriptive elements in the riddle. More on this shortly.

Having explicated the enigma for the audience by recounting how Jack set up his riddle at an earlier point in narrative time, the narrator provides a second explication, this one for the King and his retainers within the narrated event, by having Jack repeat each descriptive element in the riddle, in sequence, revealing the referent of each as he proceeds, the first and second by physical demonstration, the third by verbal explanation, and the fourth in an unspecified way. Significantly, in the riddle text itself, the four descriptive elements are presented additively, without temporal juncture; the riddle is not in itself a narrative. In recounting the explication of the riddle to the King and his knights, though, the riddle is narrativized, Jack's presentation of the descriptive elements and the accompanying explanatory actions following one upon the other. Here, then, the structure of the compound riddle question determines the structure of the ensuing narrative: first descriptive element followed by answer/explication, followed by second descriptive element plus answer/explication, and so on. It is worth noting that the function of the riddle in accomplishing a status inversion between Jack and the King resonates nicely with the inversions that make up the constituent enigmas of the riddle, namely, reversing the spatial relations of the earth and leaves in relation to human space and inverting birth and death.

In summary, then, the riddle is narrativized in three ways. First, it is simply presented as a riddle, inset into the narrative action as quoted speech, preserving its full formal integrity. Second, it is explicated for the audience by recounting the actions by which Jack has laid the groundwork for the riddle in the order in which those actions were carried out, a sequence different from the way in which the respective descriptive elements based upon those actions are presented in the riddle. Finally, after the King and his retainers fail to guess the answer, Jack disassembles the riddle descriptive element by descriptive element, following each line of the riddle with its referent-cum-explication as he embodies the enigma. The interactional structure of the riddle encounter spans that portion of the tale from the posing of the riddle to the unsuccessful attempt of the King and his knights to guess the answer to Jack's revelation and explication of the answer to the royal entourage.

Stories About Riddles

Now that we have examined closely the ways in which riddles and other enigmatic questioning routines are integrated with folktales in our two texts, we may ask what this analysis might suggest in more general terms about the resultant blending. Stated in other terms, what might be the grounds for suggesting that riddle tales constitute a secondary genre in Bakhtin's terms? Two texts from a single narrator, supplemented by two more from his brothers, cannot constitute a basis for the comprehensive designation of generic conventions, but they can help us to identify in a preliminary way some of the lines along which further analytic and comparative work might fruitfully be pursued.

To begin with, our two texts suggest some of the motivations for the blending of folktales with riddles and other enigmatic interrogative routines. The first salient point, bearing on what enigmatic routines might offer to storytellers as an expressive resource, is that such routines highlight, intensify, and formalize interactional skill and the cleverness that underlies it. As we have noted, both the ability to come up with an unanswerable enigma and the ability to solve an apparently unanswerable enigma represent displays of interactional skill and are thus exercises of interactional power. Given the thematic prominence in the Märchen and novella of status reversal, the triumph of the lowly hero and his or her accession to high status in the face of resistance by those of higher power and status, riddles and related forms offer themselves as mechanisms for the accomplishment of the transformation. On the one hand, they offer a contrast to institutionally grounded power, the counterposition of institutional and interactional power providing the tension that drives the tale. In addition, however, riddles and related enigmatic forms rest centrally on transformative tropes, such as metaphor, metonymy, personification, inversion, punning, and the like. This is the strongest warrant for Kernan, Brooks, and Holquist's provocative suggestion that "A riddle is a plot the end of which must be guessed" (1973:319). These devices disguise or conceal the referents of the routines, the answers that must be provided, obscuring the relationship between appearance and reality. In like manner, the Märchen and novella also characteristically turn on disjunctions between appearance and reality, especially in regard to dramatis personae who are not what they seem to be, of whom the unpromising hero or heroine is only one manifestation. Still further, the enigmatic routines may themselves be functionally transformed in the course of the narrative, as in the first text, where Jack treats the King's questions as more riddle-like than they were intended, in order to answer them successfully. Thus, the enigmatic routines provide an effective symbolic correlative to basic thematic business in the folktales, as transformational forms in the service of a transformation of status and as forms that problematize the relationship between appearance and reality in the service of other generic forms that do likewise. And all of these functions are merged, of course, when the hero or heroine is made to embody the enigma that brings the contest of interactional power to a climax, as occurs in both of Andrew Stewart's narratives and in his brothers' texts as well. At these points, the enigmatic routines and the folktale are fully integrated.

Given the functional compatibility of the riddle and the folktale, in terms of the ways in which riddles lend themselves to the fulfillment of significant thematic and plot conventions of the Märchen and novella, how is the blending of the genres accomplished in formal terms? The two narratives we have examined evince a range of possibilities for the narrativization of the riddle.

At the most basic level, the dialogic question–answer structure that constitutes the core of the riddle is inherently sequential and thus lends itself naturally to narrative. A simple recounting of the question and answer riddle exchange constitutes a minimal narrative in its own right. The core structure, of course, may be elaborated upon by recounting additional constituent acts of the riddling encounter, such as unsuccessful guesses followed by provision and explication of the answer by the poser of the enigma, and so on, as exemplified in both texts we have examined. Still further, the interactional sequence of the riddling encounter may receive additional narrative extension by repetition, through the multiplication of the number of riddling exchanges recounted, typically by threes as in our first text. In a related manner, when the riddle consists of multiple descriptive elements, as in the second text, the presentation and explication of the referents lends itself to narrative sequencing as well. It should be noted here that the recounting of the riddling interaction is subject to further transformation, for example, by spreading the full sequence out across successive narrated events, as in our first tale, where the first posing of the enigmas and the provision and explication of the answers are separated by a year and a day, but the interactional structure of the riddling exchange remains a structuring element in the construction of the overall narrative.

At another level, the enigma may be narrativized – and the folktale riddlized – by basing the riddle or other enigmatic form on some enabling narrative action. There are several possibilities here. In the first text, for example, Jack's disguising of himself as the miller transforms him into the embodied solution to the King's third enigmatic question. In the second text, the process is more complex. Here, Jack's actions in killing his father's mare, removing her unborn foal, making a whip of her hide, and concealing dirt in his hat and oak leaves in his shoes constitute the basis of his compound riddle.

A final dimension of the generic blending of enigmatic routines and folktales may be approached by examining how the resultant forms operate in overall functional terms. At various points in the chapter, I have laid out a range of grounds for considering our two textual examples essentially as folktales that encompass enigmatic interrogational routines. There are three points, however, at which the storytelling gives way momentarily to what we might call a breakthrough into riddling. One such breakthrough is manifested in the second text by the explication of the riddle to the storytelling audience in terms of the actions by which Jack has set up the four parts of the riddle. From a functional perspective, this explication is what would occur in a riddling event at just this point: after the riddle has been posed and the riddlee(s) have been unable to answer it. Here, the posing of the riddle and the failure to answer are reported as part of the narrated event. But Stewart's audience has also heard the riddle and – we may well assume – tried unsuccessfully to puzzle it out. They too, like the King and his retainers, will want to know the answer. What Stewart does, then, in his explication, is to give priority to his audience's curiosity, transforming the narrative event momentarily into a riddling event before returning his discourse to the narrated event. Then, at the very end of both texts, Stewart offers his own evaluation of Jack's riddling prowess ("And it was very clever, wasn't it?" and "It's very good, isn't it?"), which again reframes the situation as a riddling event. That is to say, Stewart's performance is generically hybrid at the most general functional level – basically storytelling, but with breakthroughs into riddling.

Thus, we return again to the initial enigmatic question with which we began: what is the riddle tale in generic terms? Close examination of our sample texts has given us at least parts of the answer: sometimes folktale, sometimes riddle, largely a complex fusion of the two. For a Traveler audience, such a functional as well as formal blending of story and riddle is especially captivating. The importance – and virtuoso cultivation – of storytelling among the Travelers has been widely documented, and Braid has argued convincingly that storytelling plays a critical role in the formation and negotiation of identity among Traveling people in a larger society that has historically been hostile to their way of life. A common theme of Traveler narratives is the power of quick wit and a clever tongue in gaining advantage or turning the tables in situations of adversity, threat, or, perhaps, opportunity. A resonant passage in a story told by Duncan Williamson, a master storyteller, about a quick-witted servant threatened with punishment by a laird he has publicly embarrassed, sums up the theme with pungent directness:

> And the laird came and he shook hands with the cook.
> And he said, "You know, my man," he said,
> "your wit has saved you," he said.
> (Braid 2002:19)

In a more scholarly vein, Sheila Douglas observes that "Travellers, of course, like Jack," the apparently unprepossessing hero of many of their tales, including Andrew Stewart's "The King and the Miller," "because, like him, they have been looked on as feckless, but because they are 'traveller-brained' they are really jumps ahead of the 'country hantle' – their name for the settled population – when it comes to surviving" (Douglas 1987:9).

At the same time, Travelers have traditionally cultivated an active riddling tradition (Goldstein 1963; MacColl and Seeger 1986:136–140), involving displays of verbal wit in posing, interpretive wit in answering, within an overall framework of contest and competition. Riddling foregrounds and routinizes the exercise of wit that Travelers value as an adaptive quality in their own encounters with the dominant society and exploit as an expressive resource in their stories. Both riddling and storytelling are potent means of engaging the participative involvement of an audience. Andrew Stewart's hybrid, shape-shifting performances, then, are especially felicitous in combining the representational poetics of narrative with the presentational and interactional dynamics of riddling in the affecting affirmation of the saving power of wit and words.

Appendix[8]

The King and the Miller, told by John Stewart
Once upon a time there was an old miller and he had a lovely daughter, one of the nicest, fairest girls in the land. Now he used to go up round the dam for a walk every summer's evening. He made it his point just to see everything was right, round about the dam and the mill. So this afternoon he was up round the dam, walkin wi his hands at his back and his auld white baird blawin in the wind, when down comes the king.

"Good evening," says the king.

"Good evening," says the miller.

"Well," says the king, "I'm doon here, miller, tae see ye aboot something."

"What's that?" says the miller.

"They tell me," says the king, "ye've a lovely fair daughter. I've seen her once or twice an I've fallen in love wi her an mean tae marry her. I'm gonnae gie ye three questions tae answer, an I'll gie ye a year an a day tae find the answers fir them. If you don't anwer the questions, I'm marrying your daughter."

"Well," says the miller, "what's the questions ye want tae ask me?"

"Well," he says, "I'll meet ye here in a year an a day an ye've tae tell me three things: the weight of the moon, plus how many stars are in the sky and at the time I'm speakin tae ye, what I'm thinking, at that present moment. Good day tae ye miller."

So the king turns and gallops away. The old miller comes round the dam and danners doon intae the house. He was very sick-lookin when he cam in an his daughter's at him, "Tell me father what's wrong wi ye, tell me this?" But no, he would tell her nothing an he says, there was nothing at all wrong. Now this young girl, the miller's daughter, was courting another miller's son from several miles away an now, when the boy comes across at the weekend, he saw an awfu difference in the auld miller. He says tae the lassie, "What's wrong wi your father?"

"I don't know," she says. "He'll no tell me."

But about a month or so afore the year an the day were up, the fellow says tae the lassie, "We'll hae to get him tae tell us what's wrong wi him. The mill's goin all right. He's getting plenty o corn an wheat tae grind an the market's no bad. It canny be money that's wrong. If I thought it was money, we'd help him oot, oorsels."

"It's no that," she says. "It's something that's on his mind an he'll no tell us."

That night at supper, the two o them gets at him an argues an argues an argues till the auld man tells them aboot the king comin doon an that if he didnae answer the three questions, he was gonnae marry the daughter. Right, wrong or any other way, he was goin tae marry her.

"What's the questions, miller?" asks the young fellow.

He says, "I've tae tell the weight o the moon – an impossibility – an I've tae tell him how many stars are in the sky – another impossibility – and at that minute, I've tae tell him what he's thinkin!"

The young man lookit at him. "They're hard enough questions," he says, "but I wouldnae bother aboot them, if I wis you. Just leave it tae me."

So time goes by, weeks go in an days go in, and at the finish up, the auld miller's wanderin roon the mill dam, wi his hands behin his back an his auld white baird blawin in the wind, when the king arrives doon on his charger.

"Good evening, miller," he says. "I suppose ye know what I'm here for."

"Och," he says, "I hardly thought aboot it. It was some questions, was it not?"

"Aye," he says. "Have ye got the answers?"

"I canny mind," he says. "What was your first question?"

"Ye had tae tell me," he says, "the weight o the moon."

"Well, that's quite easy, your majesty," he says. "There's four quarters in the moon an four quarters make a hundredweight. The weight o your moon's a hundredweight. If ye don't believe me, weigh it for yourself."

The kind scratchit his heid. "The next one will get ye," he says. "How many stars are in the sky?"

"Well," says the miller, "the last time I countit them, there was fifty-six billion, ten hundred thousand million, four hundred an sixty-seven thousand an four. If ye don't believe me, start an count them yourself."

"Very good," says the king. "Very good. But now ye're tae tell me, what I'm thinking."

"Well," he says, "you think you're speakin tae the auld miller. But ye'll fin oot, it's his guid-son." An he pulled the false beard an moustache off. "I married his daughter yesterday!"

(Douglas 1987:83–84)

The Miller and His Daughter, told by Alec Stewart

Once upon a time there was a miller and his dochter and they stayed on the banks o' the Ayr. They had a mill and they took corn in and they made it into meal. One day the miller was walkin' up the banks o' the river Ayr and just aboot a field-breadth fae his hoose was the hoose that the laird used tae bide in.

Well, on this day, the laird come walkin' doon the river and he met the auld miller. "Ah, miller," he says, "I see you're takin' your walk."

"Oh yes," the miller says, "I'm takin' my walk."

"And where is your dochter the day?"

"Oh she's warkin' i' the mill."

And the laird says, "Is she no' thinkin' aboot gettin' married yet?"

"Oh no, not yet," he says, "She's all I've got, and I've naebody tae look after the mill but her."

"She's a very bonnie lassie," the laird says. "I wadnae mind tae marry her mysel'."

"Oh, I dinnae ken her mind," the miller says. Well, he knew that the lassie was carryin' on wi' a shepherd that bade awa' in a hoose on the side o' the hill.

So time rolled on and he met the laird again, and the laird says, "I think I'll tak' that dochter o' yours for a wife."

"Na na," says the miller, "ye cannae dae that because she's carryin' on wi' the shepherd."

"Well," says the laird, "I dinnae ken but if you willnae gie me your dochter, I'll hae tae put ye oot o' your hoose."

"Oh," the miller says, "is that so?"

"I'll tell ye whit I'll do," the laird says. "I'll gie ye three guesses and if ye cannae answer the three guesses ye'll get oot and I'll tak' your dochter. But if he *can* answer the three guesses ye can stay on in the mill without rent, and ye can keep your dochter."

"What is the three guesses?" said the miller.

"Well," the laird says, "the first thing ye've tae tell me is the weight o' the moon. And the second thing is ye must tell me, hoo many stars is in the heavens. And the next one ye must tell me what I'm thinkin' on."

"My, my, my," the miller says, "they's terrible three hard ones ye've given me."

"Well," the laird says, "ye maun find the answers. If ye cannae guess them I'll tak' the mill fae ye and your dochter as well."

So the auld miller he's awa' hame noo, thinkin' aboot these three guesses. A' his wark was fa'in behind – the corn was lyin' there and he couldn't hardly do onything. His dochter asked him three-four times whit was wrang wi' him, but the auld miller said, "Och, I cannae tell ye. Ye couldnae help my onyway," he says.

Well, one day, she's awa' up tae the shepherd – that's the laddie she was carryin' on wi' – and she says tae him, "There's something wrang wi' my faither. He's fa'in back wi' his wark."

"What can be wrang wi' him?" he said.

"I don't know," she says, "I don't know what's wrang wi' him."

So he says, "I'll come doon when I get my tea and I'll hae a talk wi' him." So the dochter gaed awa' back and she's sittin' waitin' on the shepherd. When he comes in, he lookit a' roond aboot the mill and he seen a' the corn lyin' and he says, "Whit's wrang wi' ye, miller? Look at a' this corn lyin' here."

"I dinnae ken whit's wrang wi' me," the miller says. "I met the laird up the river and he gied me three things tae dae and I dinnae ken hoo tae get owre it."

"Whit things?"

"Well," he said, "the laird wants Annie for to be his wife."

"Oh," the shepherd says, "he cannae dae that."

"He's gien me three guesses," says the miller, "and I cannae answer them he says he's gau tae put me oot o' the mill and tak' Annie awa'."

The shepherd thocht a while and says, "Tell me the three guesses."

"Och," he says, "there's nae use me tellin' ye, for ye wad never ken them."

"Let me hear them onyway," the shepherd says. So the miller told him aboot the weight o' the moon, hoo many stars was in the heavens and what he was thinkin' of. "Och," the shepherd laddie says, "never mind. Never mind him at a'. Just get on wi' the wark," he says. "When hae ye tae meet the lairdie?"

"On Sunday night," the miller says, "when it's getting' gloamin' dark."

"Well, come on and I'll help ye tae get this corn done." So the shepherd gied him a help and he got the corn grinded and he made the meal. Time rolled by till it come tae Sunday. The shepherd come doon tae the miller's hoose aboot an hour before he had tae meet the laird. "Miller," says the shepherd, "gie me a suit o' your auld claes and I'll gang as you."

The miller says, "Whit d'ye mean?"

"Well," says the shepherd, "I'll go in your place if ye gie me your claes." So he got the miller's auld claes on and he's march up this riverside wi' his hands behind his back. And he met the laird, wha was just comin' doon.

"Ah," says the laird. "Ye didnae forget, miller."

"Forget what?" he says.

"Ye didnae forget tae meet me the nicht and tae answer the three guesses."

"No," he says, "I didnae forget, but I've no' thocht much aboot them," he says. "What was the three guesses again?"

"Well," the laird says, "the first one ye must tell me the weight o' the moon."

"Oh that's easy told," he says. "The weight o' the moon's a ton-weight. There's four quarters in the moon and there's four quarters in a ton."

"That's so," the laird says, "but the next one'll catch ye. Ye cannae tell me hoo many stars is in the heavens."

"Och," he says, "that's easier done. There are twenty-four million, five-hundred-and-fifty-thousand. Ye can coont them yoursel' if ye dinnae believe me."

"My goodness!" says the laird, "ye catched me there. But you'll no' ken the next one."

"And what is that?" he says.

The laird says, "Ye'll nae ken what I'm thinkin' o'."

"Oh ay," he says. "Ye think ye're speakin' tae the auld miller, but you're speakin' tae the shepherd." So the miller got the mill, the dochter married the shepherd, and they're livin' there still. The last time I was past the hoose I got a cup o' tea and some breid, and that's the end o' my story. (MacColl and Seeger 1986:114–117)

4

"What Shall We Give You?": Calibrations of Genre in a Mexican Market

Then the tumult of the thousand different cries of the eager dealers, all shouting at the top of their voices, at one and the same time, is almost bewildering.
Mayhew (1985 [1851–2]:13)

The Language of Selling in a Mexican Market: The Generic Baseline

Open-air markets are display events par excellence in Roger Abrahams' (1981) sense of the term, "public occasions . . . in which actions and objects are invested with meaning and values are put 'on display.'" In common with festivals, fairs, and spectacles – other display events to which they may be attached – markets are characterized by qualities of scale, heterogeneity, semiotic proliferation, abundance, and effervescence that make for a special intensification and enhancement of experience and social value. Small wonder, then, that markets have exercised an enduring attraction to literary artists from Villon and Rabelais to Mayhew, Thackeray, and Proust, and to graphic artists as well, such as Marcellus Laroon, who included the verbal elements of market language in his enormously popular engravings of the Criers and Hawkers of London (Shesgreen 1990). The literary and other artistic attractions of market language point up the expressive availability of language for the intensification of experience and the enhancement of value in market settings, not only on the part of market vendors, but of other verbal performers as well, such as the religious preachers and political orators who are drawn to markets to work the crowds.

In the marketplace, the verbal creation and enhancement of value is in the service of value of a particular kind, namely, commodity value. There is a small but growing and suggestive literature on such form–function interrelationships in the language of markets and related venues, from Mitchell's pioneering article on the language of buying and selling in Cyrenaica (1957) and Bakhtin's stimulating chapter on the language of the marketplace in Rabelais (1984 [1965]), to the more recent work of Dargan and Zeitlin on American commercial talkers (1983), my own writings on the discourse of dog-traders (1986), Kuiper on auctioneers (1992; Kuiper and Haggo 1984), Lindenfeld on the performances of French market vendors (1978, 1990), Kapchan on language, genre, and gender in Moroccan markets (1993, 1995), and – especially relevant in the present context – Flores Farfán's study of social interaction and power in Otomi markets in Mexico (1984). This chapter is intended as a contribution to that line of inquiry. It is based upon a small field project I carried out in San Miguel de Allende, in the state of Guanajuato, Mexico. On occasional Tuesday mornings, I wandered through the weekly market in San Miguel with a tape recorder running, yielding a small corpus of market-soundscape recordings from which I have drawn the materials I will discuss in this chapter.[1] In addition to the market tapes, I gathered further data in the form of observational fieldnotes, interviews with vendors and shoppers, and reflexive monitoring of my own participation in the market as a regular shopper.

Sound is one of the semiotic resources that is intensified and elaborated in the construction of the market ambience of abundance. The boomboxes of cassette vendors blare out ranchera and rock, an aged man plays thin music by blowing on a piece of cellophane to coax coins from passersby, the hammer blows of carpenters selling furniture punctuate the air. And a prominent feature of this market soundscape is the cacaphony of calls and spiels of market vendors crying their wares. I borrow the terms "call" and "spiel" from Lindenfeld (1990). The local term for call in San Miguel is *grito*; older people also use the term *pregon*. These are relatively brief, formulaic, formally economical and condensed utterances designed to attract the attention of potential customers, inform them about the commodities for sale, and induce them to buy. Spiels perform some of the same general functions and employ some of the same formal elements and devices, but are longer, continuous rather than bounded, less stereotyped, and marked by more elaborate devices and structures of argumentation. While local people recognize the distinctiveness of spiels, there does not seem to be a commonly preferred name for this genre; the terms I was offered include *propaganda comercial, plática comercial,* or simply *comercial,* the latter by extension from radio and TV commercials.

I should make clear here at the outset that the verbal genres I will examine in this chapter constitute but one part of the overall repertoire of verbal forms employed in buying and selling in the marketplace. Functionally, they are preliminaries to the more dialogic interaction of vendors and customers in the actual conduct of the sale. The calls and spiels are intended to draw customers in to the point of negotiating the sale itself.

Calls

The elementary forms of independent, free-standing calls feature either of two essential kinds of information, the identity of the commodity or the price, as in examples 1–4.[2]

1	Jícamas,	Jícamas,
	jícamas.	jícamas.
2	Nieve, nieve.	Ice, ice.
	Nieve, nieve.	Ice, ice.
3	Cien pesos,	One hundred pesos,
	cien pesos.	one hundred pesos.
4	A veinte	At twenty,
	a veinte	at twenty.

Example 1 is an irreducible minimal form, for in calls that include only the name of the commodity for sale it is repeated at least twice. Example 2 doubles that, yielding two lines of two nominal repetitions each. Minimal calls of price only also require repetition, as in 3 and 4.

Note the extreme economy of these elementary forms. The goods are announced by a single noun (*jícama, nieve*; or, in more complex forms to be discussed later, article plus noun), and the prices by two-word combinations consisting either of a quantifier plus a unit of currency (e.g., *cien pesos*) or by a preposition plus a quantifier (e.g., *a veinte*). This expressive economy is characteristic of calls generally. The functional constituents of the calls – commodity, price, or the others to be identified in a moment – are all characteristically condensed, generally realized by one or two words and lean syntactic structures.

It is worth noting, however, that there is a significant non-verbal dimension to the vending of the commodities that adds a further semiotic component to the process, namely, the common resort to ostension, holding up or pointing to an example of the commodity being offered for sale. Thus, it should be borne in mind throughout that even the most condensed calls are part of a multi-semiotic and multisensory process that combines verbal and visual appeal. I will come back again a bit later to the sensory dimension of market talk.

Returning, though, to the identification of verbal constituents, we may observe that both item and price may be elaborated, the former by proliferation of commodities for sale and/or syntactic extension in the form of declaratives, as in example 5, and price by multiple pricing of different objects, as in example 9, or again by syntactic extension as in example 6.

5   Hay aguacates,   There are avocados,
    hay las limas, aguacates,   there are limes, avocados,
    hay aguacates.   there are avocados.

6   A doscientos,   At two hundred,
    valen a doscientos.   they cost two hundred.

Again, the declaratives of 5 and 6 are condensed, syntactically lean: "There are avocados" or "they cost 200." Nevertheless, already in these elementary forms, the calls are marked by a degree of formal elaboration that draws the poetic function toward the foreground by means of such devices as repetition, phonological and grammatical parallelism, and prosodic patterning of pause and intonation. Such devices likewise serve as means for further expansion beyond the minimal forms, making for more complex poetic patterning, though still featuring a single factor, as in example 7.

7   A ciento cincuenta, a ciento cincuenta,
    a ciento cincuenta y a ciento cincuenta le valen 'ora.
    A ciento cincuenta, a ciento cincuenta, a ciento cincuenta,
    a ciento cincuenta, a ciento cincuenta.

    At one hundred fifty, at one hundred fifty,
    at one hundred fifty and at one hundred fifty they cost now.
    At one hundred fifty, at one hundred fifty, at one hundred fifty,
    at one hundred fifty, at one hundred fifty.

Here we have a parallelistic structure of

aa
a + ab
aaa
aa

The highly condensed formulaic language and poetic structuring that characterize even the simplest calls has at least three functional effects. For one thing, it enhances fluency, allowing for the rapid production and extension of calls. As the preceding example shows, it is a simple matter to extend a call building on a preposition plus a quantifier into a more extended, multi-line compound by the use of relatively elementary parallel structures. Second, it endows the calls with a high degree of cohesion, an insistent tightness of textual organization. The lines are tied closely to each other in a web of formal and semantic interdependencies. In addition, as with the exploitation of the poetic function generally, its mobilization here sets up patterns of formal anticipation and fulfillment that elicit the participatory involvement of the passers-by, catching them up in the formal regimentation of the call (Burke 1968 [1931]:124).

Beyond the elementary forms, a range of other extensions is possible. For example, the two basic constituents, commodity and price, may be combined, as in example 8.

8   A cien la canela,   Cinnamon at one hundred,
     a cien.   at one hundred.

Now, in addition to the two free constituents of commodity and price, there are a number of "bound" ones that figure as part of the basic discursive and functional vocabulary of the calls. The inventory of bound elements includes: quality of the commodity, unit quantity in relation to price, directives, declaratives (introduced already in examples 5 and 6), questions, and terms of address. By "bound," I mean to indicate that they are not used by themselves to constitute fully free-standing calls, but occur only in combination with other constituents.

There are two ways that these constituents may be bound to others. Some can appear as complete turns in situations where more than one person is calling the same goods, but are always accompanied by other call-turns to which they are tied in these collaborations. Others lack even this degree of semi-independence, appearing only in combination with other constituents within free-standing calls or calls that constitute turns. The following examples, numbers 9–12, illustrate combinatory possibilities in free-standing calls.

9   A trescientos, doscientos, y cien, mire.
     A trescientos, doscientos, y cien los globos, mire.
     A trescientos, doscientos, y cien los globos, mire.

     At three hundred, two hundred, and one hundred, look.
     At three hundred, two hundred, and one hundred the balloons, look.
     At three hundred, two hundred, and one hundred the balloons, look.

10   Piña fresca,   Fresh pineapple,
     piña fresca,   fresh pineapple,
     platano maduro.   ripe banana.

11   Hay limas,   There are limes,
     lleve limas.   carry away limes.

12   A cien las bolsas,   At one hundred the bags,
     de a cien,   at one hundred,
     ciento cincuenta, Señó, one hundred fifty, Ms.,[3]
     ciento cincuenta.   one hundred fifty.

Example 9 introduces one of the most common directives, *mire* 'look'; I will have more to say on this in a moment. Number 10 introduces qualities of the commodities, the adjectives *fresca* 'fresh' and *maduro* 'ripe.' And example 11 features the declarative *Hay limas* 'There are limes' in combination with the directive *Lleve limas* 'Take away limes.' Finally, number 12 includes a term of address, *seño*, to a potential customer and a statement of unit quantity, *la bolsa* 'the bag' or 'per bag' (two sizes of bag are offered). Note the use of the vocative term *Señó* for *Señora* here and of *bara* for *barato* 'cheap' in example 14 (lines 2 and 12), which condense the language of the calls still further.

The next example, number 13, is a collaborative co-performance between two men selling sewing materials.

13   Vendor 1:
     Hilos, agujas, cierres.   Threads, needles, snaps.

     Vendor 2:
     Escójale, oiga.   Choose, hear.
     Hilos, aceite para máquina,   Threads, sewing machine oil,
        cintas métricas.   metric measuring tape.
     Escójale, oiga.   Choose, hear.

Vendor 1:
Acérquese, conózcalo, mire.   Come close, check it out, look.

Here, the first vendor cries out some of the principal commodities for sale: thread, needles, snaps. His partner continues the catalogue, tying his call to his partner's in terms of the first commodity, thread, but extending it to sewing machine oil and metric measuring tape and framing the catalogue with one-word directives. One type of directive, here represented by *oiga* 'hear,' works to engage the sensory involvement of potential customers. The other directive in turn 2, *escójale* 'choose,' elicits the participatory engagement of customers by inviting them to make a selection of the products in a way that suggests that the goods may become theirs. Then the first vendor comes back in the following turn with a set of additional one-word directives, 'come close, check it out, look,' that extend the compulsive force of the calls. *Mire* 'look' is a companion directive to *oiga*, adding another dimension of sensory engagement. While *oiga* demands auditory engagement with the vendor's call, *mire* elicits visual engagement with the goods. *Mire* makes explicit what the ostensive display of commodities, mentioned earlier, leaves implicit: a demand for the gaze of the potential customer.

Example 14, an extract from a pitch for medicinal powder that "cleans the stomach and washes the intestines," extends the sensory reach by soliciting olfactory engagement with the product:

14   Tenga el papel,   Take the paper,
      andele, mire,   go ahead, look,
      huele a menta,   smells like mint,
      huele a anís.   smells like anise.
      Señora, señora,   Ma'am, ma'am,
      ponga el papel,   apply the paper,
      venga, güerita,   come, blondie,
      ándele, huélele,   go ahead, smell,
      y verá que bonito huele.   and you will see how good it smells.
      Huélela.   Smell it.
      A menta, a anís,   Like mint, like anise,
      no amarga y no sabe feo.   it's not bitter and doesn't taste bad.

And to look ahead for a moment, *agárrele* 'take hold' in lines 1, 13, and 18 of the next example adds tactile engagement to the range of sensory modalities activated by the vendor. Finally, returning to the last turn of example 13, *acérquese* and *conózcalo* amplify *escójale* in drawing potential buyers into engaging with the commodities for sale, spatially and cognitively.

Turns such as this last one, consisting only of directives, occur only in conjunction with other turns.

The following example, number 15, is a stretch of call-collaboration among three vendors selling used clothing, to illustrate further how constituents may be bound up into turns that are tied to other turns.

15   Vendor 1:

1	Agárrele, agárrele,	Take hold, take hold,
2	bara, bara, mire.	cheap, cheap, look.
3	Le doy barato, escójale,	I give it to you cheap, choose,
4	escójale si hay.	choose if it's here.
5	Sueter barato,	Cheap sweater,
6	pantalon barato,	cheap pants,
7	escójale.	choose.

Vendor 2:

8	Escójale, escójale,	Choose, choose,
9	todo barato, mire.	everything cheap, look.
10	De regalo y de remate, escójale.	Giving it away and finishing it up, choose.
11	Ándele, escójale,	Go on, choose,
12	todo es bara, bara, mire.	everything is cheap, cheap, look.

Vendor 3:

13	Agárrele, agárrele,	Take hold, take hold,
14	baratos, andele.	cheap, go on.
15	Qué le damos?	What shall we give you?
16	Qué le damos, oiga?	What shall we give you, hear?
17	(wd.?) por estos pantalones.	(?) for these pants.
18	Ándele, agárrele, barato.	Go on, take hold, cheap.
19	Barato, ándele.	Cheap, go on.

Here, I want to call attention especially to lines 3, 15, and 16, which add the dimension of explicit social engagement with the vendors to the directives like *escójale, agárrele, conózcalo* that elicit engagement with the commodities being offered or the insistent *ándele* 'go on' in lines 11, 14, and 19 that urge the customer to action. *Le doy barato* 'I give it to you cheap' in line 3 sets up a relationship of giving and getting, of exchange, that is at the heart of the commercial transaction. *Qué le damos?* 'What shall we give you?' in lines 15 and 16 builds upon the same dynamic of exchange, adding the compulsive power of the question, which has the pragmatic conversational force of demanding – if only tacitly – an answer. Terms of address, for their part, are phatic gestures toward potential customers, also drawing them into interaction.

Thus, we find built into these very highly condensed, stereotyped, and formulaic utterances an impressive range of functional capacities. The constituents or building blocks allow for the economical identification of the commodities, specification of their salient qualities and unit price, and elicitation of the participatory involvement of potential customers in terms of visual, auditory, olfactory, tactile, spatial, cognitive, and behavioral engagement with the goods and social engagement with the vendors in a relationship of exchange. The latter devices – directives and declaratives or questions concerning exchange – have a special rhetorical power in establishing in the potential customer's mind a virtual identification with the commodities and vendors that is a crucial prerequisite for accomplishing the sale that will make the virtual identification an actual one. "They are yours, if not yet yours." "You are in an exchange relationship with me, if not yet in an exchange relationship with me." And the poetic structuring of the calls enhances this rhetorical efficacy by building up patterns of formal expectation that again elicit the participatory energies of the customers. Note in the preceding example, for instance, the heavy use of lexical repetition, phonological parallelism (e.g., the saturation of the cries with /a/ in *agárrele, bara, barato, escójale, pantalón, regalo, remate, ándele, damos*), and syntactic parallelism. Yet all this functional business is accomplished in a highly economical way that allows for great fluency and cohesion and lends itself to smooth collaboration in the joint production of extended calls.

In fact, the production of these calls is so simple that even a child can do it. The team that produced the foregoing example, number 15, was occasionally joined by a young boy of about ten who contributed calls like the one given in example 16.

16   Escójale doscientos lo que guste.   Choose two hundred what you
                                           like.
        Aquí está la barata, doscientos.   Here is the bargain, two
                                            hundred.

And just to take one other example, an even younger boy of about eight produced the call given as example 17:

17   Cincuenta el montón de brocoli,   Fifty the pile of broccoli, fifty.
     cincuenta.
     Cincuenta el montón de brocoli,   Fifty the pile of broccoli, fifty.
     cincuenta.

Acquisition of competence in the production of such calls does not require overt instruction. Children are exposed to the calls from babyhood, as they are carried through the market by parents or siblings or accompany parents who are vendors, and they pick up the formal patterns by observation and imitation.

Spiels

Now, while my discussion thus far has emphasized the basic constituents, relatively elementary forms, and ease, simplicity, and fluency of production that characterizes the majority of calls in the San Miguel Tuesday market, as I suggested earlier there is a type of market cry, the spiel, that contrasts with these in interesting ways. These are produced by selling specialists called *merolicos* in some areas, who, consistent with Santamaría's (1983:717–718) definition, tend to sell "artifacts of rare and marvelous properties, in loud voices and verbose language in order to call the attention of the passers-by." Unlike the general run of market vendors, who tend to stick to selling the same commodities, these *merolicos* purvey a variety of goods, principally specialty items like jewelry, small appliances, or other commodities that require more considered purchasing decisions. They don't have to rely on the kind of aids to fluency or persuasiveness that characterize the economical calls I have described earlier, because they are practiced verbal virtuosi, true men of words. They also often put on a bit of a show to accompany the pitch. The following example, number 18, is a stretch of a spiel by a man selling a batch of Cannon Mills panty hose, certainly a specialty, luxury item in a market that caters principally to *campesinos* and laborers. His little performance involves running a hair-rake across the stockings stretched out between him and a young boy acting as his assistant; that's what's going on in lines 31–5.

18
1   Vale la pena.   It's worth it.
2   Vea usted las medias de.   Examine the classy stockings.
    categoría

3	Cannon Mills,	Cannon Mills,
4	Cannon Mills.	Cannon Mills.
5	How many? I got it.	[How many? I got it.
6	Too muche, too muche.	Too much, too much.
7	Panty hose.	Panty hose,]
8	la Cannon Mills,	the Cannon Mills,
9	Cannon Mills,	Cannon Mills,
10	para la (?) Cannon,	for the (?) Cannon,
11	calidad Cannon Mills.	Cannon Mills quality.
12	Sabemos de antemano	We know to begin with
13	que una mujer sin medias	that a woman without stockings
14	es como un hombre sin calzones.	is like a man without underpants.
15	Vea usted las medias de Cannon.	Examine the Cannon stockings.
16	[Customer]: Y esto?	And this?
17	Mil pesos, nada más, señora.	A thousand pesos, no more, ma'am.
18	Cannon Mills,	Cannon Mills,
19	la Cannon Mills.	the Cannon Mills.
20	Señora, vea usted,	Ma'am, examine,
21	que se atoró con la canasta,	whether it got snagged by the basket,
22	con la bolsa, no importa.	by the bag, it doesn't matter.
23	Fibra de vidrio Galilei,	Galileo fiberglass,
24	la versátil magia de la nueva ola,	the versatile magic of the new wave,
25	vea usted.	examine.
26	ás elástica y más resistente que cualquier media.	More elastic and more resistant than any stocking.
27	Vale la pena.	It's worth it.
28	Vea usted las medias de categoría	Examine the classy stockings
29	Vale la pena,	It's worth it,
30	vea usted.	examine.
31	Jalale ahí, niño.	Pull it there, son.
32	Jala más para allá,	Pull more over there,
33	eso ahí así.	right there.
34	Y mucho cuidado con caerse al hoyo	And be very careful about falling in the hole
35	porque ya saben que caerse al hoyo es muy delicado.	because we already know that to fall into a hole is very delicate.

36	Cannon Mills.	Cannon Mills.
37	Senora, vea usted.	Ma'am, examine.
38	Vale la pena.	It's worth it.
39	Vea usted las medias de categoría,	Examine the classy stockings,
40	unas medias mucho muy diferentes a todas las medias.	some stockings very much different from all the stockings.
	. . .	. . .
41	. . . arboles,	. . . trees,
42	(?) unas tunas,	(?) some prickly pears,
43	y se atoraron alli con nopales,	and they got snagged there by nopales,
44	y a la media no le pasa nada.	and nothing happens to the stocking.
45	Ayer una mujer me dijo, me dice,	Yesterday a woman said to me, she says to me,
46	"Ay mire nomás que hoyote me hice hice ayer,	"Ay, just look at what a big pock mark I got myself yesterday,
47	por ir al cerro,	going along the hill,
48	y me hice una llagota,	and I got a wound,
49	y a la media me quedó enterita."	and the stocking remained whole."
50	[Customer]: Sí.	Yes.
51	Nomás (?),	Only (?),
52	a ella le pasó,	it happened to her,
53	y a la media no le pasó nada.	and nothing happened to the stocking.
54	Calidad Cannon Mills.	Cannon Mills quality.
55	Señora, vea usted las medias.	Ma'am, examine the stockings.
56	Quiere clarita o quiere oscurita,	You want light or you want dark,
57	tengo cuatrocientos cincuenta mil colores	I have four hundred fifty thousand colors
58	Calidad Cannon Mills.	Cannon Mills quality.
59	Que se atoró con la canasta,	Whether it got snagged by the basket
60	con la bolsa, vea usted,	by the bag, you see,
61	a la media no la pasa nada,	nothing happens to the stocking,
62	porque está elaborada a base de acetato, rayon y nylon	because it is manufactured on a base of acetate, rayon and nylon

63	como las llantas Goodrich, Euzkadi	like the Goodrich or Euzkadi tires.
64	Más elástica, más resistente	More elastic, more resistant
65	que cualquier media.	than any stocking.
66	Medias hay muchas,	There are many stockings,
67	cómprelas adonde usted quiera,	buy them where you like,
68	pero medias de estas	but these stockings
69	Nomás conmigo.	Only from me.

What I want to emphasize in the spiel of this vendor is that his sales pitch is in significant ways more elaborated than the calls we have examined in terms of syntactic structures, rhetorical constituents and structures, and formal devices. Certainly, we can identify in his spiel some of the elements now familiar to us from the cries of the vendors we have already analyzed, such as terms of address to potential customers (lines 17, 20, 37, 55), descriptions of the salient qualities of his merchandise (e.g., line 26: "More elastic and more resistant than any stocking"), or appeals to the senses (lines 2, 15, 20, 25, 28, 30, 37, 39, 55, 60: "*vea usted*"). Condensed and formulaically repetitious elements are prominent in his spiel, as witness his insistent repetition of "Cannon Mills," "*calidad* Cannon Mills," "*vale la pena*," and "*vea usted*." Lines 25–30 are especially dense in this regard, and by themselves might approximate closely to a call of the kind we examined earlier:

vea usted.	examine.
Más elástica y más resistente que cualquier media.	More elastic and more resistant than any stocking.
Vale la pena.	It's worth it.
Vea usted las medias de categoria.	Examine the classy stockings.
Vale la pena,	It's worth it,
vea usted.	examine.

Note, however, that the repeated elements in the spiel grow longer than those of the more condensed cries, which are notably lean. Take lines 21–2 and 59–60, for example: "whether it got snagged by the basket, by the bag, it doesn't matter" and "Whether it got snagged by the basket, by the bag, you see." But look also at the closing lines of this extract (lines 66–9):

Medias hay muchas,	There are many stockings,
cómprelas adonde usted quiera,	buy them where you like,
pero medias de estas	but these stockings
nomás conmigo.	only from me.

This is a complex sentence, with multiple clauses, spanning four lines of the spiel, in marked contrast with the two- and three-word sentences of the calls.

With regard to the rhetoric of the spiel, recall that the rhetorical efficacy of the briefer calls resides especially strongly in a combination of directives eliciting sensory and cognitive engagement with the goods (e.g., *escójale, agárrele, mire, oiga, lleve limas*) and the evocation of a social relationship, especially a relationship of exchange, between vendor and customer (*qué le damos? le doy barato*), as well as in the formal appeal of the utterance residing in its poetic form (e.g., repetition, parallelism). The spiel, as we have established, certainly depends upon a similar formal appeal, but we can see new and more complex rhetorical mechanisms at play as well. Among the rhetorical devices employed by the pantyhose pitchman is an epigrammatic statement, a *dicho*, syntactically complex and slightly risqué:

Sabemos de antemano	We know to begin with
que una mujer sin medias	that a woman without stockings
es como un hombre sin calzones.	is like a man without underpants.

This statement is framed as conventional, axiomatic knowledge, socially given, and takes the form of a parallel construction. Here, the central appeal is to identifications of class and respectability: the image of a man without underpants evokes associations of poverty, low-class status, unhygienic disrespectability. A respectable woman would want to avoid having such associations attached to her, and buying brand-name "classy" pantyhose, indices of modern bourgeois consumerism, offers the means to do so. But the *dicho* gains further efficacy from its risqué tone – pantyhose and underpants are intimate matters, all the more so by the rather prudish moral standards of the market's general clientele. This risqué tone carries through to the double entendre of the pitchman's admonition to the young boy assisting him in the demonstration of the stockings' durability by stretching them out while the vendor draws a sharp hair-rake across them (lines 31–5). Warning the boy to avoid tripping over a depression in the ground, he says,

Y mucho cuidado con caerse al hoyo	And be very careful about falling in the hole
porque ya saben que caerse al hoyo es muy delicado.	because we already know that to fall into a hole is very delicate.

The boy's footing takes on the overtone of sexual intercourse. Ultimately, to speak thus of intimate sexual matters is to evoke a relationship of seductive intimacy which can be consummated by making a purchase – buy my pantyhose. And, of course, the epigram derives still further weight from its purported axiomatic status and from the formal appeal of its parallel construction.

In addition to the *dicho*, the vendor also builds into his sales strategy a reported testimonial narrative, a *caso*,[4] in lines 45–9:

Ayer una mujer me dijo, me dice,	Yesterday a woman said to me, she says to me,
"Ay mire nomás que hoyote me hice ayer	"Ay, only look at what a big pock mark I got myself yesterday
por ir al cerro,	going along the hill,
y me hice una llagota,	and I got a wound,
y a la media me quedó enterita."	and the stocking remained whole."

The narrative is rendered in a different stylistic mode than the other portions of the vendor's spiel. Where the majority of the spiel is characterized by a declamatory mode of delivery that is louder and more rhythmic, with marked intonation contours and stress patterns and nasalized, lengthened vowels, the narrative is delivered in a more conversational, less measured style. It is directed not to the crowd at large, but to a specific individual, though intended to be overheard by the others in attendance. Notwithstanding the difference in delivery, which makes it more accessible to verbal response on the part of a customer than the relatively less permeable declamatory sections of the spiel, its rhetorical purpose is similar to that of the epigram, that is, it is intended to elicit identification. This time, however, what is elicited is not status identification, but experiential identification, a mapping of the experience of the woman whose narrative is reported onto those of the women in the market. Note how the narrative elicits an affirmative response from a woman in the crowd. Both dimensions of identification are virtual; they call upon the women to consider that a particular status or experience might be theirs if they wear Cannon Mills stockings.

In addition to the *dicho* and the *caso*, the pitchman indexes a third genre, the radio and television commercial, first in lines 23–4 and again in lines 62–5:

Fibra de vidrio Galilei,	Galileo glass fiber
la versátil magia de la nueva ola	the versatile magic of the new wave
porque esta elaborada a base de acetato, rayon y nylon	because it is manufactured on a base of acetate, rayon and nylon

como las llantas Goodrich, Euzkadi.	like the Goodrich or Euzkadi tires.
Más elastica, más resistente	More elastic, more resistant
que cualquier media.	than any stocking.

These elements are significant in their invocation of brand-name products – Galileo fiberglass and Goodrich and Euzkadi tires – which complement the brand-name identification of Cannon Mills pantyhose. Note also that all of these products offer the wonders of modern technology – "the versatile magic of the new wave" – to the public: fiberglass, acetate, rayon, nylon. These materials render the pantyhose more elastic and more resistant than any other, introducing the trope of "new and improved" that is so characteristic of contemporary marketing. The cumulative effect of these metonyms of media commercials is to convey elements of the modern economy of bourgeois consumerism into the traditional marketplace and thus within reach of its clientele, primarily laborers and peasants.

We may observe, then, that one of the distinctive features of the spiel, by contrast with the briefer calls, is generic incorporativeness: the spiel is a secondary genre that incorporates other primary genres and styles within it, exploiting their particular rhetorical capacities. And the spiel is stylistically heterogeneous in other respects as well. Beyond the incorporation of the *dicho*, the *caso*, and the commercial, the spiel is marked by switches in key (Goffman 1974) and even code. The vendor engages in speech play of various kinds, for example in his hyperbolic statement that whether you want light or dark he has four hundred fifty thousand colors (lines 56–7), and in his playful bit of code switching into English (lines 5–7), directed at me:

How many? I got it.
Too muche, too muche.
Pantyhose.

Space constraints preclude the presentation and analysis of additional texts. The example I have offered is typical of the genre, however, demonstrating the far greater formal and rhetorical complexity of the spiel as against the calls we have considered earlier in terms of constituent elements, formal structures, generic incorporativeness, sytlistic heterogeneity, and rhetorical devices and strategies.

Now, to a significant degree, the contrast between calls and spiels is correlated with the kinds of commodities that are offered for sale and their cost. Calls are employed in the selling of basic necessities like food and ordinary clothing, the kinds of things for which people regularly come to the market. The customers for these commodities come with a predisposition to buy and there is little need to elaborate in the crying of these goods, as people are primarily concerned with locating the specific food-stuffs or clothing they need in a market whose spatial arrangements shift somewhat every week and with determining how much they cost in a market affected by the rapid inflation of the Mexican economy. These elements may be bolstered by a bit of poetically enhanced rhetoric to help impel people toward a purchase, but more would be unnecessary and even counterproductive. Likewise for small and inexpensive optional items like ices, a little treat to enhance the experience or to keep the kids quiet. But luxury and specialty items, like pantyhose or fitted sheets, require more persuasion. And while people are making up their minds on whether or not to splurge, it helps to keep them around with a good show. Accordingly, spiels are more adaptive in the vending of such special and more expensive goods.

Bridging the Generic Gap

Our considerations thus far have been devoted to establishing in terms of form–function interrelationships the conventional organization of the two standard genres of market language, calls and spiels. Though only one of the two, the call, has a commonly used label, *grito*, the contrasts between them are recognized and serve as orienting frameworks for vendors and customers alike. Each is regimented toward the accomplishment of a routine marketplace task, calls toward the selling of nominally priced everyday goods and other small commodities for which consumers regularly come to the Tuesday market, and spiels toward the vending of more expensive commodities, luxury goods, and other items that require more considered consumer decisions. The conventional forms we have considered up to this point are generically transparent, closely related in inter-textual terms within each generic type.

Having established the generic configuration of the widely recognized genres, let us turn to the consideration of several further examples that render the generic landscape somewhat more complicated.

Example 19 is an extract from a recording from the beginning phase of a pitch made by a snake-oil salesman – yes, literally selling snake-oil – just after he had finished setting up his exhibit of a caged rattlesnake, with an iguana tethered to the outside of the cage.

| 19 | Lleve pa' los callos, | Take for calluses, |
| | mire pa' los mezquinos, | look, for warts, |

riumas, calambres, torceduras.	rheumatism, cramps, sprains.
Conozca la grasa,	Become acquainted with the grease,
el aceite de de la víbora cascabel.	the oil of the rattlesnake.
Mire pa'l riumatismo,	Look, for rheumatism,
para dolores musculares,	for muscular pains,
un dolor de espalda,	back pain,
un dolor de cintura, riumas, calambres,	waist pain, rheumatism, cramps,
grasa, aceite de víbora cascabel, mire,	grease, oil of rattlesnake, look,
para riumatismo,	for rheumatism,
para dolores musculares.	for muscular pains.
Untada, frotada en cualquier dolor,	Spread, rubbed on any pain,
cualquier molestia que tenga.	any discomfort you may have.

This is a well formed, if extended, call, stretched out by a formulaic catalogue of ailments that may be treated effectively by the application of snake-oil. It exhibits the repetition and parallelism we have come to expect of calls and incorporates various devices for eliciting the engagement of potential buyers, including directives, "mire," and so on.

After listening to this medicine vendor for a while, I continued my wanderings through the market, to return approximately twenty minutes later to the snake-oil salesman's location. By that time, he had gathered a small crowd, listening to his pitch and contemplating his herpetological exhibit. His pitch at that point sounded like this:

20   Esto sirve también para los niños que se orinan en la cama.
Nada más hay que untarlo o frotarlo,
abajo del ombliguito del lado izquierdo por las noches,
bien untado, bien frotado.
No es caro.
Dos mil quinientos o se lleva tres por cinco mil.
Tos bronquios, riumas, calambres, frialdad,
se cayó, se torció.
Úntelo, frótelo,
le contiene la grasa de la iguana para riumatismo, calambres,
riumas, calambres, golpes, torceduras.

Cualquier dolor,
cualquier molestia.
Dos mil pesos uno, y dos por cinco mil.
Y el día que usted lo llegue a necesitar
no lo vaya a buscar en una farmacia,
porque en la farmacia no lo haya.
Aquí lleve su domicilio.
Centro Botánica Guadalupe de Léon, Guanajuato,
para cuando usted lo necesite.
Dos mil pesos uno.
Se pone por las noches, eh?
De preferencia por las noches,
para que no se le entre el frío en la mañana.

This also works for children who wet the bed.
There is nothing more [to do] than spread it or rub it
below the belly-button on the left side at night,
well spread on, well rubbed.
It's not expensive.
Twenty-five hundred or take three for five thousand.
Bronchial cough, rheumatism, cramps, chills,
falling down, getting a sprain.
Spread it, rub it,
it contains iguana grease for rheumatism, cramps,
rheumatism, cramps, blows, sprains.
Any pain, any discomfort.
Two thousand pesos for one, and two for five thousand.
And the day that you come to need it
don't look for it in a pharmacy,
because it won't be in the pharmacy.
Here, take it home.
Guadalupe Botanical Center of Léon, Guanajuato,
for when you need it.
Two thousand pesos for one.
Put it on at night, eh?
Preferably at night,
so that cold won't get in in the morning.

The elaboration of the inventory of ailments (bronchial cough, chills, blows, etc.) and the indication of price represent devices with which we are familiar for the expansion of calls. Observe, though, the way that the vendor expands the catalogue at the beginning of the excerpt: a syntactically complex declaration about how the snake-oil may be used as a treatment for bedwetting, with precise instructions of where and when to rub it on, below the belly-button, on the left side, at night. Note also the extended cautionary admonition about not looking for the product at a pharmacy, but buying it to take home from this authorized Guadalupe Botanical Center vendor, and the advice about applying the remedy preferably at night, to avoid the morning cold that is a ubiquitous feature of this high-altitude region. That is to say, the call is here fleshed out with more spiel-like characteristics. The snake-oil vendor has shifted from the earlier phase of attracting customers with his words and his display – what Dargan and Zeitlin's American pitchmen call "building a tip" (1983:17) – to the more complex rhetorical task of persuading them to buy, overcoming their caution by means of more elaborate expository and instructional discourse. This latter phase is analogous to what Dargan and Zeitlin's pitchmen call the "bally" (1983:18–19). There are clear ties of co-textual cohesion between the first phase of the pitch and the bally-like later one, but a creative, adaptive transformation as well.

Let us consider one final example. This is an extract from a longer stretch of sales talk produced by a vendor of kitchenware: dishes, utensils, pots and pans, and the like. Here, he is hawking dishes, by means of a pitch in which he adds plates, one after another, to the stack to emphasize just how much the buyer will get for a thousand pesos:

21	1	Se lleva otro,	Take another,
	2	por mil.	for a thousand.
	3	Tenga otro,	Have another,
	4	por mil.	for a thousand.
	5	Otro,	Another,
	6	y otro por mil pesos.	and another for a thousand pesos.
	7	Deme mil,	Give me a thousand,
	8	y échales otro,	and choose another,
	9	y así todo el bonche por mil.	and thus the whole bunch for a thousand.
	10	Aquí está el otro como regalo de año nuevo.	Here is another as a New Year's present.
	11	Así todo el paquete,	Thus the whole package, package,
	12	mil pesos.	thousand pesos.
	13	A ver, a ver, a ver quién se los lleva,	Let's see, let's see, let's see who takes them away,
	14	quién se los gana.	who gains them.

15	Nadie a la una,	No one at one,
16	nadie a las dos,	no one at two,
17	porque esto se lo está perdiendo este paquete de platos.	because you are missing this package of plates.
18	Así todo por mil.	Thus all for a thousand.
19	Son diez platos, mujeres, por mil pesos.	They are ten plates, ladies, for a thousand pesos.
20	En la feria de allá de Celaya,	At the fair over in Celaya,
21	se está cotizando a nada menos,	it is priced at no less,
22	que a mil quinientos.	than one thousand five hundred.
23	Y allá hasta las mujeres se agarran del chongo	And there the women almost tear their hair out
24	para pagar los mil quinientos.	to pay one thousand five hundred.
25	Son mil quinientos,	They are one thousand five hundred
26	mil quinientos tienen que vender así.	one thousand five hundred they have to sell them thus.
27	Por todo el paquete de platos,	For the whole package of plates,
28	por diez platos,	for ten plates,
29	dies platos de lujo,	ten deluxe plates,
30	diez platos decorados,	ten decorated plates,
31	por solamente mil pesos.	for only a thousand pesos.
32	Nadie a la una, nadie a las dos,	No one at one, no one at two,
33	entonces la oferta va para abajo.	then the offer is going down.
34	Todo por mil.	All for a thousand.
35	Nadie mil, nadie?	No one a thousand, no one?
36	Bueno, no ruegues,	OK, don't beg,
37	echalo para abajo este paquete de platos.	put down this package of plates.
38	Vamos a vender las cubetas.	Let's sell the buckets.

At first glance, lines 1–19 appear in formal terms to be consistent with our characterization of cries: condensed, formulaic, stereotyped, full of repetition and parallelism, with constituent elements that identify commodity and unit price and elicit the engagement of potential customers with directives and identificational elements such as *a ver quien se los lleva* 'let's see who takes them away.' But note that lines 1–12 do not consist solely of a series of smaller cry units, but are in fact tied together sequentially by the cumulative device of including additional plates in the package, making for an overarching cohesive structure. Then, in lines 20–8, there is a stretch of syntactically more complex comparison pricing, reporting humorously how the women at the Celaya market would tear their hair out to buy an equivalent set of dishes for 1,500 pesos, followed by a return, in lines 29–34, to his own lower price in the manner of the earlier section. Finally, in lines 36–8, the vendor offers a nicely self-reflexive transition from pushing the dishes, for which he has attracted no immediate buyers, to hawking plastic buckets. These are all features that are more characteristic of spiels than calls: longer, more extended structures of cohesion, syntactic complexity, comparative references to other markets, reflexivity. Thus, in formal terms, this pitch emerges as a stylistic hybrid, blending features of call and spiel.

This stylistic calibration makes sense in functional terms as well. The dishes and other kitchen goods that make up this vendor's wares are not foodstuffs for daily consumption or nominally priced items like needles and snaps; nor are they specialty items of a bourgeois cast, like brand-name pantyhose. Rather, they are relatively durable household items of a kind that are purchased only occasionally. Every household needs these things, but purchases involve considered decisions, balancing utility against relative quality and cost. I am suggesting, then, that as consumer goods, these wares fall between the low-end necessities and high-end specialty items. A simple, terse call will not suffice to capture and hold the attention of potential buyers, but a more elaborately performed spiel is not necessary either. Hence a sales pitch that falls somewhere in between. Thus, this vendor, faced with the task of selling goods that differ in nature and cost from those for which standard calls and spiels are designed, draws upon the orienting frameworks of both routine genres to bridge the gap, producing an emergent hybrid adapted to his particular task. Though he was not immediately successful in this particular instance, which occurred late in the afternoon when only a few customers were left, he did manage to sell a fair number of dishes with a similar pitch earlier in the day.

Calibrations of Genre

The open-air market is an arena of profusion, a concentrated time and space packed with people and goods brought together for the purpose of exchange. One of the principal means to bring sellers and buyers together is language, packaged in the cries of vendors declaiming their wares in order to attract customers and induce them to buy. The epigraph to this chapter, from Henry Mayhew's vivid description of London markets in the nineteenth century, testifies to the cacophony of cries that threaten to over- whelm the market-goer. This is the intertextuality of tumult, an auditory jangle of textual juxtaposition through which the shopper must navigate a course.

Vendors and buyers in the San Miguel de Allende Tuesday market are oriented to two contrastive genres of market cry, which I have labeled – following Jacqueline Lindenfeld – calls (*gritos*) and spiels (*plática commer- cial, pregones*). Calls, as we discovered, are formally condensed, made up of a relatively lean inventory of formal components and devices mobilized to identify the commodity for sale, recount its salient attributes, state its cost, and solicit the sensory, cognitive, and social engagement of the customer with the product and its vendor toward consummation of the sale. Calls are adapted to the routine task of orienting the potential customer to basic commodities, food staples, everyday clothing, small necessities such as sewing notions, batteries, and the like. The insistent fluency, redundancy, and repetetiveness of their construction and delivery is highly effective in capturing and holding the attention of market-goers. Even now, many years after I last visited the Tuesday market in San Miguel, I can still call them up: "*Escójale! Agárrele!*" "*A cien! A cien! A cien la bolsa!*" Granted, I have a predilection for oral poetry, but there is no denying the rhetorical potency of the calls while you are in the market itself, and respondents uniformly acknowledged their affecting presence and were able to imitate at least some of their salient features.

Spiels, on the other hand, are attractive and memorable as perfor- mances. Declaimed by true verbal virtuosi, they are longer, more complex, heteroglossic utterances, which incorporate other primary genres and speech styles in an insistent cascade of poetic and persuasive words designed to attract and hold an audience of potential buyers for more expensive, less routinely purchased goods. To enhance the show still further, the *merolicos* who are masters of the spiel may include other ele- ments of performance and display, such as a demonstration of the dura- bility of pantyhose, resistant to the snags of a hair-rake, or a live rattlesnake and iguana, sources of medicinal oil. Spiels are adapted to getting customers to buy goods that they had not, perhaps, intended to buy when they came to market, or goods that are costly enough to require more considered decisions.

The functional ends to which calls and spiels are formally adapted are not categorically exclusive. There is, in fact, a gradient range of functional middle grounds between the selling of low-priced staples and quotidian goods for which people regularly and routinely come to market and the vending of specialty items that are more expensive and demand more considered purchasing decisions, such as the dishes and snake-oil we have considered. Vendors may thus calibrate their pitches accordingly between the contrastive poles of cry and spiel as situational conditions may require. The addition to the basic call forms of more complex syntactic and rhetorical structures, more extended networks of textual cohesion, other primary genres such as sayings or stories, speech play or other forms of style switching, and so on, gives the sales pitch variably more spiel-like coloration or character. It is largely by means of these verbal calibrations that vendors orient buyers to the ecology and economy of the market. The calls and spiels and their variant siblings, then, establish the oral/aural cartography of the marketplace which guides buyers and sellers onto convergent paths toward exchange. *Qué le damos?*

5

"Bell, You Get the Spotted Pup": First Person Narratives of a Texas Storyteller

Narrating the Self

Discursive forms – especially narrative forms – for the construction and representation of the social self have risen to unprecedented prominence in anthropology, linguistics, folklore, and psychology in recent years. This turn has been stimulated by the burgeoning of interest in such convergent phenomena as subject formation, reflexivity, agency, the intersubjective construction of knowledge and experience, the dialogic construction of the self, conversation analysis, and related vantage points on social life as discursively constituted and discourse as socially constituted.[1] Disciplinary differences of orientation and emphasis notwithstanding, however, there are marked tendencies in the scholarly literature surrounding personal experience narratives to exclude or bracket on principled grounds precisely those discursive organizing principles that are central to this book: performance, genre, intertextuality.

First, there is a common restriction of interest to the unpolished personal narratives of ordinary people, as against the practiced, "polished narrative performances" (Ochs and Capps 2001:2) of "expert storytellers" (Labov and Waletzky 1967:12). The motivations for these restrictions of focus center around the understanding – perhaps something of a just-so story in itself – that such "ordinary," "unpolished" stories of personal experience represent the elementary form of narrative expression (Labov and Waletzky 1967:12; Ochs and Capps 2001:3). As such, it is suggested, these "prototypes of narrative activity" (Ochs and Capps) exhibit the "fundamental structures" of narrative discourse (Labov and Waletzky 1967:12) or of narrative in interaction which are occluded in expert storytelling by the formal complexity of artfully wrought texts or the extended holding of the floor that characteristically attends performance.

This predisposition toward the unpracticed narration of ordinary speakers tends to orient attention away from intertextuality, if not to discount it outright (Keller-Cohen and Dyer 1997). If artful performers develop their stories into artful set-pieces, and we want to exclude such practiced narratives on *a priori* grounds, we foreground the "original," "contingent," locally produced, for-the-first-time qualities of the stories on which we do center our attention (Labov and Waletzky 1967:12; Ochs and Capps 2001:2; Polanyi 1989:47–50). Even folklorists, who have a greater disciplinary appreciation for "twice-told" tales and who are more inclined than scholars in adjacent disciplines to rerecord the stories of their subjects, emphasize the individual-based nature of personal experience narratives, as mitigating against the web of intertextual relationships in which traditional folktales are enmeshed by virtue of their social and historical distribution (Stahl 1977).

Certainly, students of narrative self-fashioning have been preoccupied with defining and specifying the generic features of the personal experience narrative, and to this extent orders of intertextuality established by generic orienting frameworks figure clearly in this line of inquiry. The very concern for definitional precision and specificity, though, makes for a concomitant resistance to intertextuality in narrative constructions of the self that extends across generic categories. The inventory of adjacent genres ruled out of court is extensive (see, for example, Labov and Waletzky 1967:12; Ochs and Capps 2001:2; Stahl 1977). Stahl (1977), again with a folklorist's comprehensive generic frame of reference, identifies and surveys a whole range of oral narrative genres that converge with or ambiguate the boundaries of personal experience narrative as she and the others define it, including tall tales and jokes told in the first person, but her effort is principally in the service of firming up the generic distinctions, preparatory to zeroing in on stories that are clear-cut personal experience narratives by her definitional criteria.

In this chapter, however, I want to explore an alternative strategy, one that redresses an imbalance that results from various exclusions and omissions I have just outlined, that takes into account the interrelationships linking the expressive forms individuals may employ in representing their lives to others, however these forms may be generically packaged, presentationally keyed, or semiotically encoded. One way of framing this task is to consider the ways in which discursive productions may employ life experience as an expressive resource, using it to shape and present the social self in dialogue with others. Pursuing this line, I will explore some of the ways Ed Bell, a traditional Texas storyteller, casts his life in his narrative performance and in related expressive routines.

I want to make clear at the outset that I will not be concerned here with life history materials as conventionally and narrowly understood, as auto-biographical accounts of an informant's life-course elicited by a researcher. To be sure, various fieldworkers, including myself, have elicited such material from Ed Bell, much of it, as might be expected, in narrative form, and some of it, as again might be expected from a skilled storyteller, artfully rendered, that is, performed. Instead, I will be dealing with stories that were part of Ed Bell's active performance repertoire, narrative set-pieces that he told in full performance on repeated occasions. I should make clear also that while all of the stories I will consider are first-person narratives in which Ed Bell is the central protagonist as well as the narrator, not all of them are the kind of "told for true" personal narratives that generally count as life history. Rather, I will be bridging conventional generic boundaries and at times extending my purview beyond verbal genres. The point I wish to develop is that a systemic interrelationship ties together Ed Bell's first-person narratives, however they may be generically framed, and links them as well with other expressive forms in his performance repertoire. Some of his stories are offered as factual accounts, while others emerge ultimately as fictions, but their first-person framing and their common place in Bell's performance repertoire mark them collectively as expressive transforma-tions of the same life. I propose to explore the linkages that bind the corpus together.

Ed Bell, Virtuoso Storyteller

Ed Bell was precisely the kind of "expert," "renowned" storyteller that the seekers after "fundamental" or "prototypical" narrative structures insist upon excluding from their corpora (Labov and Waletzky 1967:12; Ochs and Capps 2001:2), and devotees of verbal art and virtuoso performance eagerly seek out (Bauman 1986:78–111; 1987; Jasper 1979; Mullen 1976, 1978, 1981). Bell was born in the Texas Hill Country in 1905, to a family that relocated several times during his early years before settling in Caldwell County, in Central Texas. In reflecting upon his penchant for storytelling, Bell identified several formative influences, including a desire to make a place for himself in a succession of childhood peer groups as his family moved from community to community and his ample exposure to stories in fishing and hunting camps during his teenage years in Caldwell County. He came into his own as a storyteller, however, during the four decades he spent as a fisherman and proprietor of a fishing camp at Indianola on the

Gulf Coast, from the early 1930s to 1972, when he retired to the family place in Central Texas. Bell's reputation as a virtuoso storyteller extended up and down the Texas Coast, and was a strong factor in attracting clients back to his camp year after year and in capturing the attention of folklorist Pat Mullen, who recorded him on several occasions – the first of several scholars to document his life and his art over the last 20 years of his life until his death in 1986.

Ed Bell greatly valued the attention of scholars, and not simply because those of us who worked with him were an eager audience for his stories. Nothing pleased him more than to see the scholarly articles and chapters written about him and to perform for my university classes, for he loved and admired teaching and learning. Although his own formal education was limited by his life circumstances, he was a man of the liveliest intellect and imagination, fascinated by knowledge and always intellectually engaged with the world around him. His lively mind and fertile imagination animated his life and his art, shaping his reflections on experience, knowledge, and reality. His stories reflect these life concerns in a variety of ways.

Personal Experience Narratives

Let us begin with Ed Bell's personal experience narratives, those autobiographical stories, told as true, that recount episodes of his own life experience. When I speak of personal experience narratives told as true, I do not suggest that they are fully and completely true in some objective, factual sense. I have multiple recordings of most of the stories, and even a superficial comparison reveals discrepancies among the texts – the product of creative embellishment, imprecise memory, and a range of other formative influences. Notwithstanding these departures from or improvisations upon full factual historicity, these narratives are intended as accounts of actual experience, are essentially credible (Labov 1997: 407; Ochs and Capps 1997:83), and are taken as true by his audiences. Thematically, formally, functionally, these stories have many dimensions worthy of exploration, but for present purposes I want to draw attention to the complex of elements related to teaching and learning, the power of knowledge and skill, and the problematics of appearance and reality.

The first narrative, about "Ed's First Horse" (Text 1 below), relates an experience that marked a significant transition point in Bell's life, the functional equivalent of a rite of passage. For young men of Ed Bell's generation in Texas, the ownership of one's first horse was a mark of adulthood: "I was right at sixteen when I got this horse. I was topping out there somewhat of a man . . . Back in those days that was the tops if a boy had a good saddle pony. It's just the same as if you have the finest roadster ever built now." Bell had earned his first significant sum of money raising cotton, and on a trip to a nearby town where there was a horse trader, his father told him he could buy a horse. Ed's first choice was a pretty white horse, "as sleek as a button," but his father, who himself had been a horse rancher and trainer, vetoed this horse as physically unsound, and directed Ed's attention to another horse as ugly as the first one was pretty. Despite his strong initial reluctance, Ed was persuaded to follow his father's recommendation, and to his surprise when he mounted his new horse, it underwent an almost fairytale-like transformation, becoming a handsome and stylish mount on which Ed could display himself in the full glory of his young manhood.

Text 1: Ed's First Horse (recorded Austin, Texas, 1982)
My daddy took me down to Luling one day, and there's a horse trader in there, and he done told me I could get me a horse. Have my own saddle horse and get my own saddle.

Well, I got rich. I raised three quarters of a bale of cotton that year. Man, I's makin' the money.

So we got down there and I picked my horse out. Great big ol' white horse, just as sleek as a button. Pretty as you could imagine. And I says, "Papa, that's the horse I want."

Papa says, "No, Buddy, you can't have that horse." Says, "That feller's just tryin' to beat you on that horse." He says, "He's not only been fistuloed, but he's fattened on soda."

[Interviewer: He could tell.]

I didn't have no idea what the . . . how to fatten a horse on soda, but I found out later that they overfed the horse, then they put a bunch o' soda in, it'd keep it gentle on his stomach, he'd use all that food. And he got fat quick.

And he showed me this old gangling cow pony, great big knees on his front legs and a big ol' white flowin' mane. Kinda ewe-necked. That means that the horse's, uh, neck don't arc away from his shoulders. It means it comes out kinda straight, like.

And, uh, I looked at that ol' horse, and he sure wasn't pretty. He wasn't pretty at all. In fact, he's about as ugly a horse I ever saw.

I said, "Papa, I don't want that horse."

He said, "Son, you can't ride that horse to death. You'll kill that horse over there the first day." Said, "Way you handle a horse, you'll kill him first day."

Finally, I listened to Papa and agreed to get that horse. And you know, that ol' horse when I got on him he was a different horse entirely. He's out there in that pen and his neck stuck out that way, and he'd run around the pen to keep from bein' roped and all that kinda stuff, and he wasn't a bit pretty. When you got on him, if you touched him with your heel, he'd arc that neck awaaay over, and he looked like those Arabian horses. He was grey colored, and he'd feel o' the ground when he pranced down through town.

"There comes that big shot, Ed Bell, comin' into town on his white stallion." Course, he wasn't a stallion, but they'd call it that, you know.[2]

I want to point out especially three elements in this narration. First, note the differential of knowledge between Ed Bell and his father. Ed has "no idea . . . how to fatten a horse on soda" or how to detect other flaws in a horse, and thus makes a naive choice based on superficial appearances alone. His father, on the other hand, is a man of knowledge and experience, wise to the tricks of horse traders and to the true qualities of horses, and thus able to discern the pretty horse's defects and the ugly horse's virtues. The two major exchanges between Ed and his father, highlighted through direct discourse, are instructional ones, in which the elder schools the younger in the selection of a horse, echoing that phase of a rite of passage in which the elders school the initiates in the wisdom of society. This account is about teaching and learning and the power of knowledge and experience.

A second major theme centers on the problematics of appearance and reality. To a significant extent, the story turns on the potential discrepancy between what things appear to be and what they really are, as realized in the contrast between the pretty horse, which is seriously flawed, and the ugly horse, which nevertheless has strong but not readily apparent virtues. The narrative argues that things are not always what they seem; and in the story Ed Bell reflects on this epistemological principle and invites his audience to do likewise.

Finally, the story addresses the manipulability of appearance to suggest or to counterfeit particular realities. In identifying the flaws of the pretty horse, Ed's father unmasks the deception of the horse trader, a figure who embodies deceit and the mastery of fabrication in American folk tradition (Bauman 1986:11–32): "That feller's just tryin' to beat you on that horse." In this regard, the story points up a special interactional concern of Ed's expressive production, that is, the dynamics of fabrication, the art of inducing a false impression in others.

Thus far, I have treated in thematic terms a particular complex of concerns expressed in this story – the power of knowledge and experience, the conduct of teaching and learning, and the problematics of appearance and reality – but an additional dimension of these concerns warrants attention, namely, the social relational and social interactional dynamics by which they are played out. The lived experience that constitutes the story stuff of this narrative, the narrated event in Jakobson's term (1971[1957]), consists of social interactions: between Ed, his father, and the horse trader as more or less informed buyers and devious seller respectively, and between Ed and his father as elder teacher and younger learner. It is these social relations and social interactions and their epistemological implications that engage Ed's interest, that are endowed in his mind with sufficient significance to mobilize his expressive energies. I make this point here, where it may seem rather obvious, because I develop it in perhaps less obvious directions later in the chapter. In the story of Ed's first horse, the social relational and social interactional elements of interest to us provide the narrative content; in other instances, they are realized in other ways.

The next story I want to consider features Ed Bell in another guise. In the story of "Joe Hamilton's Redfish" (Text 2 below), Joe Hamilton, a patron of Bell's fishing camp from Dallas (and thus a city man), asks Ed's advice about how to catch a big redfish. Ed instructs him; Joe does as instructed, and sure enough he catches a redfish. Thrilled by his catch, he wants to show it off, and he excitedly tells Ed that it is as long as an oar, innocently indulging in a bit of tall tale-like exaggeration. When Ed goes out to see the fish, it turns out to be less than two feet long – not extraordinary at all for a redfish.

Text 2: Joe Hamilton's Redfish (recorded Luling, Texas, 1983)
I would like to tell you a little bit about old Joe. That ol' boy come down from Dallas, and he was born on the wrong side o' the tracks. Well, he was a good friend o' mine, I guess. We talked and laughed together, and he was always comin' around to me and askin' my advice.

He says, "Ed, how can I catch a fish?"

I says, "Why, Joe, that's easy. All you do's just set a trotline over there, start it at the grass and run it out in the water almost anywhere, but in West Pocket's a real good place. And I don't believe you can set it over there where you couldn't catch a redfish."

He said, "Good, good, good. I'm gon' catch me a redfish."

So he went over there and he set that trotline out, 'bout like I told him to, and he caught him a redfish. And he run around all over that beach showin' it to everybody he could, and he come over to me and he didn't have it in his hand then – he got tired o' carryin' it, it was layin' out in his old car.

He says, "Ed! That redfish is as long as that oar!"

I said, "Aw, Joe, it couldn't be that big, could it?"

He says, "It's as long as that oar!"

I went out there and looked at it and it was about twenty-two inches long, and it sure woulda been a short oar.[3]

Here again, the story turns in part on a differential of knowledge and experience, but this time with an adult Ed Bell in the superordinate position, the possessor of expert knowledge. Joe Hamilton, the city dweller, is unschooled in the ways of catching fish, and thus, in the words of the story, "was always comin' around to me an' askin' my advice." This relationship sets up the teaching and learning encounter recounted in the story, with Ed as instructor and Joe as pupil, again highlighted by direct discourse. The ensuing encounter, also realized as direct discourse, implicates once again a gulf between appearance and reality, but in a somewhat different configuration than before. Whereas the discrepancy between the appearance of the two horses in the first story and their true qualities turns on the difference between overt appearance and covert attributes, the case of Joe's redfish is a matter of Joe's distorted conception of his catch and its objective size. The discrepancy is of his own making, born of his excitement and his lack of experience, but it is also another dimension of the problem encountered by Ed vis-à-vis the horses. A lack of knowledge and experience induces a flawed assessment of the true nature of things – the horses in one case, the fish in the other. There is an element of self-delusion in both instances, though with the horses it is fostered by the overt appearance of the two animals and the manipulations of the horse trader; with the redfish it is wholly self-induced. Ed Bell, as an experienced and knowledgeable fisherman, is able to see the fish for what it is, just as his father was able to recognize the true qualities of the horses. Taken together, then, the two stories play out the same issues, though in a somewhat different configuration. At the same time they chronicle a developmental transformation in Ed Bell himself, from the young, naive, subordinate figure in the horse story to the mature, competent, superordinate figure in the story of Joe Hamilton's redfish.

The third story, and the last example of Ed Bell's true personal experience narratives we will consider for the moment, is longer and more formally complex than the other two, but it implicates the same issues. This narrative, here entitled "The Big Storm" (Text 3 below), is made up of two sequentially linked clusters of episodes, both having to do with Ed Bell's experiences in a powerfully destructive storm on the Gulf Coast. In the first part, Bell is out fishing for shrimp with a new and inexperienced deckhand when the weather worsens and he resolves to set out for shore. The deckhand asks him about waterspouts, which he has never seen and which he naively calls "rainspouts." Bell instructs him about these aquatic cyclones and then observes that they are about to encounter three of them. In a display of masterful seamanship, Bell steers their boat between two of the waterspouts and brings them safely through the storm.

Then, on their approach to shore, they come upon a scene of astonishing destruction, with disabled boats strewn around the bayou. Notwithstanding his astonishment, Bell sizes up the situation and once again rises masterfully to the occasion, setting off to rescue the stranded victims of the waterspouts though the storm is still raging. Another inexperienced boatman offers his assistance, but Ed warns him not to set out. When he does so anyway and wrecks his boat, Ed rejects this new victim's plea for aid, telling him that he will be the last to be rescued. The chastened victim ultimately acknowledges that Ed has taught him a difficult lesson.

Text 3: The Big Storm (recorded Luling, Texas, 1983)

I was . . . I took a boy that was . . . wanted to work for me one time as a deckhand, and, uh, we got out there to the shrimpin' ground, caught a few shrimp, and I got worried because with a new hand on board and he didn't know what to do. So I decided it might be some rough weather, and it was about five miles in to home, I better go home.

Well, I got about two thirds o' the way in, and I was hollerin' at him, "Lash that down! Lash this over here down!"

And he was workin' pretty good at it, and he says, "Mr. Bell, I've always heard about these, uh, rainspouts and so forth," says, "what in the world are they?"

I says, "Well, we've got about three comin' across the bay now. They're little cyclones, but they drag water up from the water; they call 'em waterspouts." I said, "We're gonna get three of 'em in just a minute. Now, grab that mast and hug it and hold on for dear life, 'cause I don't know whether the boat's gon' stand or not." 'Bout a twenty-two foot shrimper.

He grabbed that and I watched the other stuff, and I was steerin' the boat. At one time, my shirt was stretching two ways at one time. I'd steered the boat right between two o' those waterspouts, and the boat leaned waaaay over on the starboard side until there was eighteen inches o' the deck already under water, and it turned us loose, and we evened up, so he says, [panting] "I . . . I sure got to see 'em, didn't I, Mr. Bell?"

I said, "Yeah, you saw three of 'em at one time. Now we got to get in."
I said, "Might be somethin' more that we couldn't ride out."

As we drove on down to the bay, just takin' it easy along, kinda, and
we looked in that bayou, and on the wrong side of it, for the big boats
was aaall out in the grass on the south side – there was boats layin' everywhere you looked! I just couldn't believe my eyes. I looked over on the
other side, and they's some sheet iron blowin' off the buildings, and one
thing and another.

Well, I hadn't seen a waterspout that big, because most of 'em . . .
those three that came by us – really two that hit the boat – were small
enough to hit a sixteen foot boat. That means they're really small. The
other one, I hadn't paid much attention to it, and it mighta grown in
that distance from there to the house.

But anyway, that camp was tore all to pieces, and I got in there and
that wind was increasin' all this time till she was blowin' eighty or ninety
miles an hour.

I looked over there, and there was people hollerin' for "Help, help,
help!" Some of 'em was in those boats when they blowed over there.
Some of 'em blowed plum outa the country, though, those sixteen foot
Lone Star aluminums . . . fourteen foot Lone Star aluminums. One of
'em blew a mile.

So, I pulled into the pier, and my wife says, "Don't you want a cuppa
coffee right quick?" She'd come out the back door, and I said, "No, honey,
I've got to get in the skiff. I'm goin' over there and pick them people up,
there's about two dozen people marooned over there that blowed outa
the bayou!"

And another fella says, "Hey, Bell, I'll go help you. I'll take my boat."

I says, "You stay where you are! Don't you move that boat, feller! That
wind's blowin' about ninety miles an hour. If you . . . if you'd had experience out in a ninety mile wind, I'd say, 'Yeah,' but you can't handle it.
There's no way."

I went on across to the other side, and the first boat I didn't have
much trouble gettin' out, except this feller run into me and I had to shove
him away, and then he run sideways into the shoreline and sheared a
pin, and he was settin' over there pretty soon, it was rainin', gettin' cold,
beggin' and pleadin' for somebody to do somethin' for him.

Well, I got this fella in and he had a great big, uh, boat, a kind of
landing craft they'd used during the war, and a fifty horse motor on it,
and it blowed in fifty feet from the water's edge, back out in the grass.
Well, he had a heart attack, I saw he was in bad shape, so I got him and
two other fellas to help him. We got him in the boat and carried across,

and let my wife work on that fella with the heart attack. She was pretty good at that.

So, I went on back over there and started haulin' these people in, and this other fella's just beggin' me to tow him back or to let him ride with me. I said, "Fella, I told you to stay put where you were. You are last, l-a-s-t last." And! let him wait till last, too. He was the last one I moved from over there, and he said, "Bell, I guess you taught me a lesson, but it was a hard one."

Yup.[4]

By now, the focal elements of the story should stand out for us in clear relief. Here again, as in the story about Joe Hamilton's redfish, Bell presents himself as the mature, knowledgeable, and skillful figure, a master of the fisherman's skills, in counterposition to the two naive neophytes, the deck-hand and the would-be rescuer. Whereas Bell can handle his boat with impressive mastery in the storm, the deckhand "didn't know what to do," has never encountered waterspouts, and doesn't even know what to call them, while the second boatman has no "experience out in a ninety-mile wind" and "can't handle it." Both, consequently, are in need of in-struction, which Bell provides, informing the deckhand about the nature of waterspouts and demonstrating how to cope with them and then teaching the overeager boatman the "hard lesson" that he should listen to those more knowledgeable than he – two encounters of teaching and learning in which the power of knowledge and skill is dramatically played out.

The story also raises yet again the problematics of appearance and reality. When Bell recounts the destruction wrought by the storm, he says, "I just couldn't believe my eyes"; the scene he witnesses defies belief. Can what he sees really be true? But notwithstanding this challenge to under-standing, Bell can immediately arrive at a realistic and practical response to the situation and act masterfully because of his deep nautical compe-tence. His would-be assistant, by contrast, cannot perceive the true nature of the situation, underestimating its danger and overestimating his ability to cope with it. He must learn the hard way about the discrepancy between his hasty assessment, rooted in naivete, and a realistic, well-founded response.

In sum, the events and interactions recounted in this narrative, as in the others, represent Ed Bell's deep concern with the dimensions and corre-lates of full adult competence. The stories are expressive explorations of the power of knowledge and skill and the dynamics of teaching and learning, contrasting knowledge, skill, judgment, the ability to discriminate between appearance and reality and to act appropriately, with naivete, incompetence, and the inability to distinguish the apparent from the real. Taken together, these personal experience stories also chronicle Ed Bell's own social development from his youthful naivete and need for instruction to his mature competence and his ability to teach others. And of course, they all in their ways portray Bell himself in a favorable guise, in realization of what Ochs, Smith and Taylor (1989) call the Looking Good Principle. In the story of the first horse, while Bell starts out as naive and gullible, he emerges at the end as the striking figure of admiration, riding stylishly down the street on his handsome steed. In the latter two stories, he is already the figure of superior wisdom and skill, in command of the situation and the social relations he recounts.

Tall Tales

As indicated earlier, however, personal experience narratives of the kind we have considered do not represent the full range of first-person narratives in Ed Bell's active performance repertoire. The real showpieces of his repertoire were tall tales of the classic American type, which he also told in the first person, casting himself as the central protagonist.[5] Numerous folklorists have commented on the relationship between personal experience narratives and tall tales, centering on the common feature of first-person narration (Halpert 1971; Stahl 1977). This body of scholarship, however, has been concerned with the problem in typological terms, that is, as a problem in genre classification.[6] I want to show instead the systemic interrelationship between personal experience narratives and tall tales in the repertoire of this individual storyteller. Ed Bell's first-person stories not only commonly use the first-person voice and point of view, but also draw upon elements of his actual biography and implicate the same complex of thematic concerns. More specifically, like his true personal experience narratives, Ed Bell's tall tales are vehicles for the expressive exploration of his epistemological, ontological, and interactional concerns as manifested or realized in the confrontation of competence and naivete, appearance and reality. Nevertheless, the tall tales allow for the exploration of these concerns from other vantage points and by other means than in the narratives of personal experience. An examination of several further texts will reveal these commonalities and differences.

Let us look first at a tale in which Ed Bell portrays himself at a youthful stage in life more or less corresponding to the time when he bought his first horse, as recounted in the story examined earlier, "The Bee Tree" (Text 4 below), one of his most frequently performed tall tales. It relates how the young Ed discovered a prodigious bee tree while out hunting near his boyhood home and how he determined to cut it down for the honey. His father responds to his request to take the wagon and team into the woods with paternal skepticism; he does not believe Ed's account of the huge tree, attributing the description to Ed's overactive imagination and expressing doubt that he could cut down a tree of that size in any event. Nevertheless, the boy's father is willing to indulge him, and he sets off for the bee tree with two friends who share his amazement once they see the tree for themselves. Ed and his friends finally succeed in chopping the tree down, aided by another team of boys who have been chopping on the other side, believing that they were the first to discover it. When the tree is finally felled it yields a vast amount of honey, plus an abundance of grey squirrels. When all of their vessels are filled, the tree continues to pour out honey, which fills an entire creek bed and forces the boys to take a long route home. And as far as he knows, Bell relates in closing the story, "that creek is still runnin' bank full with honey."

Text 4: The Bee Tree (recorded Austin, Texas, 1982)
You know, folks, over at, uh, near Luling, Texas, where I come from, uh, there's, we got woods out there, big lots o' woods, but not very many big trees. A tree that's three feet in diameter's a big tree. It's sure big.

One year I was huntin' possums or something, and oh, off down on Rock Water Hole Branch. That was about two miles below our place and it's a dry branch, it just . . . it doesn't run any water or anything.

Well, I looked over across that branch and I saw the biggest tree I've ever seen in my life. You've heard o' those big ol', uh, trees in California, you know, bein' so big. Well this tree was so big, couldn't even see either side of it. Course it was kinda hid with brush too. And I stared at that tree and I looked all around. Well I couldn't believe that a tree was that big would be down there. Never had seen it. Sure hadn't.

And while I was lookin' up to see the heighth of it, I could see something moving up there [looks up]. That's bees. That's bees goin' out and in! Folks, there was a place about six inches across, a little knothole and the bees were just swarmin' through that hole, just ZZZzzzzzzzzzz.

Well, you know I was really intrigued by that bein' a bee tree. I thought, you know I'd like to get that honey. That's what I always think of, get some honey, you know, or get whatever's there to be gotten.

So I went home and asked Papa if I could take the wagon, team, go down there and chop that bee tree down.

He said, "Buddy, you got the strongest imagination of anybody I ever heard tell of." He said, "You know there's not any tree that big down there, and if it is that big you couldn't cut it down."

I says, "Papa, I'll get Alec Moore and Parm Williams to go down and help me."

So Alec and Parm promised to go and Dad said, "Well, you can take the wagon team, I won't need 'em this week. How long you gon' stay?"

I says, "Papa, it's gon' take several days to chop that tree down."

So he says, "Better get your Mama to fix some food."

Well, Mama's done fixed it. She heard about me gon' be gone three or four days, and I was Buddy, I'm the oldest boy. And you know, it's a funny thing with these women, really think their oldest boy is somethin' special, whether he is or not.

Anyway, I went down there to chop this tree, takin' the beans Mama'd cooked and the biscuits she'd baked, and Parm, and Alec. We got down to Rock Water Hole Branch. And by the way, while you're goin' down there from the house, you have to cross this branch twice. Or, you've got to go about two miles around the big bend. Well, why go that bend? We just cut across and it was two miles down there.

We got down there and those boys was . . . were enthralled. I'm tellin' you, they couldn't believe it. They said, "Ed, we've been here for years and we've never seen that tree. We still don't believe it's a bee tree."

I said, "Well, I don't either. We're all even."

So we got off over there and we looked that tree over. Yup, it's a bee tree. And there's my mark, big ol' X on there, and E. B. right under it. Well, that made it legal.

So we went on back, unhitched that team, put 'em away out there, way off from the place, so the tree wouldn't fall on 'em when we got it chopped down. Course we was thinkin' about choppin' it down right quick.

We started choppin' on that tree, and we hadn't been cuttin' very long until I got kinda tired. I stopped, I listened, I hear a "chop, chop, chop." Now my goodness. That's . . . I believe that's somebody choppin' on the other side.

Oh man, my hackles raised right quick and I was gonna see what's wrong. So! told those boys, I said, "Listen, if y'all don't mind I'm goin' on the other side'n see, I believe there's somebody choppin' on the other side o' this tree."

Well Parm says, "Go ahead, Ed, you done all the findin' o' the tree, so we'll just keep on choppin'."

Well I went 'round the side o' that tree and back on the other side, and there's three o' those ol' Harwood boys, they'd found this tree and they was choppin' on the other side.

Well, we had a little argument at first, but they showed me there was their mark right up there on that bee tree. That made it legal. So, I said, "Listen, let's just all cut it down and divide the honey."

"OK, that's fine."

Went back and went to choppin'. We chopped for two or three days, and every once in a while I'd look up at that hole, them bees swarmin' out and in. And I got to noticin' one o' those limbs up there kinda swellin' and settlin' back down. I said, "What in the world's the matter with that? Never saw a tree do that." Well, I dismissed it, just a crazy tree anyhow.

Went ahead choppin', finally we got that thing cut down. I think it was about five days we chopped on that thing. And it fell right across Rock Water Hole Branch. And it was about ten foot deep and that made the hole up above the Branch quite a piece and one o' the limbs broke open down there just about four inches wide, just below where the bees went in, and do you know they's just a solid stream o' honey started runnin' out o' that thing?

Well, we was all excited over that and one of 'em hollered then and says, "Look, look, look!" Great big ol' limb about three feet in diameter'd broke off, and that was the limb that had been givin' it out and in, kinda like a bellows, and there's a row o' gray squirrels come outa that limb for three days and nights. There'd been so many in there every time they took a deep breath they'd swell the limb up.

Well, we had the gray squirrel t'eat, we had beans, and we had biscuits, and we was fillin' up all of our vessels. We brought tubs, buckets, fruit jars, pitchers, everything we could find we brought along with us to put that honey in.

Those other boys had too. They was camped way over on the other side o' the Branch, the other side o' where the tree was at. So, we was all fillin' up. I didn't kinda like it 'cause those other boys had more vessels really than we did, and they got more honey'n us. I really thought I found the tree first.

But anyway, why, we's gettin' all this honey gathered up, we got all the squirrels we could eat, why, we couldn't stand to eat a squirrel any more. So we decided to go home.

That honey, now folks, was still pourin' outa that six-inch hole, into Rock Water Hole Branch. And it was just f-f-f-fooooo in there, like that [flowing gesture].

Well, we got in this old wagon, hitched the team up; got in the wagon, started out home. We got to the first crossin' of Rock Water Hole Branch and it looked like it was level full. I . . . well, what in the world? It hadn't rained in weeks.

Parm jumped out and run over there and he hollered, "Ed, it's honey. It's full o' honey!"

Well, I couldn't, uh . . . uh, couldn't believe that, but I . . . it had to be. And we went on two miles around now, three, whatever it was – it was a long ways. We got up to the other crossin' and it was full o' honey too.

Now folks, this was *upstream* from where we cut that bee tree. It wasn't downstream, it was upstream.

And folks, as far as I know that creek is still runnin' bank full with honey.[7]

I have discussed this story at length elsewhere (Bauman 1986:78–111) and will not attend here to some of its most engaging stylistic features. Rather, I will confine myself to pointing out some of its significant thematic and rhetorical features vis-à-vis the personal experience narratives we have examined. In particular, the story of the bee tree displays some notable parallels to the account of Ed's purchase of his first horse. Bell portrays himself once again as young and naive, reinforced by the wide-eyed persona he adopts in the tale (cf. Mullen 1978:145–148). And his father, once again, represents the voice of reason and reality, chiding Ed for his overactive imagination. But here a significant transformation takes place. In this story, by contrast with the earlier one, Ed's vision of the hyper-real bee tree is the true one. The tree does exist; it is not the illusion that his father believes it to be. Bell's narration creates a world in which the nature of reality and true experience is renegotiated, in which mature, rational knowledge and practical experience are not fully reliable guides. In this sense, the tale of the bee tree inverts the theme of the story of Joe Hamilton's redfish as well; it portrays a world in which a redfish might be as big as an oar, unbelievable as that might seem to a practical fisherman. The tall tale is thus an expressive exploration of appearance and reality, innocence and experience, from the other side of the lens, yielding an inverted image. It provides a vehicle for Ed Bell to give voice to another dimension of his life, the side of imagination and speculation, to portray another reality that is fully as important to his identity as his more overt acquisition of practical mastery over his external existence.

But the efficacy of the tall tale as a vehicle to express Ed Bell's preoccupation with the lability of appearance and reality extends beyond the textual capacity of such stories to convey other visions of the world and to renegotiate the relative power of practical knowledge versus imagination. The special quality of the tall tale resides in its interactional effect, in the way in which the audience's response is exploited by the genre. The tall tale is manipulative in distinctive ways (Bauman 1986:20). Tall tales told in the first person masquerade as personal experience narratives, all the more so when they utilize circumstantial elements drawn from the real life of the teller, as in Ed Bell's performances. They aim to elicit the kind of belief accorded to personal experience narratives. But tall tales are ultimately fabrications, in Goffman's sense, manipulations of understanding that induce in the hearer a false sense of what is going on (Goffman 1974:83). At some point in their telling, tall tales begin to challenge the belief of the hearer as they transcend the bounds of credibility and shift into the hyperbole central to the genre. They move the hearer from a sense that "this is true" to a stage of wondering "is this true?" to the conclusion "this is not true," helped along by such metanarrationally loaded statements as "Well, I couldn't believe that a tree was that big would be down there. Never had seen it. Sure hadn't." To this extent, then, Ed Bell's tall tales carry the hearer along the same trajectory that he himself followed in buying his horse, from susceptibility to the fabrications of the horse trader, to doubt, to enlightenment. Bell's tall tales do *interactionally* what his personal experience narratives do thematically: they explore the tension between appearance and reality and the ways of apprehending, comprehending, and manipulating those readings of the world. They elicit and manipulate the interpretive energies of his audience and induce in them the same kind of intellectual experience that most engages his interest and imagination in recounting his own life experience.

A look at the second and final example in our tall tale corpus, "The Fast-Growing Watermelon" (Text 5 below), will allow us to observe how additional elements of the personal experience narratives are given expression in Ed Bell's tall tales. In this story, Ed's younger brother, Artie, asks Ed's help in raising a big watermelon as a school project. Ed willingly agrees and instructs Artie on how to fertilize and water the plant so that it will thrive, insisting that the boy must be responsible for its care. In the beginning, Artie is even a bit overzealous, but one morning, he forgets to water his plant, so Ed has to do it and that makes him so angry that he dumps the whole water barrel onto the plant. When Artie later checks on his watermelon, he is astonished to find that it has taken off cross country, leaving behind an ever-widening furrow. The two brothers chase the melon, with Ed directing the chase, and when they finally catch up with it, it has grown to huge proportions. Ed determines that the only way to stop it is to cut through the vine with an ax. Once stopped, the melon is so large that Ed has to send Artie back for a trailer to haul it home. They eat all they can, but make hardly a dent in it. Finally, Ed instructs his brother to dump it in the hog pen, where an old sow and her nine piglets "made the winter right there in that watermelon rind."

Text 5: The Fast-Growlng Watermelon (recorded by Patricia Jasper, Luling, Texas, 1979)
You know, folks, I just can't help but tell you about my kid brother and his watermelon. That happened years ago and that kid brother was a good deal smaller than I am. Right now we're about twins. But that boy had a project in school. And I just wanted to help him out all I could. That boy was a pretty good kid and wanted to learn, and always I'm gonna help anybody to learn.

So he said, "Ed, I've got a project."

"Uh, what is it, Artie?"

He said, "The teacher wants me to raise a big watermelon, one of the biggest ones."

And I said, "Well, Artie, I can do it. Now, what are you goin' to do with the watermelon?"

"Oh," he said, "just raise it and tell her how big it was, is all she wants to know."

I said, "Well, OK, we'll raise you a big watermelon."

We had a goat pen right off to my left out here a little piece from where I'm sittin' and it was full of goat manure. That is one of the best plant foods that I know of in this world. It was just about eighteen inches deep. I told Artie he could go out there and dig off all the crust of that, about four inches deep and get to the harder stuff that was more rotten. That is really best.

So Artie goes out there and digs out all that top, you know, and gets everything ready. And I show him how to cut it into the soil. And right out west of the house was a nice little spot to plant a watermelon. In fact, we planted two or three hills, so be sure to get one hill to grow.

All right, he cut that stuff into there, and then you had to water it, 'cause when you put hot fertilizer on this ground out here it requires a lot more water than what we get from the rain. So I showed him how to build a old slide made out of a forked tree with, uh, it came together like a 'V' and then part of the tree went on ahead. Nailed two boards across that, and that way, then, you can tie on to it with a pair of mules or horses, and just tow it along on the ground full of water. I would go down to the tank and get a load of water and bring it up there and set it right by that watermelon.

Well you know at first it didn't need very much water. A little bitty plant like that, you know, it just don't take much. But that watermelon started growin'. And that boy had put in, I guess, about three times too much water, uh, too much fertilizer. And then he was overwaterin' it too, which didn't hurt anything 'cause it was in the sand. That watermelon started growin' and the vine just started runnin' out everywhere.

Well, Artie's just a kid. And you know, they lose interest about things like that. And they don't take the right care o' them. One morning I went out there and that watermelon vine was beginnin' to wilt. I got plum mad at that boy. Darn it! He'd forgot to water that watermelon, the day, the eventin' before when he came in from school. Well I told him he had to do all that work. But I looked at that watermelon vine and I said, "Well, I'm afraid it'll just about be gone by night. Artie won't get in from school till late," 'cause they rode burros to school and they went four miles. "I, well I just got to water that watermelon."

So I got out there and got the bucket and I poured about two buckets over there on it, and that just made me madder and madder, 'cause I don' like doin' anybody else's work! When they're supposed to do it, they should do it. I just went over to that barrel and I just turned it over, poured all that water out on those watermelons. "Well," I said, "you're well watered now." Left his barrel layin' down.

Artie came in from school and I said, "Artie, what in the world is the matter with you? You didn't water that watermelon yesterday. You got to learn to take better care of your watermelon."

He said, "Well, Ed," he says, "there's a pretty good size vine out there." He says, "I thought it was doin' all right."

I says. "That don' make no difference. You're supposed to water that watermelon every day when you come in from school."

He said, "I'll go right now, Ed."

I said, "Ha, ha, ha! You goin' to have to haul a barrel of water first."

Well, he didn't like that much. But he went out there and hauled a barrel of water. And he got back around there and he looked at that watermelon, and he kinda got astonished.

He come back in and says, "Say, Ed, that watermelon's gone and done somethin'. I don' know what it's done."

I says, "What's the matter?"

He says, "There's a vine goin' up due north from the house." He says, "That's a long ways across our place." And he says, "It's goin', and it looks like somethin's draggin'." Says, "It's just a little scooped out place, about like that" [scooping gestures]. And he said, "I don' know what to do about it. Won't you come out and show me?"

I went out there with him, and sure enough there was a scooped out place and there was a watermelon vine, and I've never seen a watermelon vine doin' that before. It looks like it was stretchin' and gettin' bigger at the same time. And it was just growin' like wildfire.

I says, "Artie, we got to follow that and see where it goes to. I believe that's a watermelon that's draggin'."

So we got to followin' that drag. And when we got up to the north string of fence, which was a half mile away, that thing had gone through the fence and it broke three barbed wire. Ah, my goodness! That drag then was gettin' about that wide [gesture] and it's deeper.

I said, "That watermelon's growin' fast, Artie. Never saw anything grow like that. But it's growin' fast. And it's travelin' fast. We'd better go back and get that old Model-A of mine."

Went back and got that Model-A and we cut off up north and went a mile past the place on the road and then we took a, an L-turn off. And, uh, we run down that road a piece. And there was a watermelon vine that big around [gesture] layin' right across the road.

I says, "Artie, listen. We, uh, we, we way behind that watermelon."

So we drove back and down that main road and a mile further come to another offset. Went down it, and there was the watermelon vine still bigger. And it was goin' across the road and it done drug all the fences down. There wasn't a sign of a fence left.

We cutout and went a mile further, and went down there. And we looked out across country and there come that watermelon. We're makin' pretty good time. And it just knockin' weeds, fences, and everything down as it comes. But we didn't know hardly what to do.

But I told Artie, I said, "You grab that double-bitted ax out of the rumbleseat of that Model-A and run back there and chop that vine off behind the watermelon. That's the only way we can stop it. Don't dare get in front of it 'cause it's got terrible speed."

He went back there and went to choppin', and you know, when he chopped it off, the watermelon's right in the middle of the road. Well, that blocked all traffic. And I knew somebody'd try to steal that watermelon if they could. We couldn't put it in that Model-A rumbleseat. There wasn't no way! It was just a powerful big watermelon.

So I told Artie, I said, "You take the car and run back down to the house and get that two-wheel trailer." I was gonna make him do what work I could.

And he didn't know how to drive that Model-A, so he's back in just a little while with that big ol', great big ol' two-wheel trailer. But he didn't bring any skidboards to load the watermelon with. We had a powerful hard time gettin' that watermelon on there. Well man, that watermelon stood way higher than my head. And long! It was twenty, thirty foot long! Looked to me like it was still growin' some. So we got it around there and we had to shovel dirt up by the trailer and skid that thing on. We finally got it up on there though. And when we got it on that trailer, we took out for home.

Well, we got home and I told Artie, I said, "I believe that watermelon's ripe, Artie, let's eat it."

So we cut off one end of it. Sure enough, it was ripe. We got all the family out there and we started eatin' that watermelon. We ate all we could. And we just puffed out all over. I says, "We can't eat any more o' that."

Well, we left it sit out on the trailer that day, and the next morning I said, "Artie, you gonna have to take that watermelon out there and dump it in the hog pasture where the hogs are, because it'll get bad pretty soon. A watermelon gets sour, you know."

So we hadn't eaten, oh, about two or three foot of the end of that watermelon. And that was the little end. Took it out there and we just slid it out of that trailer, in there where those hogs were. I had an old sow with nine pigs, and whipped all the other hogs away. And you know, her and those nine pigs made the winter right there in that watermelon rind.[8]

In this story, Ed is the adult, the knowledgeable figure in the relation-ship, while his younger brother, Artie, is the inexperienced neophyte. This relationship between them is clearly cast as one of teacher and learner when Artie asks Ed's help. Ed reports his response as follows: "I just wanted to help him out all I could. That boy was a pretty good kid and wanted to learn, and always I'm gonna help anybody to learn." Moreover, when the watermelon gets out of control, Artie comes back to his older brother for help, admitting, "I don't know what to do about it." Ed himself has never encountered anything quite like this, but he immediately sizes up the situ-ation, hits upon appropriate action, and takes charge in a fine display of practical problem-solving. In this text, there is no direct questioning of the hyper-reality represented by the watermelon, as in "The Bee Tree," but the melon's appearance and behavior clearly challenge the brothers' sense of reality: Artie "kinda got astonished," and Ed is moved to exclaim, "I've never seen a watermelon vine doin' that before." Although Ed and Artie go on to cope with the hyper-real watermelon in eminently practical ways within the story world, their reactions of astonishment and unfamiliarity serve as devices to help induce the tall tale response pattern, the shift from the "this is true" of the personal experience-like opening of the tall tale to the "is this true?" of its transitional phase. Like all of Bell's tall tales, this story engages the hearer in contemplating the ambiguities of appearance and reality.

To this point, then, we have examined Ed Bell's intellectual and imaginative concern with the getting and giving of knowledge, the contrast between inexperience and mastery, and the puzzle of appearance versus reality as expressed in his personal experience narratives and his tall tales. In generic terms, the personal experience narratives are the base form, intended by Ed Bell and received by his hearers as basically true accounts of actual experience, though with some allowance for creative license, artistic effect, or self-aggrandizement. The tall tales are generically more complex, double-voiced (Bakhtin 1981: 301–305), playful transformations of personal experience narrative. In crafting a narrative fabrication that is ultimately something else, they exploit our generic expectations of personal narrative.

Practical Jokes and Stories About Them

Now consider one last story, "Ed Wins the Spotted Pup Award" (Text 6 below). Taken as a textual whole, the story may be seen as a personal experience narrative recounting a practical joke Bell played on some of his fellows down on the coast. Driving home in a thick fog, he is forced to stop because he can no longer see the road. When he gets out of his truck, he spies some pieces of sheetrock in a roadside ditch, and gets the idea for a trick. The next day he tells his friends that while driving home in the fog, he was forced to a halt because his truck had been pushing the heavy fog ahead of it and compacting it to the point that it became impenetrable. To free himself, he told his friends, he had to chop away the fog with an ax (his ax figures in several of his stories) and throw the sheets off to the side of the road. When one of his hearers is duly skeptical, because of Ed's large repertoire of tall tales, Ed challenges him to go see for himself. He does so, comes back full of admiration for Ed's stunt, and in effect enters into collusion, helping Ed to maintain the fiction before the others by offering to take them to see for themselves. When they all return, they confer the "Spotted Pup Award" on Ed – not a real dog, but a metaphor that recognizes a highly creative expressive fabrication.

Text 6: Ed Wins the Spotted Pup Award (recorded by Patrick Mullen, Washington, DC, 1976)

Well, I was comin' in from Port Lavaca one night – I'd been up to see my wife, and she was in town. Had to go back to the beach and the fog was immensely heavy. Oh, it was thick and bad. I had my head out the window, lookin' at that white stripe in the pavement. That's the only way I could get along.

Well, I got out to the bend o' the road and my eyes just nearly went out. So I got out there, wonderin' if I was outa the road. I got out and looked and I was in the road all right.

Then I saw a buncha that stuff out to the side o' the road and here was a I, uh . . . I had a double-bitted ax in there and I just started to hit all the fog and the mist, just like that [chopping motion].

So when I got down to the beach, I told 'em that the ol' V-8 Ford panel job had stalled outright in that bend where the road turned to go to Alamo Beach. "Why, the wheels just started spinnin', and it set and wouldn't move at all." And I said, "You know, the fog got so bad I could-n't see the road at all.

"I got out to see what was the matter. Thought maybe there was a cow layin' in the road or I'd dropped off in a big hole. But I found I couldn't get around the front of it – somethin' in the way.

"Well, I could feel around there and it'd give just a little, not much.

"Well, I just reached back in there and got that ol' double-bitted ax and started slashin' in that stuff, and I said, 'Huh! Kinda funny, kinda like sheetrock only it darn sure wasn't – it was fog.'

"And I . . ., when I got a hole chopped in there I could see the lights of Magnolia Beach down ahead of me about two, two and a half miles, and even see stars out in the sky. I . . . then I realized what'd happened. I'd been pushin' that fog along in front of me that way and it just pushed it all together and finally, why, uh, it just stopped the truck, because that stuff had got so solid it formed kinda like rubber and it was hangin' on other stuff and it stalled the truck out."

So I said, "I just went ahead and chopped all this fog out, great big sheets of it, and just throwed it over in the ditch. Well, I got a pretty good bunch of it outa there; I guess it looked to me like there was about half a trailer load of that stuff I chopped out so people, other people could get by too, 'cause I cleared the whole pavement."

I come on down to the beach. Feller down there said, "Bell, I'll be doggoned if you can't tell the biggest ones I ever heard of, but," said, "you usually cover it." Said, "You've got a backup. I'm afraid you have this time, but I don't believe you could possibly cover that one."

"Well, didn't you say you was goin' to town today?" That was the next day, of course, that I was tellin' 'em about it.

Says, "Yeah, I'm goin' to town in just a few minutes."

I said, "When you get up there to where that Alamo Beach road turns off, the road turns gently back kinda toward Port Lavaca. You look in the ditch on the left side. That's where I threw that fog, those sheets of fog I chopped out. Now, it didn't seem to me like they was gonna melt."

He went on to town and come back down there and he pulled his hat off and bowed real low. He says, "Hey, folks! Come on over. Pull your hat off and bow to the chiefliest chief liar of all peoples, he's always got a backup."

Some of 'em come over there and said, "What in the world's the matter with you, what're you actin' so crazy about?"

"You's listenin' when he told that fog tale to us."

"Oh, yes, but that was ridiculous."

"Well," he said, "them sheets of fog're layin' in the ditch just like he said they are. You don't believe it, I'll take you up there and show you."

Well, some of 'em really wanted to go up there and look at it. They got back, and they'd all lift their hats off and bowed and said, "Bell, you get the spotted pup." Says, "He's yours till somebody takes him away from you."

Well, down our way when a man wins the spotted pup, he's the top liar. So I happened to get that spotted pup.[9]

We observed in the first story we considered, about Ed's acquisition of his first horse, that the horse dealer's fabrication represents attractive subject matter for Ed as a means to explore the tension between appearance and reality and the susceptibility of appearance to manipulation in order to impart a false sense of reality. Like the horse story, the Spotted Pup narrative recounts a fabrication, but here the trickster is Bell himself and the fabrication is a playful one. What is the nature of this reported trick? A close look at the fabrication itself reveals that it consists largely of the telling of a tall tale. The account Bell gives to his friends about encountering a fog so thick and compacted that he had to chop his way through it with an ax has all the lineaments of a tall tale in the classic mode: it starts out framed as a true personal experience narrative, builds upon the occurrence of a heavy fog of a kind familiar to all residents of the coast, and then proceeds to extend the severity of the fog into a dimension of hyper-reality that requires extraordinary action, ultimately carrying the account to a level where it can no longer be believed. The story even resonates intertextually with another of Bell's favorite tall tales about red-fishing in a fog bank

(Bauman 1986:106–108; Mullen 1978:139–40); both are about thick fog and both recount the driving in a heavy fog by watching the line painted on the road. The Spotted Pup story is thus essentially a metanarrational story about the telling of a story, involving as well a doubly laminated performance about a performance. That is to say, one way that Ed Bell performed his life was by using his own storytelling performances as the stuff of further narrative production.

But this is only part of the picture, for the fabrication recounted here extends beyond the telling of a tall tale insofar as Ed introduces yet another dimension into his trick. Not only does he play with the ambiguities of appearance and reality in the tall tale, but he also compounds the trick by providing pseudo-verification of his lie in the form of the scrap sheetrock, which he recasts as sheets of compressed fog. His fabrication thus takes on an element of practical joking, involving a playful manipulation of the non-verbal, material environment in a further dimension of fabrication. Here, then, Ed uses a further, non-narrative vehicle as a means for the expressive exploration of his intellectual concerns, a complement to the narrative forms employed for the same purpose. And indeed, Ed Bell was an accomplished practical joker.

But let us return to the narrative sphere once again, for there is yet a further dimension of complexity played out in the text before us. For presentational purposes, I have treated this story of how Bell won the Spotted Pup Award as a personal experience narrative about the telling of a tall tale and its associated element of practical joking. Taken as a whole, that is what it is. In the actual performative unfolding of the story, however, the situation is more complicated. A careful examination of the text reveals that as this story was performed in the narrative event in which it was recorded, it is full of generic ambiguity. In fact, the story appears more like a tall tale than a personal experience narrative. Note that in the third paragraph, Bell sets us up, as he set up his audience of friends on the coast, by not specifying what the "buncha that stuff out t'the side of the road" is, only suggesting later that it was "kinda like sheetrock," and by telling us, *before* the account to his friends – that "I just started to hit all the fog and the mist, just like that," with accompanying chopping gestures. Then, although the full-blown account and explanation of the event to his friends is framed as an account of an account ("I told 'em that . . . ," "And I said . . ."), the framing recedes into the background as the devices for reporting speech drop out, and his quoted narration about discovering the nature of the compacted fog and chopping his way through it appears to be a direct narration of the event to us. In other words, in that section of the text between "I got out to see what was the matter" and "I came on down to the beach," the effect of Bell's narration is to make it appear that the present audience, not his friends at home, are the direct recipients of the account, notwithstanding the one quotational frame in the line "So I said, 'I just went ahead and chopped all this fog out . . .'" To this extent, then, we are targets of his tall tale fabrication in nearly equal measure with the story-internal audience of Ed's fellows on the coast. The Spotted Pup story is not simply a personal experience narrative *about* the telling of a tall tale – it actually oscillates between the two in the narrative event in which it was performed. The text is thus a wonderfully multi-voiced interweaving of all the expressive forms by which Ed Bell explored his preoccupation with innocence and enlightenment, appearance and reality – personal experience narrative, tall tale, practical joke – all in the service of underscoring how intellectually and experientially complex and engaging these ontological and epistemological problems can be.

Intertextuality and Narrative Self-Fashioning

Ed Bell performed his life in multiple guises: in true personal experience narratives, in first-person tall tales, in practical jokes, in narrative performances about his narrative performances. All of these expressive creations and recreations of the performed self are systemically interrelated, formally, functionally, and thematically. Each expressive vehicle – the personal experience narrative, the tall tale, the practical joke – has different capacities, and these differences add texture to Ed Bell's use of his life and his art to give voice to his intellect and his imagination. No single genre alone would suffice; together, they provide him with the means to figure himself in a variety of alignments to a remarkably consistent and coherent set of epistemological and social-relational concerns.

Bell's personal experience narratives center on situations and social encounters in which the relationship between appearance and reality is ambiguous and there is a clear asymmetry of knowledge and experience in the protagonists' abilities to resolve the ambiguity. Resolution is achieved in a display of expert knowledge and mastery, which serves both pedagogical and practical ends. The nomic calibration of these stories, in Silverstein's (1993) phrase, is to the real world; the resolution favors a naturalistic, empirical, and most of all, knowing orientation to reality. The narrative plots trace a developmental trajectory from naivete, gullibility, or ignorance to informed knowledge, a kind of *Bildung*-in-brief. Bell traces his own development with a series of stories keyed to stages in the life-cycle, here illustrated by the story of his first horse, which chronicles his own youthful naivete, to the stories of Joe Hamilton's redfish and the big storm, which portray him in the full power of mature adulthood.

Bell's tall tales, by contrast, provide an expressive vehicle to keep the wonder alive, to indulge in flights of epistemological fancy that education to this-world realities would otherwise displace. In these stories, he narrates himself in a world of hyper-reality, not necessarily governed by the ontological realities of his personal experience narratives. The alternative nomic calibration of these tall tales, however, still allows for the displays of knowledge and practical mastery that portray him in an advantageous light. Moreover, the tall tale offers a mechanism for play with the epistemological lability of reality not only in the narrated events that the tales recount, but in the narrative events in which they are told: they are generic fabrications that ambiguate the framing of the communicative event for the tall-tale audience. Practical jokes extend the same kind of play into the broader experiential environment of their victims.

The *representational* self-aggrandizement of the story content in both the personal experience narratives and the tall tales, in which Bell portrays himself as looking good, is complemented and enhanced by the *presentational* looking good of virtuosic performance; the mastery portrayed in the stories is highlighted by the communicative mastery displayed in the telling of the stories. Likewise, the social-relational dominance of the knowledgeable figures in the stories – Ed's father or Ed himself – as they are portrayed in the encounters represented in the narrated events is matched by the social-interactional power of the master performer in the narrative event, skilled at eliciting and manipulating the participative energies of the audience in both the personal experience narratives and the tall tales and the experiential world of his interlocutors in the practical jokes.

As a figure animated in his stories, as a performer in his storytelling, and as a social-interactional trickster in his practical jokes, Ed Bell had a strong predisposition toward being in control and toward looking good in exercising that control. His performances themselves, as well as his practical jokes, became narrative resources in their own right, as in the Spotted Pup story, recycled in metaperformances of his mastery of people and situations. This narrative blends all three of the self-fashioning expressive forms we have considered – personal experience narratives, tall tales, practical jokes – into a complex intertextual blend of genres and enactments, exploiting all of the capacities they offer for self-aggrandizement. Wining the Spotted Pup Award simply corroborates and ratifies that he was looking as good to his friends on the Gulf Coast as he was in performing the story for me.

6

"That I Can't Tell You": Negotiating Performance with a Nova Scotia Fisherman

Performance and Other Presentational Frames

Ed Bell was a virtuoso performer, one of the most artful storytellers I have encountered in several decades of field research. He was precisely the kind of master performer to which students of verbal art are attracted: the orientation of performance studies to artfulness and virtuosity tends to predispose many students of oral poetics toward the most artful texts and fully realized performances as objects of presentation and study.

At the same time, however, the more general scope of the ethnography of speaking, with which the study of verbal art as performance has been closely allied, and especially the detailed attention to form–function–meaning interrelationships and to the situated management of framing and voicing that are central concerns of that line of inquiry, lead us to recognize that performance is but one mode of discursive production among others within the communicative economy of a discourse community and to the concomitant recognition that texts – even those that are the most poetically marked and conventionally performed – may be rendered in other communicative modes. Indeed, Dell Hymes' foundational treatment of performance as a special mode of communicative display in his "Breakthrough Into Performance" (1975b) rests upon a close formal analysis of alternative, shifting, and negotiated frames – report, translation, performance – for the voicing of poetic texts by his Chinookan consultants in the emergent course of his ethnographic work with them. Hymes' seminal essay is one of a number of works in the ethnography of performance, from Lee Haring's pioneering essay "Performing for the Interviewer" (1972) to Michael Silverstein's "The Secret Life of Texts" (1996), that have illuminated variously the selection, entextualization, framing, and voicing of oral texts within the ethnographic encounter as one significant order of situational contexts in which our textual corpora have been produced (see also, for example, Basso 1996; Briggs 1985, 1986; Darnell 1989[1974]; Paredes 1993[1977]; Tedlock 1983). Still, the central problem that he poses – how does performance, as a mode of textual production and reproduction, relate to other such modes? – remains underexplored. This chapter represents an effort toward filling that gap.

I take as my point of departure the understanding that performance resides in the assumption of responsibility to an audience for a display of communicative competence, subject to evaluation for the skill and efficacy with which the act of expression is accomplished. In these terms, performance is a variable quality, depending upon the degree to which a speaker assumes responsibility for such communicative display, from sustained, full performance to a fleeting breakthrough into performance, with hedged or negotiated performance lying somewhere in between. My purpose in this chapter is to analyze the dynamics of this continuum, the discursive processes by which the assumption of accountability for communicative display are negotiated in a particular ethnographic encounter revolving around the reproduction of traditional narrative texts.

Storytelling and Sociability in the La Have Islands

The materials I shall treat are all drawn from a single afternoon's work (July 27, 1970) with one individual during my fieldwork in the La Have Islands, which lie off the shore of Lunenburg County on the southwest coast of Nova Scotia, between the mouths of the La Have and Petite Rivers. The group includes about twenty named islands, fourteen of which have been inhabited at one time or another since the late 1840s by the largely Irish and German forebears of the present inhabitants. The islands vary considerably in size, from little more than exposed rocks to several square miles in area, with the houses ranged around the shore in settlements of from one to more than thirty households per island. Local communities are not confined to single islands, for segments of some adjacent islands are connected, rather than separated, by the channels that flow between them, while various parts of other islands belong to different communities. The region has always been one where people are oriented as much to the water as they are to the land.

The settlement and growth of the La Have Islands were fostered by the development of the Lunenburg County fishing industry. With the depletion of the inshore fishery and the mechanization of offshore fishing, the industry has undergone a steady decline. At the time of my fieldwork, lobstering was the mainstay of the economy, supplemented by some inshore fishing, but economic opportunity was severely limited in the area and most of the young people were leaving. At the height of island prosperity, between 1890 and 1925, there were approximately 100 households on the Islands; at the time of my visits, a number of formerly inhabited islands were deserted and the permanent population numbered about 150 people.

A central concern of my fieldwork in the La Have Islands was to explore the locally defined aesthetic of spoken language, which led me to a focus on the principal marked occasion for speaking in traditional island culture, namely, evening sessions of male sociability at the general store (Bauman 1972). During the early decades of the twentieth century, when island population was at its fullest, the La Have Islands were served by two general stores, both located on the same island, but at opposite ends and serving different communities. The one in which I was particularly interested was Sperry's store, a typical general store in the great North American tradition of general store, stocked with an enormous range of merchandise, including hardware, soft goods, tea, sugar, flour, canned goods, fishing supplies, kerosene, clothing, housewares, and so on. In general, the store filled those needs of the people that fell between what they produced for their own subsistence and the special items that were purchased on infrequent trips to Bridgewater or Lunenburg.

Shopping at the general store was never a completely utilitarian activity, for all the islanders took pleasure in the opportunities for sociability that the store afforded. With the exception of a few old, retired men, however, who occasionally congregated around the store during the day, or young men who sometimes gathered there on stormy days in winter, daytime visits to the store were chiefly for the purpose of buying something. On winter nights, though, the situation was otherwise, with sociability – the association with others for the sheer pleasure of the interaction – becoming the primary purpose of visiting the store. As a people who depended upon fishing for their livelihood, the La Have islanders had little leisure time during the spring, summer, and early fall months when the weather allowed them to be on the water. It was only during the fall and winter months, when the days were too short and the weather too cold for fishing, that they could enjoy the luxury of leisurely evenings, and it was on these fall and winter evenings that the men congregated at the general store. Every night in this season, from early evening until 11 or 12 o'clock, the store at the north end of Bell's Island was filled with men who gathered to enjoy one another's company in card playing and conversation.

The gathering at the store was an exclusively male activity, although both men and women recognized it as the premier speech situation of the community. Women might come in to buy something in the evening, but they preferred to leave the store to the men, and those few women who did come did not stay. Children, too, were excluded from attendance, largely because their parents did not want them out at night. Once again, though, those who did come were not allowed to linger, because the language and conversation of the card players often became too rough for their tender ears. By his early teens, a boy might be permitted to listen to the conversation from the fringes of the group, but it was not until he reached the age of seventeen or eighteen that he would be allowed to take the floor, though only infrequently would he think of doing so. From the early twenties, eligibility for active participation increased roughly with age and worldly experience. The younger men did not say much, but listened with interest to the "old fellers that knowed everything" and "had it further back," who dominated the conversation.

One of the major genres that figured in those storytelling encounters was the *yarn*. In La Have Island usage, a yarn was a narrative, the principal feature of which was that it dealt with personal experience: "each person would tell of his own experience, whichever way it happened; one feller seen it, he experienced it, then he'd tell it." Yarns were told and accepted as essentially true ("most of them fellers, you could believe what they said"), though with some license for creative embellishment ("Maybe somebody would add a little bit onto it – make it sound better – but most of it was true"), about something that transcended common knowledge, experience, or expectation. Yarns dealt for the most part with unusual work experiences (e.g., catching a halibut "as big as a barn door"), travels to distant places ("The ones who traveled the most could tell the most and best"), encounters with the supernatural ("them times you wouldn't go out the door without seein' things; every yard of road had its ghost"), and memorable local occurrences. Although yarns were told and accepted as essentially true accounts of actual events, it is clear that some at least of the tales of encounters with the supernatural were traditional legends, also found elsewhere but localized by the islanders.

The true focus of the gatherings at the store was the presentation of personal experiences and individualized points of view. That is, the evening sessions of sociability represented an occasion in which the display, maintenance, and development of personal identity were of paramount importance, through the exploitation of a conversational resource in personal terms. Nevertheless, the interplay between the individual and social dimensions of the storytelling events gave shape to the internal organization of the gatherings themselves. Each participant's contribution was a personal one, with emphasis upon the individuality and uniqueness of his experience. At the same time, however, these individual contributions were bound together by a chain of association, a process in which each story was elicited by an emergent intertextual link through some sharing of a common ground with the preceding one, each individual making his personal contribution by drawing on a common conversational resource. One consultant explained the dynamic in these terms: "some feller would tell a yarn, and by the time he was finished the next one would have one that led off of it – something that he had heard or saw." For example, "one man would mention a port and another man would have been there and that's how the yarns came out." In this way, the tension between the individual and the communal provided the energy by which the event proceeded.

Negotiating Performance

Now, at the time of my fieldwork in 1970, the last general store had been gone for thirty-odd years, and the heyday of the evening sessions had waned even earlier, so, like many ethnographers, I was studying memory culture and my sources were of middle age or older. On the particular afternoon in question, I was working with one of the best of them, a man named Howard Bush, of Bush Island, then eighty-seven years old. My goal was to record examples of the kinds of yarns that figured so prominently in sessions at the store. While Bush had been present at many of those sessions, he had never been prominent among the active participants in the storytelling there, partly because pride of place was given to older men and he had still been comparatively young when the period of active storytelling entered its decline. He remembered a fair number of stories from the tellings of others – on that afternoon I recorded fifteen narratives from him – but a number of factors bore heavily on his recounting of them to me, relating to his willingness to assume responsibility for a display of competence in telling them.

First of all, while yarns were understood to be narratives recounting personal experience, my interest in the stories told at the general store constrained Bush to dredge up and retell what were not for the most part his own stories, but rather ones that had originally been the personal narratives of others. Furthermore, as I have mentioned, one of the basic conventions of yarns was that they be told and accepted as essentially true, with corroborating detail and other devices of verisimilitude, such as direct claims of veracity, appeals to eye-witness knowledge, and so on. Bush was at an obvious disadvantage here, telling the stories of others called up from distant memory at a remove of up to seventy years or more. Not surprisingly then – I say this with hindsight and hindsight is rarely surprising – our recording session became an extended negotiation about performance (see Briggs 1986). I propose to look here at four of the yarns I recorded to illustrate some of the dimensions and products of that negotiation.

The first text I shall examine is also the first narrative that Bush told me during our afternoon session. In arranging my visit with him, I had indicated that I was interested in yarns of the kind told at the general store and when we began our conversation he told me that he had recalled one that he had heard his uncles – participants in the narrated event – tell "dozens of times."

Text 1: The Monkey in the Pickle
There was an old fella, years ago, he lived in La Have River and he kept a shop, a small shop, and he had a small vessel. And every . . . about every week he'd come down here trading, uh, goods out of his shop for fish. And he had a monkey.

[RB: A pet monkey.]

He had a pet monkey. And he'd always bring that with him.

Well, uh, I get kinda worked up, and I can't think about what I want to say. [eleven second pause].

The people would salt their fish in butts, you know, puncheons we call them. And when the fish was forked out it would leave the . . . it would leave the pickle about half, half in the butt.

And, uh, the people used to bring cod oil and bring, uh, fish and trade it for these shop goods, you know. And he was always three parts drunk himself. He sold . . . he sold some and he was always about three parts, and he'd be in the cuddy and when the people would bring this oil – they'd tell him they was here with some oil – well, uh, he'd say, "You go measure it." Well they'd measure one gallon of oil and two of water. They sold him more, uh, more water than what they did oil. But he didn't know it at the time.

And the boys – my father then was one of them at that time, but he must've only been a small boy, and his brothers – they was anxious to try to dump this monkey into the puncheon, into the puncheon of pickle (laughs).

So they rigged up a scheme. They took a board and they put it, uh, just on it . . . on a . . . so it wouldn't take much to tip it, you know. But this monkey's jumping around everywhere, like some dogs is. So when he jumps on this board it'll tip him into the pickle.

Anyway, it did. That's 'cause it . . . it dumped him in the puncheon of pickle one day. This old man was three parts drunk. He heard the monkey hollering and, uh, he couldn't find it right away, where it was.

And at last he did find it.

And I don't know how he got it out. That I can't tell you. He mighta maybe put the board down with a slant, and maybe he crawled out. I imagine that's the only way he would get it out.

And, uh . . . I don't know if I can tell you very much more about that or not. I don't think there's very much more to it.

This is a story about a practical joke, of a kind widely told in rural North America; practical jokes and narratives about them are, in fact, part of a unified expressive tradition, and we have already encountered one such story told by Ed Bell (Chapter 5; see also Bauman 1986:33–53). Notwithstanding his having heard the story of the monkey in the pickle dozens of times and having planned to tell it to me in advance of our session, Bush expresses his difficulty in actually recounting it at two points in the text, once near the beginning, and once at the end. In the first instance, after a reasonably adequate orientation to the story by island standards, introducing the dramatis personae, locating the action in terms of place, and presenting the potentiating conditions for the narrated event, the narration breaks down quite decisively, signaled by Bush's statement, "Well, uh, I get kinda worked up, and I can't think about what I want to say," followed by an eleven second pause before he resumes the story. Then, at the end of the narrative, he encounters further problems in producing a satisfactory ending. After indicating that the old trader finally did locate his distressed monkey, he runs out of information concerning the narrated event and shifts into a confession of his difficulty in bringing the story to effective closure:

And I don't know how he got it out. That I can't tell you. He mighta maybe put the board down with a slant, and maybe he crawled out. I imagine that's the only way he would get it out.

And, uh . . . I don't know if I can tell you very much more about that or not. I don't think there's very much more to it.

These two trouble spots and Bush's metanarrational comments concerning them invoke both aspects of communicative competence. The earlier one indicates a breakdown in his *ability* to sustain the narrative line and the flow of narration, while the second implicates his lack of *knowledge* concerning the outcome of the narrated event and thus of the conclusion of the narrative. Bush's confession of nervousness and inability to think of what to say after the opening orientation section constitutes a disclaimer of performance on the grounds of an incapacity to continue the very act of narration, though the story was familiar to him from repeated hearings. The problem, apparently, lay in constructing an adequate narration for me, as an outsider. I base this interpretation on the information presented as Bush resumed the narration after his disclaimer and the lengthy pause that followed, namely, the explanation of the practice of salting fish in barrels. Every adult islander would be expected to know all this, but Bush appears to have realized that I might not. Because the nature of the pickle is so central to the point of the story, he felt the need to provide the relevant information as his uncles never had to do, and I believe this realization was sufficient to undermine his narration, never strongly confident to begin with.

The difficulty that Bush encounters at the end of his yarn is of a different nature. Whereas the early breakdown stems from a lapse in his ability to sustain the narration, the problem at the end implicates the other aspect of communicative competence, that is, his lack of knowledge concerning the features of the story that he feels are necessary to an appropriate telling. The problem, as noted, has to do with bringing the narrative to effective closure. Bush apparently senses that the eventual finding of the monkey in the barrel of pickle, the last thing he recounts with assurance, is not an effective point on which to end the story. A comment on the appearance of the pickled monkey or the reaction of the drunken old trader would have been effective here, exploiting the potential for burlesque provided by the monkey's immersion in the strong brine or the trader's inebriated state, but we cannot know how Bush's uncles ended the story, or whether he had forgotten what they said. We can observe, though, that Bush fulfills the need he feels for more detail by speculating, rather anticlimactically, on how the monkey was extricated from the barrel, concerning which he has no definite knowledge. Having suggested what might plausibly have happened, he still feels a lack of closure, and so confesses to a lack of anything else to tell. This, then, is a disclaimer of performance on the grounds of insufficient knowledge. In both instances, whether on the basis of a lack of ability or knowledge, he excuses himself from full competence and thus from full responsibility in recounting the story. The first yarn, however, is the only one in which Bush's disclaimers of performance invoked his ability to narrate; all subsequent disclaimers appealed to insufficient knowledge, as his nervousness in the encounter diminished.

In the second example (Text 2, below), I had asked Bush if he had heard a story told to me by another man, the father of his son's wife. This is, in fact, a localized version of a widely told traditional treasure legend,[1] of

special sociolinguistic interest because of the core motif in which successful recovery of a buried treasure, associated with the devil or other forces
of evil, can be achieved only by the strict maintenance of silence; when one
of the diggers speaks, an expression of his humanity or a reaffirmation of
his human social ties, the treasure is lost, reclaimed by the devil:

Text 2: The Loss of the Buried Treasure
RB: Did you hear . . . [the story about the treasure]?
HB: I don't . . . I can't tell any story about it. But, uh, I know . . . I
       know I heard the story about where they went to dig this chest
       of money, and, uh, they was down to the chest of money, far
       enough for to see the handle on it. And they hadn't, uh, they
       wasn't to speak. There wasn't a word to be spoke. And they had
       the rope through the handle . . .
RB: Mn hmm.
HB: . . . for to snake it up out of the ground. And one fellow spoke,
       and tore the handle right off the chest. They had the handle.
       They had the handle on the rope. Now I . . . now that's the story
       I heard, now.
RB: Yeah. That's . . . who . . . who was it told that story?
HB: I don't know. I don't know. I can't say.
RB: Do you recall how they found that money? Was it in a dream?
HB: No, I don't think . . . I don't think so. They lost the money. The
       money went down. The Old Fellow to- . . . took it back again.

Howard Bush's opening response to my request for this yarn is a disclaimer
of his ability to "tell any story about it." But then he proceeds to recount
precisely the narrative I was asking about, but framed at both the beginning and the end as a *report* of his having *heard* the story: "I know I heard
the story," and "Now that's the story I heard, now." The narrative itself is
very lean, containing none of the locational, motivational, or personal ori-
entational information that conventionally opens a yarn: where it happened, what motivated the action, who was involved. Thus, Bush's opening
disclaimer is not a denial that he knew the story, at least in its outlines, nor
a breakdown in his capacity to narrate, but a statement of his lack of competence to tell it as a yarn should properly be told. He is unwilling to assume
responsibility for an adequate narration, an appropriate telling in island
terms. He does produce a narrative, but won't undertake to perform it
because he does not know it well enough.

Moreover, the narrative he does present is not even a full outline of the
story as he recalls it. He ends his account initially with the tearing of the

handle from the treasure-chest. It is only in response to my further questioning – though not in direct answer to my question – that he provides the additional information that the money was lost, reclaimed by the devil. Thus, consistent with his professed unwillingness to perform the story, resorting rather to a report of having heard it, Bush's initial report is restricted to what is in effect a metonym of the full story, sufficient to identify it but short of a complete account.

In examining the formal features of the narrative, we may observe that the text is marked by a number of parallel syntactic constructions which become more apparent when it is set out in lines determined by breath pauses. I have indicated one set of parallel constructions by italics, a second by boldface:

> I know I heard the story about where they went to dig this chest of money, and uh,
> they was down to the chest of money far enough
> for to see the handle on it.
> And they hadn't, uh,
> *they wasn't to speak.*
> *There wasn't a word to be spoke.*
> **And they had the rope**
> **through the handle**
> for to snake it up off the ground.
> And one fellow spoke
> and tore the handle right off the chest.
> **They had the handle.**
> **They had the handle on the rope**.

I draw attention to the parallelism in the text because this device is frequently employed in oral poetics as a key to performance. The question must arise, then, of why parallelism should be so evident in this text when Mr. Bush has clearly disclaimed responsibility to perform it. The answer, I believe, is that parallelism is not here as a marker of artfulness, but is rather an artifact of the narrator's insecure command of the story line, a means of nailing down successive bits of the story as he recalls them, and as he tries to call up what happens next. The parallel constructions represent a reuse of already proven constructions in lieu of providing new information of which Mr. Bush has relatively little at hand. Parallelism is, after all, a basic device of cohesion in a discourse which can serve, as here, to maintain discursive continuity in the absence of other means to do so. This is an instance of what Silverstein (1984) aptly calls "the pragmatic 'poetry' of prose," the quotation marks around "poetry" indexing the absence of purposeful artfulness. Parallelism is thus not here a key to performance, but an index of its absence.

The third narrative (Text 3, below) has certain features in common with the preceding two but contrasts significantly with them in regard to performance. This is a story that Howard Bush had from his uncle, from whom he heard it on a number of occasions. Bush's son, who had arranged our interview, suggested that I ask his father about it. Like the account of the lost treasure, this is a localized version of a widely told legend in which the devil, sitting in on a card game (here because the blasphemous participants had in effect called him into their presence by their swearing), is given away by his monstrous feet.[2] I have numbered the sections in the story as an aid to the discussion that follows.

Text 3: The Devil as Card Player

RB: I wanted to ask you also about that Solly Richards story, about the . . .

HB: Oh, about the devil (laughs).

RB: Yeah.

[I]

HB: Well, when they was in this old shop playing cards, they played every night, or near about every night outside of Sunday night. It was in Elmer Cane's shop, was called Elmer Cane's shop, well it was Elmer Cane. And they carried on the devil, they swore, you know how it went on, maybe, I suppose, half tight. And one of them was my uncle, was . . . was my wife's [*sic*: mother's] brother.

[II]

And one night they was playing and a man come to the door. I don't know if he knocked or not. There's no doubt maybe he did, for he was a stranger.

Anyway he went in, and he asked them if he could have a game of cards with them and they said "yeah." And he sat down to the table.

And after a little while one fellow looked under the . . . lost a card and he looked down under the table to get to it and he saw this funny looking foot (laughs). Looked like a horse's foot.

They knocked off playing. And he left. The man left.

But I don't remember . . . I don't know what to tell you,

what he done when he left, but I think he done something to
the shop. I think he took a chunk with him. I think he took a
piece of the shop with him or tore it to pieces or something.
    It was the devil.

RB: Yeah.

[III]

HB: And my uncle told me . . . well, he didn't tell me, he told us
within the house, all hands. He went home, he went to bed, and
he had no rest the whole night. He couldn't get asleep, he said.
He was playing cards with the devil all night. He had no rest at
all, he said. He was . . . like it seemed he was in a blaze of fire.
"That settled the card playing there," he said. It settled him and
it settled it there.

The text may be seen to fall into three parts, indicated by Roman numer-
als. The first part (I), the orientation, is fully adequate by traditional
standards, setting the scene for the narrated event by place (the shop), participants (including Bush's uncle), and potentiating action (playing cards,
drinking, and especially blasphemy).

The middle section (II) does not display the confidence of the orientation. Here Bush makes two admissions of ignorance, once with regard to
whether or not the devil knocked at the door of the shop, and later with
regard to damage caused by the devil on his hasty departure from the
premises. In the former, he is able to make some effort toward supplying
circumstantial detail of the kind called for by the genre by drawing on his
cultural knowledge concerning island etiquette: strangers are required to
knock before entering. Nevertheless, he hedges his guess by saying, "There's
no doubt maybe he did," the "maybe" undoing the apparent certainty of
"There's no doubt." Concerning the damage to the shop, his memory fails
him again, but here he has no cultural knowledge to furnish narratively relevant information. Accordingly, he confesses, "I don't know what to tell
you," that is, in effect, "I don't have sufficient information to sustain an
appropriate narrative performance at this point." Here again, the apparent
syntactic parallelism of "I think he done something to the shop" / "I think
he took a chunk with him" / "I think he took a piece of the shop with him,"
are not keys to performance but indices of insecurity, the repetition of the
same syntactic frame while trying to dredge up additional forgotten elements of the story.

In the concluding part of the narrative, however, Bush is on his firmest
ground yet. Note that here the narrated event has shifted; he is no longer
recounting the encounter with the devil in Elmer Cane's shop, but his

uncle's later account to himself and others concerning the effects of the diabolical experience. Here Bush was himself a participant and can supply a
full personal account. At this point, his mode of presentation shifts
markedly. I have set out this concluding passage in lines to make its artfulness more clearly apparent:

He went home,
he went to bed,
and he had no rest the whole night.
He couldn't get asleep, he said.
He was playing cards with the devil all night.
He had no rest at all, he said.
He was . . . like it seemed he was in a blaze of fire.
"That settled the card playing there," he said.
It settled him and it settled it there.

The passage is marked, first of all, by parallel syntactic constructions in the
first six lines and the last two lines of the above excerpt, making for two
parallel sets. This is not the hesitant, repetitive, insecure parallelism of the
earlier examples; beginning with "He went home," Bush's voice becomes
louder, more forceful, and higher in pitch, and in the seventh line the
quoted speech of the uncle's statement takes on a shift in voice, re-
enacting his emphatic delivery. Moreover, the lines display perceptible
patterns of rhythmic stress, with a single beat in the first two lines and four
in each of the remaining lines (in the sixth line, the four beats occur after
the false start):

He went hóme,
he went to béd,
and he had nó rést the whóle níght.
He coúldn't gét asléep, he sáid.
He was pláying cárds with the dévil all níght.
He had nó rést at áll, he sáid.
He was . . . like it séemed he wás in a bláze of fíre.
"That séttled the cárd playing thére," he sáid.
It séttled hím and it séttled it thére.

This is a breakthrough into performance, signaled, or keyed, by this confi-
dently rendered, mutually reinforcing set of formal devices: syntactic,
prosodic, and paralinguistic.

The final narrative we shall consider is a local character anecdote,
recounting an event at which Howard Bush himself was present. Again, it

was his son who had suggested earlier that I ask Bush for this story. As it happens, the event took place at the general store itself, in a milieu of male sociability within which such stories were characteristically told:

Text 4: Frank Bell and the Eggs

RB: One story I know you know about was Frank Bell and the eggs.
HB: Right. Yes, that I know is true. That I seen him do. I sat right, right in the shop and seen him, seen him do that.

He always used to torment Aubrey Sperry, that was the boss of the shop, 'bout he could . . . he could suck three dozen eggs and eat the shell of the last one. Well, every time he came to the shop he'd be tormenting Aubrey. At last, Aubrey got kinda tired of it.

One day he come up starting in, he says, "I could suck three dozen eggs and eat the shell of the last one, and I want a bet for five dollars." Aubrey goes to the till and he lays down a five-dollar bill and he counts out three dozen eggs.

And . . . oh, there was – I don't know – maybe seven or eight young fellows, lot though, not my age, but young, young fellows, sitting around. All hands begin to laugh. He didn't go right away, you see, and they begin to laugh. Well, he thought they was laughing at him while he didn't take right ahold of the eggs. He was going to take back water [i.e., back off], and it looked like if he was going to take back water. But we laughed at him, and then that give him . . . he went to work at it.

Now I don't know how many he sucked. He punched the holes in the ends and he . . . I guess he must have sucked pretty near a dozen the first time. Then he lit his old pipe. He had a little smoke, not very long. He took a couple more, half a dozen or so. And that's the way, till he had them all down. He'd suck so many and then he'd have a little smoke. And he talked a very, very short time, and he left. "I guess I'll go home."

He went down the road, not very far down the road, there was a man coming up while he was going – down they passed when they was coming up – and they seen where he stood right over there and vomit them up. He put his finger down, you see, and he vomit them up, so that they wouldn't make him sick (laughs).

In this story, by contrast with others, Bush is fully secure in his performance from beginning to end. The key factor, obviously, is that this yarn allows him to speak from his own personal experience as a marginal participant, as he is clear to establish at the outset: "Yes, that I know is true. That I seen him do. I sat right, right in the shop and seen him, seen him do that." Not only can he testify directly to the veracity of the story, but he can also supply abundant circumstantial detail, a hallmark of good yarn narration. The two fleeting departures from the assured and fluent narration that characterizes his telling of this story occur in his hedging about exactly how many men were in the shop and exactly how many eggs Frank Bell sucked before taking up his pipe for the first time, small lapses quickly redressed by settling on the figure of seven or eight young fellows and a dozen eggs. This is, on the whole, a confident narration. With this yarn, then, Mr. Bush is ready to take full responsibility for correct, authoritative performance, keyed by his opening appeals to firsthand knowledge and the resultant truthfulness and reliability of his account.

From Disclaimers of Performance to Full Performance

The four narratives we have examined are, as I have indicated, selected from a total of fifteen told to me by Howard Bush in the course of one afternoon. Nevertheless, I believe they serve well to illustrate the negotiated and shifting dynamics of his narration vis-á-vis performance. The first of his yarns, about the monkey in the pickle, highlights clearly the two dimensions of communicative competence on which performance rests, namely, the knowledge and ability to communicate in socially appropriate and interpretable ways. In Bush's attempt to recount this narrative, each in its turn serves as a basis for a disclaimer of performance, that is, a statement of unwillingness to assume responsibility to his audience for a display of skill and effectiveness in storytelling. Early in the story, Bush confesses an inability to proceed with the act of narration itself because he can't think of what to say, and his speech is broken off for a time until he can gather his thoughts sufficiently to resume. Then, toward the end of the story, he excuses himself from responsibility on the basis of insufficient knowledge to render the story effectively by local standards. Thus, first a lack of ability, then a lack of knowledge constitute the basis for his incapacity to perform the narrative.

In the next text, about the lost treasure, he again disclaims performance on the basis of inadequate knowledge of the story. Here Bush undertakes only to report the yarn, which he does by presenting just the core motif as a metonym of the complete narrative.

In the story of the devil as card player, by contrast, we find a more complex dynamic at work. Bush's presentation reveals a shifting hierarchy of dominance in this text, in which he is willing to assume responsibility for the correct doing of the orientation section, disclaims performance in the course of recounting the central narrated event – the recognition of the devil by his fellow card players and his departure through the wall of the shop – and breaks through into full artistic performance at the end, where the narrated event has shifted to one in which he himself was present, namely, his uncle's account of the terrible aftermath of his diabolical encounter.

In the final example, the anecdote about Frank Bell and the eggs, the narration is framed fully as performance. Here, Bush is able to assume responsibility for a display of narrative competence throughout, sustained by his own eye-witness participation in the actual event.

What implications can we draw from this sampling of four narratives and the presentational dynamics that give them shape? First, I would like to argue, on the basis of this exploration, for the productiveness of considering performance not as any doing of an oral literary text, but as one of the range of interactionally defined presentational modes, or frames, which may be more or less functionally dominant in any act of spoken communication or at any given point during its course. This perspective allows us to chart more closely the culturally shaped, socially constituted, and situationally emergent individuation of spoken art. Investigations along these lines, must, of course be founded on the ethnographically determined understanding of the standards of communicative competence that are placed on display in performance, and how the speaker signals or disclaims the accountability to an audience for a display of competence. All of these factors are to be discovered in community specific contexts; what may he accomplished by code switching in the breakthrough into performance by Philip Kahclamet, as reported by Hymes (1975b), may be signaled by certain formal patterns or claims to eye-witness knowledge by Howard Bush. Likewise, a disclaimer of performance may itself be a key to full performance, as in the Iroquois oratory described by Michael Foster (1974:84), or, as in the ease of Howard Bush's narration, it may signal a genuine unwillingness to be accountable for performance. Moreover, while there are a number of devices and patterning principles that have been widely documented as features of verbal art, the discovery of keys to performance cannot rely on *a priori* formal assumptions about what constitutes artful language. My analysis has suggested, for example, that parallelism, identified by Jakobson (1960) as constitutive in the poetic function, may be an artifact of an incapacity to perform, a signal, indeed, of the absence of performance. On the other hand, a fully crafted use of parallelism, reinforced and intensified by other formal features and evidences of presentational confidence, may in fact key a display of communicative competence in the performance of the same individual. Only by close ethnographic analysis of form–function interrelationships in situated contexts of use can such nuances be discovered.

Second, I would underscore the importance of a sensitivity to the influence of the ethnographer on the dynamics of performance. The situation and the audience may have a determinative effect on a speaker's willingness to assume responsibility for a display of communicative competence and this is no less true when the audience is an ethnographer than under conditions of so-called "natural" native performance – another problematic concept. It is evident that the texts produced by Howard Bush are, to a substantial degree, the emergent products of my casting him in the role of oral narrative performer, and of his own ambivalence about assuming that responsibility because of a sense of the limits of his competence to do so. This can hardly he a unique situation; I have observed a similar dynamic in other fieldwork encounters not my own. But just as presenters of oral texts may subtly reject the mantle of performer that we wish to impose upon them, so too may individuals from whom we seek straightforward ethnographic information perform to us without our being aware of it (Paredes, 1993[1977]). Ethnographers, like linguists, have a strong bias toward the referential function of language – we tend to believe what we are told and expect straight answers to our questions – but we are all susceptible to being performed to, and we must be able to understand when the forces of performance take precedence over straightforward referentiality. A sensitivity to performance is thus a necessary part of critical, reflexive ethnography, not only in the study of oral poetics but in fact in all instances of data gathering through verbal interaction with native sources. Thus, I submit, the more we can learn about performance, the better will be not only our understanding of artful speaking but our general practice of ethnography as well.

The negotiation of participant roles and presentational frames that we have traced through Howard Bush's narration, however, is not simply a matter of his staking out an alignment toward the production of narrative texts within the context of the ethnographic encounter in which the texts were recorded. The work of contextualization in which he and I were engaged in the course of that afternoon reached back to other events: sociable evenings at Sperry's general store, primarily, though other storytelling events as well. By asking for stories that were told at the general store, or ones like them, I established an agenda of anticipatory intertextual production, actualized when he complied with my request by narrating the texts I recorded.

In this light, Howard Bush's framing efforts become recognizable as calibrations of the intertextual relationships between his textual productions and the antecedent performances at the general store, oriented both to the thematic content of these earlier texts and – more importantly – to the generic conventions of performing a yarn. Secondarily, some of the narratives he told me are dialogically linked to discourses from occasions earlier in my stay in the La Have Islands that provided me with the basis for eliciting some stories from him on that July afternoon: a telling of the treasure story (Text 2) by his son's father-in-law and an earlier suggestion by his son that I ask him about the card game with the devil (Text 3) and Frank Bell's feat with the eggs (Text 4).

The four texts we have examined reveal different intertextual alignments to antecedent storytelling performances. The narration of the story about the monkey in the pickle (Text 1) reproduces much of the thematic content of the narrative, but emerges as a telling in which Bush disclaims performance on the grounds of incomplete knowledge of the narrated event and inability to render the story as a fully constituted performance. His rendition of the buried-treasure story is a report of his having heard the story, reproducing only the narrative core of this widely told story as an index of the entire plot, and disclaiming performance on the basis of a lack of knowledge of the whole. The text about the card game with the devil oscillates between an alignment in which Bush is willing to take responsibility for meeting the conventional expectations for performing a yarn (sections I and III) and a more qualified willingness to recount part of the narrative (section II) concerning which his knowledge is less secure. And finally, in recounting the story about Frank Bell and the eggs (Text 4), he takes full responsibility for performance, aligning his rendition with the authoritative standard represented by the performances at the general store. The dynamics of intertextual calibration set in motion by my request for yarns of the kind told at Sperry's store thus transcended the bounded speech event in which our dialogue took place, at the same time that they were grounded in our afternoon's interaction.

Performance is fraught with risk (Keane 1997; Schieffelin 1996; Yankah 1985). As a mode of communicative display, performance makes the performer accountable to an audience; it solicits the close scrutiny of an audience and invites their evaluative judgment. Any performance, then, is shadowed by the specter of failure, of being – or being judged to be – a failure. Clearly, for the most part, Howard Bush did not want to take the risk of incurring that judgment. For him, the standard of competence in telling yarns was established a generation earlier by older men with a range of memorable, narratable experiences that they could recount coherently, knowledgeably, authoritatively. Given that storytelling in the La Have Islands – as in so many other places – was a privileged means of constructing and presenting oneself as a person of social worth, what was at stake, potentially, in failed performance was a loss of face. Accordingly, when he considered that he lacked the knowledge or ability to meet the standard of competence to which he felt accountable, Bush resorted to the disclaimers that frame the texts we have examined and then went on to report the stories he had heard, but not to perform them. But when he felt that he could meet the standard – "that I know is true. That I seen him do" – he was ready to take the risk, in full, fluent, authoritative performance. Either way, however, whether as report or performance, his renditions involved the careful alignment of current telling to past tellings and the close calibration of the intertextual gaps that separated his tellings in our encounter and those of his fellows with whom he gathered at Sperry's store to pass the winter evenings with cards and talk.

7

"Go, My Reciter, Recite My Words": Mediation, Tradition, Authority

From legends about magical poets in Iceland to the cries of market vendors in Mexico, riddle tales in Scotland to tall tales in Texas, the foregoing chapters have explored the production of intertextuality in a variety of cultural settings extending from the far North Atlantic to the heart of Mesoamerica. Using genre and performance as our principal vantage points on how speakers may align their words to the words of others – other texts, other genres, other performances – we have also discovered how language ideologies, social relations, participant structures, modes of self-fashioning, situational exigencies, and functional agendas of various orders exert a shaping influence on the construction of intertextuality and reciprocally, how intertextuality serves as a means of constituting those elements of social and cultural life. The webs of intertextual resonance we have examined extend across time and space, linking discursive moments separated by a single speaker change or many decades, a few feet of interpersonal space or hundreds of miles. My perspective throughout has been ethnographic, seeking to elucidate discursive practices and relationships in terms of the orienting frameworks and discriminations employed by the participants in these acts of discursive production and reproduction. Taken together, the exploratory case studies of the preceding chapters offer – if principally by juxtaposition – a cross-cultural perspective on intertextuality as discursive practice.

This chapter is more explicitly cross-cultural. It draws together and extends the principal threads of earlier chapters in a comparative examination of a communicative regimen that has been obscured from analytical attention – even, perhaps, from full recognition – by the constrictive sway of dyadic speaker-hearer models and conceptions of the bounded speech event, productive as those constructs have been in enabling the study of language in society. More specifically, I will examine communicative routines that are regimented in such a way as to require a mediating relay, a routinized pass-it-on reiteration of a source utterance. The relay process in turn renders the participant structure of the mediational routines more complex than elementary, dyadic speaker-hearer or sender-receiver models can accommodate. My examination proceeds from a formal analysis of mediational performances to a consideration of what such routines might accomplish in functional terms, including tradition-alization, authorization, and the socialization of discourse.

Mediational Performances

In contemporary usage, mediation usually implies written and electronic technologies of communicative production; the conventional understanding is that speech is unmediated, with speaker and hearer in a co-present, face-to-face relationship, while the employment of writing and the electronic media distance the sender from the receiver. My focus in this chapter, however, will be on a dimension of communicative organization missing from this conventional framework, namely, spoken mediation, the relaying of spoken messages through intermediaries. I will focus, at least initially, on speech routines organized around the relay by a mediator of at least one utterance from a source to an ultimate targeted receiver, with the relayed message framed and understood by the participants as a replication of the original. I use the term *replication* in the sense offered by Greg Urban: the reproduction of an instance of discourse in a new context, in a relationship of copy to original (Urban 1996). Accordingly, when I employ the term "reproduction" in the pages that follow, it should be understood as synonymous with replication. Likewise *reiteration*, which underscores the verbal, "said-again" focus of my examination. I should emphasize that my frame of reference here is that of the participants. Analytically, the cases on which we will focus our attention extend from mediational routines in which the recontextualized utterance is a verbatim replication of the original, to ones in which the recontextualized utterance differs in certain lexical or formal aspects from the source, and I will take account of those dimensions of variation in my discussion. In the understanding of participants, however, all of the central cases we will examine are built upon accurate replication. Toward the end of the chapter, in order to add dimension to a consideration of the relationship between mediation and authority, I will extend the examination to mediational routines that do not involve full replication.

Let me specify more fully what I mean by speech mediation. I should emphasize at the outset that the serial transmission or relaying of a message or utterance or text by a succession of speakers, as in rumor or folklore or reported speech, does not suffice to define the phenomena I wish to explore, though it is an essential part of the processes by which they are accomplished. What I propose to examine are processes and routines in which the recontextualization is deliberately managed, conventionally regimented, in performance. The routinization of mediation in performance highlights and exploits some essential properties and capacities of the process in especially illuminating ways.

Following Judith Irvine (1996), we may say that mediation sets up implicational or indexical relationships between a sequence of dialogues. I will call the first dialogue in the sequence the source dialogue and the second and subsequent dialogue(s) in the sequence the target dialogue(s). Stated more fully, the source dialogue reaches ahead cataphorically to at least one target dialogue, involving the recontextualization of at least one utterance (which I term the source utterance) from the source dialogue, and, reciprocally, the target dialogue reaches back anaphorically to – or presupposes – a source dialogue from which the recontextualized utterance (the target utterance) is projected into the target dialogue. In this regard, the mediational routines I propose to examine involve mediation in the strong sense of the term distinguished by Richard Parmentier (1985:24–25). That is to say, the mediational structure of these routines does not rest simply on the bringing of two dialogues into articulation by means of or through the intervention of a discourse that serves as the vehicle or medium of communication between them, but rather on the synthetic conjunction of dialogues in such a way that the routine cannot be dissolved into two independent dyads. Insofar as speech mediation involves (at least) two related dialogues, either may serve as an indexical vantage point for participants (and analysts, for that matter, though I will concentrate on participants' vantage points). The implicational relationship between dialogues in the mediational sequence exerts a formative influence on both of them, shaping both the participant structures and discourses by which the dialogues are constituted in a variety of ways. The structure of this implicational relationship, then, affords us a framework for adducing salient dimensions of organization in mediational performances. How are the respective dialogues metapragmatically regimented in such a way as to establish the implicational relationship between them, from the vantage points and perspectives of the participants?

In the survey of examples that follows, we will want to pay special attention to a number of factors. First, we will want to bear in mind that the mediational forms that are the focus of this investigation are conventionalized performances, programmed to include mediational routines. Thus, participants bring with them to these events a set of conventional understandings and expectations concerning their mediational structure. The routinized, conventionalized nature of these performances constitutes a powerful aspect of their metapragmatic regimentation, a basis on which the implicational relationships between source dialogue and target dialogue may be understood.

We may also observe that some of the mediational routines we will survey are organized in such a way as to allow participants access to both the source dialogue and the target dialogue (the mediator participates in both by definition), and thus to allow for observational confirmation of the conventional expectations they bring with them to the performance. This occurs most readily in those cases where the source dialogue and the target dialogue are both encompassed within a single event. When the source dialogue and the target dialogue occur in two temporally separate events, only the mediator is necessarily present at both, though others may be as well. In other cases, though, the separation into two events may serve to limit participatory access and thus to preclude experiential confirmation of conventional understandings concerning the relationship between the implicated dialogues. The separation is especially salient when the source dialogue is not only temporally separate from the target dialogue but also takes place in a different existential realm. In all these cases, the linkage from one implicated dialogue to the other must be inferred, based on conventional understandings, indexical markers, and other available evidence.

In addition to the metapragmatic function of the conventionalized event structures, certain reflexive properties of the discourses by which they are constituted serve to index the mediational nature of the routines. Prominent among these is the textuality of particular constituent utterances. By textuality, again, I mean to identify those properties that serve to bound off a stretch of discourse from its contextual surround, to render it internally cohesive and coherent, to turn it into an object available for decontextualization and recontextualization (Bauman and Briggs 1990; Kuipers 1990; Silverstein and Urban 1996). While textuality potentiates decontextualization and recontextualization, the examples make clear that the relationship between the source utterance that is relayed in the target dialogue and its recontextualized form is a variable one.

Also central to our considerations are the participant structures and their constituent participant roles by which the performances under examination are organized. Mediation renders the participant structure of communicative exchanges far more complex than dyadic speaker-hearer models can accommodate. Performances built upon structures of mediation represent in their various ways participants' manipulations of participant roles to various functional ends. It would then be possible to compare such performances in terms of the ways in which, as routines, they pragmatically constitute and reconstitute participant roles in the mediational process.

I should make clear that I do not intend this exploration of mediational routines to yield a comprehensive or universal inventory of participant roles. Rather, we will operate with a heuristic set of participant roles sufficient to specify salient dimensions of participation in the communicative routines under examination. While all of the terms have some degree of currency in the literature on participant roles and I do rely to an extent on prior efforts at systematization (especially Goffman 1974; Levinson 1988), my usage departs in certain respects from those efforts. Accordingly, let me specify the inventory of participant roles we will employ in our investigation of mediational routines, using the structure of such routines as a definitional frame of reference. Note that some of these role classes (participant, speaker, receiver) operate at a broader level of generality than others.

> *Participant*:   any party with a ratified role in the proceedings.
> *Speaker* or *sender*: any producer of a verbal utterance.
> *Author*:   formulator of an utterance.
> *Source*:   speaker of source utterance.
> *Receiver*:   any hearer of a verbal utterance.
> *Addressee*:   participant at whom an utterance is immediately directed.
> *Overhearer*:   receiver who is not an addressee.
> *Target*:   ultimate destination of an utterance; receiver of target utterance.
> *Audience*:   receiver(s) of a performance.
> *Mediator* or *relayer*:   addressee of source utterance; speaker of target utterance.

At a minimum, mediational routines (see Figure) might be seen to involve at least two mutually implicated sets of participant roles in which a receiver in the first set, which organizes the source dialogue, becomes the sender in the second, which organizes the target dialogue. The participant structure of the source dialogue projects forward to that of the target dialogue, while the participant structure of the target dialogue projects back to the source dialogue. Further, only the first speaker in the source event is understood to be the relevant source of the message, while the second, mediating speaker is recognized as a relayer of the source utterance. Still

Mediational Routine

$$Source \text{———} (message) \longrightarrow Mediator \text{———} (message_1) \longrightarrow Target$$

source utterance   target utterance

Source dialogue | Target dialogue

←Implicational→
relationship

further, considered in these terms, mediational routines decompose addressee and target, insofar as the source utterance is addressed initially to a receiver who is not the ultimate target of the utterance, the latter being (at a minimum) the second addressee in the sequence, that is, the addressee of the target utterance. And finally, as the examples will show, the participant structure of mediational sequences may also incorporate overhearers at either stage of the sequence, who may themselves be cast or recast as targeted receivers.

This set of analytical understandings, of course, rests upon local conceptions of the various performances as built on mediation. In those cases where the source dialogue is such that of all the participants in the target dialogue, only the mediator could have had access to the source dialogue, the mediator's behavior stands as the only warrant that the source dialogue actually occurred. Performances built upon structures of mediation highlight the local constitution of participant structures in formalized and routinized ways. They place the complexities of participant structures on display, inviting the contemplation of analyst and participant alike. Insofar as each is a creative, public exploitation of locally mobilized capacities of participant structures, comparison of their participant structures opens the way toward a comprehensive exploration of participant structures more generally.

Medieval Irish Poetry

One dimension of the functional differentiation of participant roles to which mediational performances lend themselves is the decoupling of responsibility for formulation of the message, that is, authorship, from reponsibility for performance of the message. Performance, insofar as it resides in the assumption of responsibility for a display of expressive skill, foregrounds the latter function. Accordingly, mediational performances are frequently characterized by a mapping of this functional differentiation onto the phase structure of the routine, with authorship assigned to the producer of the source utterance and performative animation assigned to the mediator, who replicates the text in the target utterance. Medieval Irish poetry offers an apt case in point. The medieval Irish poet, or *fili* (pl. *filid*) of high reputation did not perform his own compositions; that role was assigned to a *reacaire* 'reciter' or bard – a role of lower status – who memorized the poem from the instruction of the fili and then delivered it in full performance.[1]

The fili occupied a high position in medieval Irish society (ca. 1250–1650), with the pinnacle of the poet's profession being the *ollamh*, or court poet to a noble chief (Breatnach 1983:77). The office was hereditary, insofar as the learned arts were the province of a particular family in each district, but it required long and arduous training in the esoteric and archaic poetic language (*Bélre na Filed*; Williams 1971:121) and complex forms of court poetry. By virtue of his office, the chief's poet belonged to the aristocratic classes (Breatnach 1983:38; Knott and Murphy 1966:62), but his privileged standing depended upon the fulfillment of the duties attendant upon his rank.

The poet's ties to his patron were notably strong; the relationship was often framed in the idiom of marriage, with the poet as the chief's wife – subordinate and dependent, but bound to the chief by mutual loyalty, respect, and reciprocity (Breatnach 1983:40–43). The element of reciprocity, frequently summarized as the exchange of *dán* 'poem' for *dúas* 'reward' (Breatnach 1983:53), called upon the chief to provide land, cattle, protection, and refuge, plus other occasional gifts to the poet (Breatnach 1983:65; Williams and Ford 1992:163, 171–172) in return for which the fili composed poetry that commemorated, celebrated, and exalted his noble patron's reputation and that of his family and line, while also serving him as counselor, messenger, negotiator, ambassador, and peacemaker (Breatnach 1983:55–59). A 17th-century account identifies the fili's principal obligations in succinct terms:

> As every Professor, or chief Poet, depended on some Prince or great Lord, that had endowed his Tribe, he was under strict ties to him and his Family, as to record in good Metre his Marriages, Births, Deaths, Acquisitions made in war and Peace, Exploits, and other remarkable things relating to the Same. (Bergin 1970:7)

Williams and Ford (1992:177) set the relationship between poet and patron in broader social terms:

> The society in which the poets functioned was rather loose in its organization, and the ties that kept it together were few in number. Most important was the loyalty of the lord to his subjects and their homage to him. One of the principal functions of the poet was to enthrone the lord as an object of loyalty. And since every lord depended upon two things for his position – his lineage and his bravery – the poets were expected to emphasize these heavily in their poems.

The importance of poetry in the maintenance and validation of noble lineages was itself a poetic theme (Williams 1971:88–89; Williams and Ford 1992:168), and of course, the more noble, generous, and brave the patron, the more poems celebrated his noblity and the higher the prestige of the poet attached to his house (Breatnach 1983:78; Williams and Ford 1992:169).

Not only were the eulogies important to the chief in life, they were also seen as the imperishable essence of his enduring fame and reputation after his death, as preserved in the collections maintained by every noble family (Breatnach 1983:54). Williams and Ford (1992:179) make this point especially effectively: "Each and every one of them would realize that the poem would exist long after they had passed on. And, in fact, the evidence is that songs like this were not only part of the tradition, they constituted that tradition." The poets themselves were also ready to make their function clear and explicit; in the words of one assertive poet, "I am your authority, your reputation, O hero of Clár" (Breatnach 1983:54).

If the poet had the power to build and sustain a chief's reputation, he could also undermine or destroy it, through the vehicle of satire (Williams 1971:116). Knott and Murphy observe that the expression *meth n-enech*, literally 'loss of face,' was in constant use in ancient Ireland. A verse like "None but gentlewomen do I satirize, the children of kings or great noblemen; so she is exempt; I never satirized your mother" (Knott and Murphy 1966:81) could strike a sharp blow to a nobleman's honor and that of his family.

The fili was responsible for the composition of a poem, but not for its performance; that role, as noted, was assigned to a *reacaire* 'reciter' (or bard), a position of lower status, but still one of privilege (Knott and Murphy 1966:64). The 17th-century account quoted above provides a revealing description:

The last Part to be done, which was the *Action* and *Pronunciation* of the Poem in the Presence of the . . . principal person it related to, was perform'd with a great deal of Ceremony in a Consort of Vocal and Instrumental Musick. The Poet himself said nothing, but directed and took care that everybody else did his Part right. The Bards having first had the Composition from him, got it well by Heart, and now pronounc'd it orderly, keeping even Pace with a Harp . . . (Bergin 1970:8; cf. Williams and Ford 1992:163)

Bergin (1970:20–21) goes on to clarify that the poems were not sung, but chanted in a kind of recitative to the harper's accompaniment, as they are for the most part in an unrhythmical syllabic meter, without regular stress and therefore unsuited to a regular melody.[2] Taken together, then, the process in which the fili instructed the reciter in the poem for subsequent performance before the patron constituted a mediational routine.

There is a 16th-century poem that is especially useful for illustrative purposes because of its centrally reflexive character; the poem is a metacommentary on the very mediational process by which it will be conveyed from the poet to his patron. The poem requires a bit more explanation. First, it should be noted that while poet, reciter, and patron might all be co-present on the occasion of performance, as above, reciters were also enlisted to carry poetic messages to distant patrons; another term for the reacaire is *marcach duaine* 'horseman of poetry' (Knott and Murphy 1966:65). It is also necessary to know that contrary to the ideal, a fili might occasionally fall into disfavor with his patron, or even be dismissed outright (Breatnach 1983:74). The former seems to be the case here. Finally, a word about the translation. The convention among scholars of medieval Irish poetry is to translate verses in running text, with lines or pairs of lines marked off by punctuation – comma, semicolon, or period.[3]

Neglected Merit

1   Go, my reciter, recite my words; depart speedily; let no weariness keep thee from going to see the head of our protection; turn again to me with tidings.

2   Take from me to Domhnall's heir earnest words in which there shall be meaning; turn thy face in friendly wise towards the fruitful branch of the blood of Ir.

3   Commend me to Mac Carthaigh: hide not from him what I say. Put into his ears that I am as I am – it is a shame to his noble blood.

4   Cattle or horses, gold or silver, I have none: tell this. Speak and make haste, give him sure tidings.

5   That I lack corn-ricks and pigs, not that alone has humbled my pride: neither of these things is within my reach – my honour likewise has fallen from me.

6   That my art is my only wealth is, I know, no prospect of fortune. Though all men now despise it, there was a time when it was precious as gold.

7   To thee it will be a reproach that I am in deep water, O descendant of Carthach who perverted no treaty. Take hold of me, if thou wilt lift me up, thou heir to the fair-sodded Fold of Art.

8   Show that I am not thy horseman, O son of Domhnall who never refused the poets, I am lost beyond all others, it is time rightly to make this plain.

9   Thou art not known to have denied any other – what character is higher? No blemish is found in thy bounty, save that thy own poet is still empty-handed.

10   The learned of the Five Fifths flock towards thee, O chief of Glandore: that I alone depart unsatisfied is marvel enough to look upon.

11   This heavy sickness in which I am – let not the time for healing it pass thee by, O cluster of the branches of Oilill and Fiachaidh, see whether thou art bound to relieve me.

12   My reciter! make known now the secret that I have kept too long. Go before me to the head of Cairbre's descendants: too slow, methinks, thou art in offering to go.
(Bergin 1970:306–307)

Let us consider how the mediational structure of the relay from poet to reciter to patron is managed in this poem. The frame established by verses 1–6 anchors the poem in the source dialogue, in which the poet instructs his reciter to carry his message to his patron. The poet's participant role as source-speaker is marked by first-person pronouns, while his social identity as a poet is indexed by the reference to "my art" in verse 6 and by the formalization of the poetic text. The opening verses are addressed to the reciter by means of the vocative, "my reciter," in verse 1, the second-person pronoun in verse 2, and the imperatives in verses 1–4. At the same time, though, these opening verses implicate the mediational process and the target dialogue as well, as the reciter is commanded to relay the poet's source utterance – "my words," "what I say" – to MacCarthaigh, the ultimate target of the poet's message, who is also designated by third-person pronouns and kinship-based praise-names ("Domhnall's heir," "the fruit-ful branch of the blood of Ir").

At verse 7, however, there is a shift of footing (Goffman 1981) that carries through verse 11, as the poet prefigures the target dialogue by means of vocatives which turn his message to the patron himself, "Descendant of Carthach," "chief of Glandore," "cluster of the branches of Oilill and Fiachaidh," and, tied to verse 2, "son of Domhnall." Note that the second-person pronouns in these verses now refer to the patron, not the reciter, though the latter remains the addressee in the source dialogue, to which the absent patron/target is not a party. Finally, with the vocative, "My reciter," in verse 12, the poet shifts footing once again, back to the source dialogue with its attendant formal features, though implicating the medi-ational process and the target dialogue as before.

In the foregoing examination, we have used the source dialogue as our indexical vantage point. From the perspective of the target dialogue, in which the mediational recontextualization of the poem is accomplished, the implicational machinery reframes the process. For example, when the target dialogue becomes the deictic center, the first-person pronouns no longer index the relayer of the poetic message, that is, the reciter, but project back to the source dialogue and to the poet as the author of the text.

Fijian Epic

If mediation may serve to extend the reach of spoken communication in physical space, as when the reacaire carries a poem to a distant patron, it serves in more complex ways to bridge gaps in existential space. This sort of transcendence, in fact, is one of the principal features of so-called spirit mediumship. In many of the world's cultures, communication between the world of the ancestors or of the dead and the living takes the form of medi-ated, poetically regimented performance which serves to reproduce the separation of existential domains in the heightened and reflexive act of bringing them into conjunction. Such performances must be distinguished from spirit mediumship, another means of bridging the gap between exis-tential domains. Raymond Firth defines spirit mediumship as "a form of possession in which the person is conceived as serving as an intermediary between spirits and men. The accent here is on communication; the actions and words of the medium must be translatable, which differentiates them from mere spirit possession or madness" (1959:141). That is to say, in spirit mediation, it is the spirit who is the source and author of the utterance, using the medium simply as an instrument of articulation, a means of giving physical voice to the utterance. The medium surrenders or is dispossessed of all agency. In spirit mediumship, by contrast with the mediational performances with which we are here concerned, there is no relay, no differentiation between source dialogue and target dialogue, source utterance and target utterance.

Examples of mediational relay between the spirit world and the human lifeworld occur more widely in the literature than one might expect, though they are often marked by a disjunction between the ethnographer's conception of the process and that of the participants themselves. An illuminating case in point is provided by Buell Quain's rich collection of Fijian oral poetry (Quain 1942; see also Finnegan 1992 [1977]). Quain's collection presents the epic songs of Velema Daubitu of The-Place-of-Pandanus village, on the island of Vanua Levu, whom Quain identifies as "The last composer of epic songs in all Bua Province" (1942:5). Song, with other performance forms, is expecially highly valued in The-Place-of-Pandanus: "Appreciation of pleasing verbal expression is so pervasive that the men who assemble for a casual evening's bout of kava drinking observe each others' delivery with self-consious envy, even though they have worked and played with their companions since infancy" (Quain 1942:5).

In terms of local understandings, Velema is less a poet than a "seer," able to communicate with the ancestors who are the source and subject matter of his songs. Velema also figures pseudonymously as Toviya in Quain's village ethnography, where he is identified as a "priest," though Quain (1948:229n) questions the appropriateness of this designation. Recruitment to the role of seer is partly hereditary, partly on the basis of temperament. Velema was chosen by his mother's brother to guard the sacred articles, an ancient war club and an axe, which serve, in effect, to open the channel to the ancestral realm, Flight-of-the-Chiefs (see also Quain 1948:30–31, 184, 236). From his uncle as well, he learned the ritual etiquette of this communicative relationship, and absorbed the formal patterns of epic song (Quain 1942:14). His uncle singled him out for this role, however, because Velema's "diffidence, his excitability and his curiosity about serious things," even as a child, marked him to the people of his village as one who was destined to become a seer (Quain 1942:13–14). While Quain identifies Velema as the "composer" of the songs that are unique to his repertoire, that ascription is plainly at odds with the Fijian understandings of the poetic process. Some songs he has learned from his uncle; others, he sings for the first time on special occasions, but Quain's own account makes quite clear and explicit that in local terms the source of the songs is the ancestors, who have taken part in the events the poems recount: "In trance or in sleep, the songs come to him, taught him by his supernatural mentors. He takes no personal credit for his compositions" (Quain 1942:14; cf. Geddes 1945:42–43), though his skill in "delivery" is highly evaluated (Quain 1942:5), indicating that the quality of a performance rests with the performer, not his ancestral source.

The performed texts carry with them metapragmatic evidence of the mediational sequence.[4] One framing device employed as a song opening is a line stating where the dream inspiration for the song occurred, before launching into the narrative action. For example:

> *Sleep lying at the Slow-Flowering-Spring*
> And a certain rumor spreads vigorously.
> It uproots the house posts and it casts them down.
> Tip-of-the-Single-Feather hears it,
> The fame of Mooring-Rope's medicine.
> Tip-of-the-Single-Feather stands up.
> (Quain 1942:76)

In this text, Velema reports that he received the song while asleep at the Slow-Flowering-Spring, a place in contemporary Fiji; the second and ensuing lines shift to a narrative set in the legendary domain, Flight-of-the-Chiefs. An additional introductory framing device is a spoken, rather than chanted, line, reiterating the words employed by the ancestor from whom Velema learned the song, in order to contextualize the poetic narrative that follows. Here, for example, the ancestral source locates the ensuing action at Flight-of-the-Chiefs:

> *During one of my sojourns at Flight-of-the-Chiefs* [spoken]
> The Eldest is calling:
> "I am calling Tip-of-the-Single-Feather
>   Calling him and Curve-of-the-Whale-Tooth.
>   Listen, Tip-of-the-Single-Feather:
>   Go bring forth the poplar mast
>   Which lies felled at the headland of Flight-of-the-Chiefs."
> (Quain 1942:21)

Note that as performed by Velema, these poems are reanimations of the ancestral teacher's voice, which itself reanimates the voice of the epic protagonists. Thus, in the preceding example, we have Velema reanimating the words of the dream-ancestor who taught him the poem and who in turn reanimates the words of The Eldest. The exception is the opening of the kind that introduces the first example, in which the performer reports the location of his inspiration in his own voice.

The primary mediational relay, however, is understood to be from the ancestral dream-source through Velema to the audience. According to Quain, the performer's relay of his source's ancestral communications represents for the contemporary audience their "only bonds with the distant past" (1942:8–9), the source of authoritative history. While Quain feels compelled to observe that "To one of Western culture such history is suspect" (1942:9), full of anachronisms, he goes on to acknowledge that "natives at The-Place-of-the-Pandanus," Velema's community, "trust the ancestral communications of seers [i.e., performers] so perfectly that those who dispute of even recent history refer to them for solution. Through such communication forgotten genealogies of the last generation can be known again with certainty" (1942:9). Thus, the song performances mediate not only across existential domains but also across gaps in time.

The importance of the seer's authoritative singing of genealogy in history becomes apparent when we recall that in Fijian social organization, the status of a kin group (*mataqali*) is decisively determined by the status of its founding ancestors, and that the village high-chief is the leader of the highest ranking mataqali in the village (Geddes 1945:37; Sahlins 1962:291, 295). The Fijian seer-singer thus played a central role in the structure of power and authority in traditional Fijian society. Quain observes that in the village he studied, the priests functioned in the past "as the special shamans of the chief," and "those who knew how to communicate with ancestors supplemented the chief's authority in social control" (1948:231–232). Moreover, Velema himself bore a chiefly title of a land-group (Quain 1948:97, 233).

In terms of the framework we have established for the analysis of mediational routines, Velema's performance to a contemporary audience is the target dialogue; the audience has no direct access to the source dialogue, that is, the singing of the song by the spirit-ancestor in Velema's dream-vision. In what ways and by what means does the target dialogue index the mediational process?

To begin with, the opening line locates the speaker at Flight-of-the-Chiefs, framing what is to follow as occurring in the legendary kingdom of the epic world. This identifies the voice of the opening line as that of the spirit-ancestor, for the contemporary singer, who animates the utterance in performance, has no direct access to Flight-of-the-Chiefs. Thus, the opening line indexes the spirit-ancestor as source and the singer as relayer; the line is recognizable as direct discourse, quoted from the source dialogue. Additional information is conveyed by the mode of delivery: the opening line is spoken, not chanted in the manner of the lines that follow (hence the framing parentheses provided by Quain). The shift from spoken to chanted delivery marks the second and ensuing lines as constituting the song text proper, a narrative of events at Flight-of-the-Chiefs. Here still, the discourse is quoted from the source dialogue of the spirit-ancestor, reanimated by Velema. In the local understanding of the epic tradition, the song is understood to have been entextualized by the spirit-source. The further understanding, however, is that the singer, Velema, is responsible for the skill and effectiveness of his performance in recontextualizing the song in the target event. His abilities and efforts as performer, though not as source, index his mediating role. Thus, from references to person and place, as well as formal markers of textuality and performance, within the larger context of local undertandings of the epic genre, Velema's sung utterance indexes a limited range of aspects of the mediational process – the source utterance, the participant roles of source and animator-as-mediator – but none of them in denotationally explicit terms.

Akan Chiefly Discourse

In our examples thus far, we have considered mediational routines that span gaps in space, time, and existential domains. We turn now to gaps of another order, namely, the social distance between people of differential position in political hierarchies of status and power. Kwesi Yankah's account of the mediation of chiefly discourse among the Akan peoples of Ghana, with examples from the royal court of the Asantehene, the "King" of Ashanti, serves as a useful example (Yankah 1991, 1995).

Every Akan chief (and Queen Mother) has one or more official functionaries, or *akyeame* (sing. *okyeame*), who serves as "the chief's orator, diplomat, envoy, prosecutor, protocol officer, prayer officiant . . . confidant and counsellor" (Yankah 1995:84–85; see also Stoeltje 2002), but whose most prominent public function is to act as mediating spokesman on formal occasions, relaying the chief's discourse to and from his interlocutors. Some akyeame serve in hereditary positions by virtue of occupying special ritual "stools." These individuals may not possess oratorical skills at the time they accede to their positions, but they are then expected to acquire those skills on the job (Yankah 1995:86). Other akyeame are appointed directly by the chief because of demonstrated skill in public speaking, though occasionally the chief may convert their offices to hereditary status as well (Yankah 1995:87).

As in the case of the Irish fili, the okyeame's relationship to his patron chief is framed figuratively in terms of marriage, with the okyeame as the chief's wife. The binding of the okyeame to the chief involves formal rites of betrothal, marriage, and – when the chief dies – widowhood, in addition to other oaths of office (Yankah 1995:89–90, 92–94). The marital metaphor conveys the intimacy, mutual accessibility, loyalty, reciprocity, and common interest inherent in the spousal relationship. The okyeame thus has a clear vested interest in upholding and protecting the sanctity and reputation of the chief he serves, for his own status and reputation rest upon those of his patron.

Yankah locates the okyeame within a speech economy in which the power of the spoken word as a social and spiritual force "calls for the deployment of various strategies of speaking that may obviate crises," including prominently "threats to face," by means of such devices as verbal taboos, politeness forms and honorifics, and various forms of indirection (1995:51). Public speaking (*dwamu kasa*) in Akan society is characterized by a markedly high density of such mitigating devices, and Yankah (1995:52–54) suggests that the role of the okyeame as an intermediary in public speaking "is a specialized functional expression of the verbal art of indirection." Such indirection takes on special salience in the management of communication in the presence of the chief, as part of what Yankah (1995:84) calls an interactional "politics of avoidance," by which the veneration of the chief is enacted. The chief must be protected from potentially threatening verbal, physical, or spiritual penetration of his royal space, and the mediation of the okyeame serves to insulate him from the risks of disgrace, embarrassment, or disrespect that direct contact with his interlocutors might entail (Yankah 1995:58, 84, 97). This protection has a dual aspect: the interposition of the okyeame between the chief and others allows the okyeame to ward off face-threats to the chief, and at the same time the relay of the chief's words through the okyeame allows them to be conveyed in their most advantageous, attractive, and efficacious guise.

In practice, the mediational regimentation of the okyeame's role works as follows. On formal occasions, the chief's speech is addressed most immediately to the okyeame, marked by a mutually oriented gaze and the occasional vocative use of the title "okyeame," preceding the body of the utterance. The chief's speech is delivered in a special register, *adehye kasa* 'royal speech,' which is typically hurried, low in volume (though usually audible to those in attendance), and marked by occasional stuttering (cf. Irvine 1975) and a slight nasal resonance (Yankah 1995:109). According to Yankah (1995:109), "The generally low-keyed nature of the chief's word is meant to signify its incompleteness as a speech act." At intervals during the chief's speech, the okyeame responds with a ratifier, such as *sio* 'yes.'

After the chief has spoken, in the simplest case, the okyeame turns to the intended target of the chief's speech and relays it to him or her. Note that the target will have overheard the speech as the chief directed it at the okyeame, but now becomes the addressee of the okyeame's relay. By contrast with the low-keyed style of the chief, the okyeame's relay involves performative display: it is louder, fuller, more lively in gesticulation and histrionics, vocally more expressive (Yankah 1995:109), subject to open, public, on-record evaluation (Yankah 1995:57).

Yankah distinguishes three modes of relay employed by the okyeame, only one of which involves replication of the source utterance in the target utterance (we will consider the other two modes later in the chapter). In this mode, the chief pauses after each sentence (or occasionally longer segment) and the okyeame relays his utterance closely as indirect discourse preceded by an attributive device. Thus, for example:

King:	I am concerned about this funeral (sio)
	Because the gentleman who has returned to his soul's origins (sio)
	Served in this palace for thirty-nine years (sio)
Okyeame:	Otumfuor, the Almighty, says he is concerned about these events,
	Because the gentleman who has returned to his soul's origins, served in this palace for thirty-nine years.
King:	We all know the role he has played in this palace (sio)
Okyeame:	He says we all know the role he has played in this palace.
King:	We would have done him no greater honor (sio)
	Than to observe his wake (sio)
	To bid him farewell (sio)
Okyeame:	He says we would have done him no greater honor, than to observe his wake, to bid him farewell.

(Yankah 1991:13–14)

And so on. In the first relay, there is a shift of pronoun and verb form, occasioned by the okyeame's use of indirect discourse, and a lexical substitution of "these events" for "this funeral"; these minor changes aside, the okyeame reproduces the Asantehene's utterances faithfully. The okyeame's departure from the chief's utterance may extend as well to clause transposition, as in the following excerpt, but the predominant feature of this first mode of relay is the close replication of the original, and Yankah makes clear that from the participants' point of view the okyeame's recontextualization of the chief's words counts as verbatim relay.

King:	You all know (sio)
	I do not haphazardly (sio)
	Observe the wakes of my akyeame (sio)
Okyeame:	He says, for his akyeame's wakes, you all know he does not
	haphazardly observe them.

(Yankah 1991:14)

In sum, the mediated performance of Akan chiefly discourse is a symbolic enactment of the chief's sanctity, of the protective distancing of the chief from others. It creates a communicative gap that symbolizes the social gap that sets the chief apart. In practical terms, of course, the doubling of utterances on these formal occasions has the additional advantage both of allowing a second hearing, which can enhance understanding, and of providing more time before speaking, which can enhance fluency and ensure a more considered utterance.

Mediation, Authority, and Power

Readers familiar with Ruth Finnegan's landmark work, *Oral Poetry* (1992[1977]), will perhaps already have noted the close correspondence between the three case studies of mediational performances I have presented and her valuable observations concerning the role frequently played by oral poetry in the service of social, political, and religious power and authority. Indeed, the Irish fili and the Fijian epic singer figure prominently in her analysis. "Oral poetry," Finnegan writes,

> frequently serves to uphold the *status quo* – even to act as the kind of 'mythical' or 'sociological charter' which Malinowski emphasized as one function of oral prose narrative . . . Court bards strengthen the position of rulers, poets act as propagandists for authority, the accepted view of life is propagated in poetic composition and, when poets are an established group, their own power and interests are often fortified by their performances. The social order is maintained through the performance of poetry in ceremonial settings, where established groups express solidarity and social obligation in song.
>
> (Finnegan 1992[1977]:242; italics in the original)

All of our mediational routines have a ceremonial locus; all uphold the authority of political and religious leaders (Finnegan 1992[1977]:189); all employ specialized, esoteric, interpretively difficult registers saturated with traditional authority (Finnegan 1992[1977]:234); all involve a degree of hereditary control over access to office (Finnegan 1992[1977]:190); one (Fijian epic singer) claims divine inspiration for his songs (Finnegan 1992[1977]:191). But why this convergence? What does mediational performance contribute to the maintenance of power and authority?

As I have suggested earlier in the chapter, my turn to routinized enactments of speech mediation stems from an interest in identifying discursive practices and processes that transcend the face-to-face speaker-hearer dyad as the frame of reference for the elucidation of spoken interaction in the conduct and constitution of social life. My strategy has been to foreground performances, reflexive enactments in which discursive practices are placed on display, and the capacities of communicative structures laid open to examination. In all of the mediational routines we have examined, at least the target utterance, and sometimes the source utterance as well, is framed as performance, and takes place before an audience which is constituted for the purpose and is an integral component of the event (cf. French 1958; Hymes 1966). In this regard, mediational routines are public enactments. Accordingly, one of the salient functional capacities of such routines is publication, in the root sense of the term: making discourse publicly accessible (Hymes 1966; Graham 1995; Urban 1991). The constitution of the audience as public, then, is a critical factor in determining the social and cultural capacities of mediational routines and I will attend to it at various points in the discussion that follows, insofar as the data will allow. My discussion will focus on three metadiscursive processes enacted by the mediational performances I have surveyed: traditionalization, the socialization of knowledge, and authorization.

Traditionalization

The concept of tradition has played a dominant role in Western understandings of oral poetics since at least the latter part of the 18th century, part of the Herderian foundation of folklore and Americanist linguistic and cultural anthropology (Bauman and Briggs 2003). Herder celebrated the capacity of poetic expression to "spite the power of time," and so to constitute "the eternal heritage" of a people, the very foundation of culture itself (Herder 1967[1877–1913], 5:164). In Herder's understanding, the entextualizing force of poetic formalization rendered poetic discourse memorable, repeatable, durable, allowed it to "be sung again for as long as men wanted to sing it" (Herder 1969:85). When a text is "sung again," an

intertextual relationship is established, the core of an intertextually constituted *tradition* of textual continuity through time.

In Herder's treatment, the concept of tradition is never far removed
from the dynamic immediacy of lived performance; the intertextual continuity of poetic tradition rests upon a succession of re-performances.
Herder's emphasis on performance aside, though, a variety of factors –
the philological preoccupation with textual history and origins, the
ephemerality of performance, and, not least, the very objectifiability and
detachability of texts that potentiates their decontextualization and
recontextualization – has fostered an abstracted conception of tradition
grounded in the reification of intertextual relations that connect a historical succession of cognate texts.

In recent years, however, there has been an emergent reorientation
among students of tradition, away from this reified view of tradition and
toward an understanding of tradition as a discursive and interpretive
achievement, the active creation of a connection linking current discourse
to past discourse – that is, from tradition to traditionalization (see Chapter
2 and Hymes 1975a). This understanding, in turn, directs our attention
toward the means and processes by which traditionalization is accomplished and by which it endows discourse with meaning. From this perspective, then, I would suggest that one of the salient capacities of
mediational routines of the kind we have surveyed in the foregoing discussion is the reflexive enactment of the nuclear structure of traditionalization. That is to say, certain of these mediational performances represent
formalized, routinized ways of foregrounding the metadiscursive practices
and processes that are minimally necessary for traditionalization to be
achieved.

Mediational routines are organized by their very design to spite the
power of time, to transcend the ephemerality of the spoken word. The
phase structure of such routines confers upon the source utterance a projected textual lifespan that extends beyond the source dialogue, at least as
far as the target dialogue and in some cases beyond it. By the convention-
alization of the mediational structure of the routines, the source utterance
anticipates repetition – detachment from the source dialogue, the source
speaker, the context and circumstances of production, and recontextualization in the target dialogue. Moreover, the shaping of the source utterance
prepares it for this decontextualization and recontextualization.

One of the principal operations in this preconditioning process is the
entextualization of the source utterance, endowing it with sufficient formal
and functional boundedness and internal cohesion to allow it to be lifted
out of its context of production and recontextualized in the target dialogue.
In the examples we have surveyed, the entextualizing devices employed

range from the minimal functional boundedness of a turn at talk to highly complex poetic structuring. In addition to entextualization, the repetition of the source text may be prepared for by such further devices as explicit directives to the mediator, such as "Tell X he is pardoned," in the words of the Asantehene to his okyeame, or deictic shifts, as between verses 6 and 7 of the Irish poem, "Neglected Merit."

From the vantage point of the source dialogue, however, the projected textual lifespan of the source utterance is only virtual; it is actualized by the mediator's production of the target utterance. The target utterance is framed as reproduction, effecting the continuity of the text through time. The act of textual reproduction by the mediator places the target utterance in tension between the source dialogue and the target dialogue, tied simultaneously to both. This double anchoring rests ultimately on the intertextual relationship between the source utterance and the target utterance. Insofar as the target utterance is framed as a reiteration of the source utterance, it is anaphorically tied to the source dialogue; insofar as it is a re-production of the source utterance under new circumstances, however, it is inevitably grounded as well in the new context of the target dialogue. Our survey of examples, limited though it has been, reveals a range of means by which this double anchoring may be accomplished and the relative strength of the ties of the relayed text to source dialogue and target dialogue may be calibrated. The ways in which such means are deployed will affect the degree of iconicity between the relayed text and the source text.

1   *Reported speech.* The target utterance may be framed as direct discourse, that is, as a faithful replication of the source utterance which retains the source dialogue as its deictic center, as in the Fijian epic songs we have examined, or as indirect discourse, with the target dialogue as deictic center, as in our Akan examples.
2   *Other indexical forms.* The target utterance may index the participant structure of the source dialogue or the target dialogue. For example, "Nana X, Otumfuor bids that it reach your ears," does both.
3   *Locative references.* Locative references may assimilate the text to the source dialogue or the target dialogue. For example, "Sleep lying at the Slow-Flowing-Spring" invokes the location of the source dialogue.
4   *Presentational mode.* The target dialogue may maintain or shift the presentational mode of the source utterance. In the mediation of Fijian epic song, both the ancestor's source utterance and the singer's target utterance are performed, while the mediation of Irish poetry

involves a shift from the pedagogical delivery of the fili to the reciter to the performance of the reciter to the chief.

5   *Interactional regimentation.* The interactional structure that shapes the production of the source utterance and the target utterance may be maintained or varied. For example, an Akan chief's utterance may invite ratification by the akyeame ("sio") after each line, while the target utterance is rendered continuously.

6   *Lexical choice.* The mediator may substitute lexical alternatives for words in the source utterance, such as the okyeame's "these events" for the Asantehene's "this funeral," in our first Akan example.

7   *Formal organization.* The mediator may maintain or alter the formal structure of the source utterance. In our second Akan example, the okyeame transposes the clause sequence of the Asantehene's utterance in producing the target utterance.

And so on. Further cases will doubtless reveal additional means and devices. The essential point, however, is that the process of traditionalization rests fundamentally on the establishment of textual iconicity through reproduction of a source text in a new context and the concomitant double grounding of the recontextualized text. Mediational routines enact the nuclear structure of traditionalization in an especially reflexive way, foregrounding, routinizing, and objectifying the process, but the same structure lies at the center of every act of traditionalization.

The Socialization of Knowledge

Not only do mediational routines affect the temporal continuity of texts, they also enact and display in elementary form the social currency of texts, their dissemination beyond a single individual source and their incorporation into the stock of usable knowledge available to others. As Schutz and Luckmann have observed, "The general and fundamental presupposition for the acceptance of subjective elements of knowledge into the social stock of knowledge is 'objectivation'" (Schutz and Luckmann 1973:264). What Schutz and Luckmann mean by objectivation is the outward manifestation of knowledge in messages communicated to others (Schutz and Luckmann 1973:286). They frame this consideration in terms of the intersubjective transmission of knowledge, a transfer from mind to mind(s). For the accomplishment of this intersubjective transfer, only a single act of communication, a single objectivation, is minimally necessary, and for this our basic speaker-hearer dyad will suffice. There are, however, circumstances under which it may be deemed necessary or desirable to confirm publicly that the transfer of knowledge has been achieved and that the knowledge in question has become a part of the receiver's usable repertoire. A display of this kind requires at a minimum a second objectivation. When this second objectivation takes the same textual form as the first, the bond between the propositional content and the textual form of the utterance is hardened, with the implication that the fusion of the two is necessary to its meaning and efficacy. Entextualization is obviously conducive to the socialization of knowledge as an element of formalization, insofar as it enhances the transferability, memorability, and repeatability of the encoded knowledge, now rendered as a text and thus as a durable unit of knowledge. In the terms we are developing, then, mediated performance routines are reflexive enactments of the core process by which the socialization of entextualized knowledge may be displayed. The objectivation of the source message, in textual form, anticipates a second objectivation of the text, confirming its social currency.

Recognition of the capacities of mediational routines to enact the socialization of knowledge in such a way as to tie propositional content to textual form helps to account for their widespread use for pedagogical and language socialization purposes, as in the *ɛlɛma* routines described by Bambi Schieffelin among the Kaluli of Papua New Guinea (1990:75–111) or the *dile* routines described by Charles Briggs among the Mexicano people of Northern New Mexico (1986:66–69). While students of language socialization, focusing primarily on the acquisition of communicative competence by young children, tend to emphasize the formal side of the process, and students of the regimentation of language in the classroom (e.g., Abagi, Cleghorn, and Merritt 1988) make more of the inculcation of content, both processes socialize children to a fusion of the two and call upon them to display their competence in maintaining that fusion.

Authorization

"An established belief in the sanctity of immemorial traditions," as established by Max Weber in his classic typology of the forms of legitimate domination, is a strong basis for claims to authority (Weber 1978[1921–2]:215). Accordingly, to suggest that mediational routines represent performative models of the nuclear structure of traditionalization is also to raise the possibility that such enactments may be related in similar fashion to the process of authorization, the process of rendering discourse authoritative. Bakhtin's conception of authoritative discourse provides a useful point of departure in this regard. According to Bakhtin:

The authoritative word demands that we acknowledge it, that we make it our own; it binds us, quite independent of any power it might have to persuade us internally; we encounter it with its authority already fused to it. The authoritative word is located in a distanced zone, organically connected with a past that is felt to be hierarchically higher. It is, so to speak, the word of the fathers. Its authority was already *acknowledged* in the past. It is a *prior* discourse. (Bakhtin 1981:342; italics in the original)

Still further, authoritative discourse is "sharply demarcated"; it allows "no play with its borders, no gradual and flexible transitions"; "It enters our verbal consciousness as a compact and indivisible mass" (1981:343).

While Bakhtin's characterization is highly suggestive, it approaches authoritative discourse as already given: "we encounter it with its authority already fused to it . . . already *acknowledged* in the past." It is prior, distanced, ancestral, removed. Missing from Bakhtin's treatment, however, is any consideration of *how* discourse becomes authoritative, the process by which it is infused with authority. As before, I would suggest that mediational performances of the kind we have examined in the foregoing pages offer an illuminating key to the process at hand; such routines, I submit, are enactments of the core process of authorization.

Consider once again the workings of these mediational performances. The source utterance in mediational routines is produced in anticipation that it will be reproduced in the process of relaying it to its targetted receiver, but framed as emanating from the source. The conventional phase structure of the routines establishes the temporal priority of the source utterance. The target utterance, the second in a sequence, is understood to be a replication of this prior discourse; it emanates from the past, all the more so when the source is an ancestor, as with Fijian epic. Moreover, in producing the target utterance, the mediator does not speak on his own, but on behalf of a specific, identifiable source who is, in all the examples we have surveyed, known to be the author of the replicated text, responsible for its formulation and entextualization.

Still further, in all of these cases, the author occupies a recognizably higher position than the mediator in a socially salient hierarchy of status and authority. The Irish poet is higher in social rank than his reciter, and his artistic skill is more highly regarded; the ancestral inhabitants of Flight-of-the-Chiefs in Fiji are spiritually more powerful than singers who learn from them in dreams; Akan chiefs are politically superior to those who relay their words. Each of these roles – poet, ancestor, chief – places the incumbent in a position of authority over the mediator, whether on the basis of social rank, artistic skill, spiritual power, or political power. Given these hierarchical asymmetries, then, one might simply view the authoritativeness of the authors' words as deriving from the authority vested in their roles. What, then, do mediational performances contribute to the process?

Such routines, I would propose, *enact* the authorization of discourse, by making its authority manifest, objectifying it in overtly perceptible ways. Observe, first of all, that these routines prescribe that the mediator replicate the author's discourse intact; the integrity of the author's text must be preserved. Agency resides with the author; the mediator is denied an active role in the formulation and entextualization of the message. Rather, he is bound by it. Note that in the Irish and Fijian cases, the mediator's words never breach the boundaries of the text as formulated in the source utterance; this underscores the textuality of the decontextualized and recontextualized utterance. Or, as Bakhtin would have it, the text remains "sharply demarcated," an "indivisible mass," allowing "no play with its borders." Textuality has its own momentum. The locational framing line that opens Velema's performance in the Fijian example lies outside the text of the epic account itself, as learned from the ancestral source. In the examples from the Akan, the okyeame's resort to indirect discourse and transposition of clauses in relaying the Asantehene's words do represent penetrations of the text, but the target utterances do not add to or subtract from the chief's message.

There is some ambiguity in the second and third of the okyeame's target utterances in the first example from the Akan. Here, although the okyeame replicates the Asantehene's words verbatim, Yankah renders the okyeame's utterances without quotation marks, that is, as indirect discourse. He maintains (personal communication) that the okyeame employs the pronoun "we" in these instances because he is a member of the Asantehene's court and thus, like the Asantehene, has a first-person vantage point on its practices and on the events that transpire within its precincts. I will have more to say below concerning the implications of the okyeame's footing with regard to authorization. For the moment, though, I would emphasize that in the preponderance of cases we have examined, the full integrity of the source utterance is preserved intact.

This is not to say, however, that the mediator contributes nothing to the process. Recall that these are performances. Not only does the mediator bear responsibility for replicating the author's text correctly, but performance also renders him accountable for reproducing it well, marking it as worthy of special communicative care and effort. Acceptance and realization of the standards that regulate the replication of authoritative discourse are an integral part of the authorization process.

To summarize my argument, then, the mediational routines we have examined play out the process of authorization insofar as they demonstrate by their very design the dominance of the temporally prior source utterance over the target utterance. The mediator's replication of the source utterance, by preserving its integrity and displaying special care in its reproduction, amounts to an act of discursive submission, the subordination of present discourse to discourse that emanates from the past. Moreover, I would suggest, submission to the *form* of the source utterance has a concomitant effect on the *rhetorical power* of the text: upholding the integrity of the form opens the way to acceptance of the validity of the message. In this way, the mediational routines we have examined are reflexive enactments of the process by which discourse is invested with authority.

In arguing that mediational performances may operate in this manner, I do not mean to suggest that this capacity is necessarily or fully realized in all such routines. I have already suggested a possible limiting factor, namely, the infiltration of the mediator's voice into the target utterance. Still further, in contexts where the full authorization of the source utterance is the norm, the mediational routine may serve secondarily as a resource for contrastive manipulation. Strict replication of the source utterance by the mediator minimizes the intertextual gap (Briggs and Bauman 1992) between the source utterance and the target utterance, thus enacting the authorization of the former in the strongest possible terms. When the source utterance is infiltrated by the mediator's own voice, by contrast, the intertextual gap is widened in the process of recontextualization. What is the effect of this transformational process? Let us consider some further examples.

The relay mode that characterizes the mediation of Akan chiefly discourse in the example presented earlier is only one of three possible modes available to the okyeame. A second, which Yankah terms analytic relay, gives far more expressive latitude to the okyeame. As characterized by Yankah, analytic relay exploits the okyeame's prerogative to embellish and enhance the chief's message by paraphrase, elaboration, or proverbial reinforcement; he is considered to have been faithful to the chief's utterance as long as he does not alter its logical focus (Yankah 1991:9). In the following example, the okyeame frames his relay as a report of the chief's speech, but his rendition elaborates upon, intensifies, and reinforces the chief's message by means of a succession of apposite proverbs to the effect that the event should move along without waiting for more participants to arrive:

Chief: I suppose the time is far spent, and we should begin the
            function
Okyeame: Friends, so says the chief. He says, as we decorate the
            corpse, we decorate it for the empty parlor (where it will
            be laid in state), and that since time is far spent, we need
            not wait till all villagers arrive. The elders say, the head of
            the clock bird is eaten in haste. Those of us gathered here
            are not too few. The elders say nothing little is too small.
            We know more delegates will arrive when we begin; little
            additions break the bottle.
            (Yankah 1991:19)

In this instance of analytic relay, as noted, only a trace of the chief's
source utterance is preserved in the wording of the source utterance,
though the logic is indeed consistent with his own. The chief's authority
remains salient, insofar as the okyeame is understood on such formal occasions to be relaying a message from the chief, and his direct references to
the chief's utterance ("so says the chief," "He says") make it explicit that he
is relaying a message from the chief. Nevertheless, by re-entextualizing the
chief's message rather than replicating it, the okyeame is authorizing the
propositional content and illocutionary force of the message, not the discourse itself, severing the meaning and illocutionary force from the form
of the source utterance. Still further, the okyeame's reformulation infuses
additional dimensions of authority into the target utterance. The four
proverbs ("as we decorate the corpse, we decorate it for the empty parlor";
"the head of the clock bird is eaten in haste"; "nothing little is too small";
"little additions break the bottle") bring the traditional authority of proverbial wisdom and the elders into play, and the okyeame's contributions to
the target utterance bring to the fore his own authority as an official of the
chief's court, while displaying his virtuosity as a performer. Of the three
relay modes, analytic relay displays the okyeame's skill to best advantage
and is the most highly valued in aesthetic terms.

If the okyeame considers the chief's utterance to be sufficiently audible,
clear, and well articulated, especially if it is lengthy, he may resort to the
third relay mode, which consists of what Yankah calls a token relay formula,
such as "the message is yours" or "it reached your ears" (1991:9, 12). The
latter device is interesting because, as Yankah points out, it gives explicit
recognition to the fact that the target of the chief's utterance is initially an
overhearer; the relay formula recasts the overhearer into an authorized
recipient (1991:12). This third relay mode is not favored; while token relay
formulas are acceptable in moderation under appropriate circumstances,

their overuse marks an okyeame as ineloquent, and such incompetence is noted and remarked upon. The token relay formula serves no discourse-authorizing function; the authority of the chief's message derives directly and solely from the political authority vested in his role.

In the analytic relay of Akan chiefly discourse, I have suggested, the infiltration of the source utterance by the mediator's voice in the process of recontextualization operates to diffuse the full authorization of the chief's words, such that the okyeame may claim authority for his own words as well, or for the words of the elders, in the service of authorizing those of the chief. The range of examples presented by Yankah and Yankah's own discussion make clear that analytical relay allows for a gradient of re-entextualization on the part of the okyeame. The term re-entextualization is appropriate here because no matter how far the okyeame's utterance departs from the chiefly source on these formal occasions, it continues to be understood as a relay of the source utterance, which itself was accessible to participants. The force of this understanding is such that even when there is no source text, and the okyeame is delivering a message of his own devising, he frames his speech as a relay of the chief's words. Yankah presents an example, a speech of 73 lines, in which one of the Asantehene's akyeame advises a new subject chief on proper chiefly comportment and service (1995:167–172). The speech is entirely of his own formulation, drawing on the authority of his office and experience to the extent that he personalizes the text with phrases like "I believe," "I request of you good service," "All I say is . . ." Nevertheless, at one point in the speech, he shifts his footing by stating: "Otumfuor says if he is convinced you are of good service / Then he will be self-assured telling you good news," thus relaying and authorizing a source utterance that the Asantehene has not spoken.

But this order of shared authorization, to be sure, does not at all exhaust the possibilities for expressive calibration of the intertextual gap between source utterance and target utterance in mediational routines. To illustrate a more extreme possibility, let us consider an example drawn from the performance of the *coloquio*, a form of festival drama in Mexico that I have investigated with Pamela Ritch (Bauman 1996; Bauman and Ritch 1994). The coloquios are traditional nativity plays, performed as the climactic event of patronal festivals. Coloquio performances are lengthy and elaborate events, up to twelve hours in duration, and based on written scripts (referred to as *libros* 'books') that may exceed 8,000 lines of verse.

The official, public standard that shapes coloquio performance is that actors must memorize their lines exactly as they are in the script; the script is the authoritative reference point for the play. Most participants strive to adhere to this standard, though in actual practice late recruitment to the cast, lack of diligence, limited literacy, or faulty memory may cause certain actors to fall short of fully accurate recitations. Accordingly, every performance features a prompter, stationed just offstage, whose function is to feed lines to actors from the script when their memory falters. It is not uncommon for the prompter to have to feed entire speeches to certain actors, line by line, making for a kind of echoic doubling of the dialogue, as the prompter's offerings are fully audible to the audience. To this extent, the prompter's supplying of a line to an actor, who then relays it to the audience, constitutes a mediational routine that is a part of every coloquio performance, though such routines may vary in their distribution from one performance to the next. The source dialogue consists of the prompter addressing the scripted line to the actor, with the audience as overhearers, while the target dialogue consists of the actor repeating the line, this time addressed directly to the target audience.

In the performances enacted in the community that is the focus of my earlier accounts, this mediational routine becomes a resource for further expressive manipulation. There is one character in the play, a holy Hermit, who is traditionally played as a burlesque figure. One of the chief devices employed by the Hermit in his comic performances is to parody the scripted lines assigned to him and thus to subvert the official ideology of strict adherence to the scripted text. Consider the following excerpt from one of his longer speeches, which occurs in a scene in which the Hermit is lost in a forbidding mountain wilderness. In the speech in question, as rendered in the script, he offers an appeal to God to deliver him to safety and reaffirms his commitment to the religious life. Here is the passage as performed; lines transformed by the Hermit are rendered in boldface (P = prompter, H = Hermit):

P: Por un lado se presenta	At one side appears
H: Por un lado se presenta . . .	At one side appears . . .
P: un risco muy elevado.	a very high cliff,
H: **Ah! tu estas bien elevado**.	Ah! you are very elevated.
P: y por otro lado un fuerte collado	and at the other side a rough hill
H: **Por aca 'ta tambien mi cuñado**	Around here is also my brother-in-law
P: desligado alrededor.	loosened all around.
H: **y tiene bigotes alrededor**.	and he has whiskers all around.
P: Ay! yo no se porque el temblor	Ay! I don't know why this tremor

H: **Yo no se ni porque temblor**	I don't even know why tremor . . .
P: a la cobardia me enseña	leads me to cowardice.
H: **Ya su senora me enseña**	Now his wife leads me.
P: que observo por este lado	for I observe at this side
H: **Ah! y mi suegro esta aca del otro lado**	Ah! my father-in-law is here on the other side
P: una muy soberbia peña	a very overbearing rock
H: **a esta breñosa greña** . . .	at this jumbled heap of grain
P: que esta pronto a despegarse.	that is soon to detach itself,
H: **hasta levantarse, [?]**	until straightening up, [?]
P: y no hay quien me defienda de mi.	and there is no one to protect me from it.
H: y no hay quien me defienda de mi.	and there is no one to protect me from it.

In the first and last lines of this brief passage, the Hermit relays the lines fed to him by the prompter exactly as given. In the other lines, however, he engages in a form of *relajo*, or license (see Farr 1994, 1998): he talks back to the authoritative script, using punning and other forms of speech play to carnivalesque effect. The paronomastic quality of his improvised lines should be apparent from the Spanish transcript, even to non-speakers of Spanish. In the course of his parodic counterstatement, he introduces various in-laws, a special focus of joking in Mexican folk humor, he portrays his brother-in-law as covered with whiskers, he resorts to a bit of sexual innuendo concerning his brother-in-law's wife, and so on. Thus, while the mediational routine represented by the prompting process in its standard guise serves as a display of textual authority, as the actor repeats the prompted line exactly as given, the parodic counterstatement of the Hermit, as he distorts the script line by line, call that authority into open question, if only until the next performer returns to a faithful rendering of his lines.

Ultimately, then, if the mediational process allows for the enactment and display of authorization by minimization of the gap between source utterance and target utterance, it allows for other calibrations of the authorization process as well. Mediational performance routines of the kind we have examined here construct a framework within which utterances may be placed in relationship to each other in a heightened and reflexively resonant way. The entextualization of the source utterance and its replication in the target utterance in such a way that the intertextual gap is minimized is a potent means of infusing the discourse with authority, and we have seen that this capacity for strong authorization is a widely exploited means for the enactment of authority that is an essential condition for its maintenance. At the same time, the infiltration and transformation of the source utterance in the target utterance, the widening of the intertextual gap while still maintaining some of the integrity of the source utterance, becomes a means of sharing or diffusing authority. And at a further extreme, the transformation of the source utterance in such a way that it continues to display its derivation but is rendered ridiculous becomes a powerful means of enacting a challenge to the authoritative word.

What I have attempted to demonstrate in this chapter is that mediational performances represent formalized, routinized communicative structures, one of the most significant design features of which is to enact and display the continuity of discourse across gaps in time, space, existential domain, and social status. In so doing, I suggest, they enact as well the core structure of processes that are constitutive of social life: traditionalization, the socialization of discourse, and authorization. But as my closing examples make clear, if mediational performances can display these core processes, they can comment upon them as well, calibrating and recalibrating their force and even – in parody – turning them upside down, reminding us yet again that what serves authority can also challenge it.

For clarity of exposition and argument, I have chosen in this introductory investigation to examine highly regimented and routinized mediational performances in which verbatim relay is a conventional expectation and performance plays a significant role. In larger scope, however, these routinized mediational performances represent but one mode of regimenting the circulation of discourse, that is, one way – or one set of ways – of configuring genres, participant roles and structures, metadiscursive ideologies, and presentational frames by which communities conventionalize and institutionalize the entextualization, decontextualization, and recontextualization of utterances. A full investigation of structures of mediation designed to transcend the speaker-hearer dyad would extend from ad hoc pass-on-the-message procedures ("When you see Mark, tell him to call me") to various routines of speech socialization, pedagogy, and spirit mediumship (touched on above, in passing), frameworks for interlingual translation between interlocutors who do not understand each others' language, the organization of performing arts in which the role of composer or choreographer or playwright is separate from that of performer (cf. the Irish fili), and an open range of additional possibilities, to be discovered, by which communities may regiment the ways by which we live in a world of others' words.

8

Epilogue

Consider one last set of mediational performances.

Writing of Paul E. Hall, a Newfoundland song-maker with whom he worked, John Szwed makes the following observation:

> He sees his talent as singular . . . he feels that his skill and accomplishment have been wasted on his listeners, and he longs to reach a larger audience. It was not surprising to him that I should be interested in his singing, for he thinks his songs are valuable and should reach a more appreciative public. (Szwed 1970:157)

Concerning ʿAwadallah, one of the epic performers she recorded in Egypt, Susan Slyomovics notes that from his point of view, "the goals of my research, as far as he was concerned, the soul of my research, should be to present the historical facts to foreigners as recorded in the epic" (1987:13).

At the end of her account of the extended conversations she had with the Mexican market woman she calls Esperanza, conversations devoted to Esperanza's telling of the story of her life, of her "sins," Ruth Behar records that Esperanza brought her confessional story to an end with the directive: "You tell them somewhere ahead so someone else can carry the burden" (1995:170).

Warodi, the Xavante elder at the center of Laura Graham's study of Xavante public discourse, "wished to position his people within a global context." Graham reports: "He freqently ended speeches by exhorting me to 'take his words across the ocean' so that people there could learn of the Xavante" (1995:16–17).

In each of these cases, the ethnographic encounter itself is revealed to be the source dialogue of a mediational process. The performers project their performances forward from the field encounter to a target dialogue in which their texts will be relayed by the ethnographer to an as yet unseen but clearly implicated receiver. As brief as they are, these examples suggest the relevance of our exploration of intertextuality to a critical examination of our own ethnographic practice.

They suggest, first of all, that "dialogic" models of the ethnographic enterprise that rest tacitly or explicitly upon dyadic, intersubjective dialogue "between anthropologist and informant" (Marcus and Fischer 1986:69) or "the ethnographer and his native partners" (Tyler 1986:127) in "the immediate situation of communication" (Clifford 1988:39), like all models of the speaker-hearer dyad in the bounded speech event, may underspecify the discursive reach and participant roles of the ethnographic event. The texts, performances, knowledge that are emergent out of the encounters described in our examples are not simply the co-creation of anthropologist and informant, for other participants and other dialogues are already implicated in the performer's discourse. In the Bakhtinian metaphor of polyphony that is commonly employed in approaches of this kind, the chorus of voices in these ethnographic encounters includes the projected voice of the ethnographer relaying the performers' texts to an ultimate target audience.

Certainly, poststructuralist critics who conceive of the ethnographic process in dialogic terms characteristically recognize that it includes at least two moments of dialogue, the first represented by the fieldwork encounter, the second by the writing of the ethnographic account addressed to an audience of readers. Our examples suggest, however, that a degree of potential distortion arises when the respective dialogues are dissociated into two separate stages. Consider, for example, Marcus and Fischer's framing of the ethnographic process "in terms of its two major stages – going into the field, that is, finding a site where the anthropologist can immerse himself in another culture, and eventually returning home to write about the knowledge he has gained from fieldwork for scholarly and, sometimes, more public readerships" (1986:35; see also 31). The cases before us demonstrate how the second dialogue may already be present in the first.

They also demonstrate how the "informant" or "native partner" may take an active hand in directing how his or her discourse may be recontextualized by the ethnographer. These performers are not at all the hapless robbery victims portrayed by Tyler, for example, in his indictment of those ethnographers who

> have tamed the savage, not with the pen, but with the tape recorder, reducing him to a 'straight man,' as in the script of some obscure comic routine,

for even as they think to have returned to 'oral performance' or 'dialogue,' in order that the native have a place in the text, they exercise total control over her discourse and steal the only thing she has left – her voice. (Tyler 1986:128)

Indeed, the performer's agenda may be consonant with the ethnographer's own – may, in fact, be based upon a fine understanding by the performer of the ethnographer's agenda and of the capacities of the ethnographic process. Many performers desire the authorization, publication, and social dissemination of their words; they want their texts to spite the power of time. By framing their performances as part of a mediational process, the performers are inviting or acknowledging the ethnographers' collaboration, just as the ethnographers have done in seeking them out. Note also, in this regard, that this collaboration has a representational component as well. James Clifford, while making a number of penetrating observations concerning ethnographies "cast as dialogic encounters between two individuals," goes on to say that such ethnographies "remain *representations* of dialogue" (1988:43, emphasis his), with the implication that such representations are in some sense etiolations of what really went on in the field interaction. It is worth pointing out, therefore, that in the cases I have cited, the representational process begins with the performer. The projection by the performer of the ethnographer's mediational relay is itself already a representation of dialogue, and insofar as all of the texts offered by the performers in our examples are reperformances of texts performed before, they are representations of prior dialogues as well. In a truly dialogic conception of ethnography, one that takes Bakhtin fully seriously, it is representational dialogue all the way down (cf. Mannheim and Tedlock 1995:3). Nor is is necessarily true, as Clifford maintains, that "a purely dialogical authority would repress the inescapable fact of textualization" (1988:43), at least in regard to the kinds of cases we are examining. The performers' words are already entextualized, and they anticipate that their texts will have a formative – even a determinative – influence on the ethnographers' texts.

To recognize the agency of the performer in attempting to exercise control over the ethnographer's future recontextualization of his or her words and to establish the terms of the ethnographic collaboration is not, of course, to assume that he or she has determinative control over the ethnographic process. Among other factors, it is well to remember that the mediational relay projected by the performer in the field encounter is only virtual. The actualization of the target dialogue in the eventual ethnographic account rests in the hands of the ethnographer, usually at a far remove from the field. The analytical perspectives I have brought to bear in our explication of the target-dialogue phase of mediational performances offer further critical tools for explication of the process of writing ethnography, especially in regard to the ways in which the attribution of authority may be calibrated in the framing of the target utterance. And it is at this stage in the relay that many of the other intertextual practices and processes we have considered come into play, for the ethnographer as much as for the performers we have encountered throughout this book: the inter-articulation of genres (how to write an ethnography about stories, for example, or songs), the calibration of intertextual gaps between the performed text and the represented text, the negotiation of authority and authorship, the assumption – or disclaimer – of accountability for artful or authoritative or correct replication, the traditionalization of the reported text.

Let me make clear that I do not want to overgeneralize my argument or my claims. The cases I have cited to frame these concluding observations all involve artful performances marked by the special qualities of poetic entextualization, display, and heightened reflexivity we have adduced throughout these pages. Once again, however, I would argue that such performances foreground and thus highlight discursive and metadiscursive practices, processes, and ideologies of more general currency and broader reach. No less is true of the cases at hand; the mediational organization of the ethnography of performance offers a productive critical vantage point on the ethnographic process in all its guises. Bruce Mannheim and Dennis Tedlock, whose linguistically and sociolinguistically informed conception of dialogic anthropology is the best we have, observe that "one of the things language does best is to enable its speakers, in the very moment they are present to one another, to breach that presence" (1995:8). The ethnographic work of John Szwed with Paul E. Hall, Susan Slyomovics with ʿAdawallah, Ruth Behar with Esperanza, and Laura Graham with Warodi allows us to confirm the truth and salience of this observation especially clearly, but it should alert us as well to the ways in which all ethnographic dialogues may escape the power of presence.

Notes

Chapter 1 Introduction: Genre, Performance, and the Production of Intertextuality

1   This discussion owes much to my extended collaboration with Charles L. Briggs. Portions of the discussion are drawn from Bauman (2000), Bauman and Briggs (1990), and Briggs and Bauman (1992). See also Foley (1997).
2   Genette uses the term "transtextuality" for this relational nexus, reserving the term "intertextuality" for quotation (1997[1982]:2–3). Allen (2000) is the most comprehensive survey of conceptions of and approaches to intertextuality.
3   For a more detailed and nuanced discussion of parody, see Genette (1997[1982]: 19–30).

Chapter 2 "And the Verse is Thus": Icelandic Stories About Magical Poems

1   For this text and related examples, see Nicolaisen (1997:186–188).
2   In Icelandic, kraftaskáld is the same in singular and plural; in this chapter, I have anglicized the plural form.
3   Motif M411.18 Curse by poet (Thompson 1955–8).
4   Motif D214.2 Winds controlled by magic (Thompson 1955–8).

Chapter 3 "I'll Give You Three Guesses": The Dynamics of Genre in the Riddle Tale

1   See, for example, Abrahams (1980, 1985), Dorst (1983), Lüthi (1976[1970]: 121–133), Norton (1942), Wells (1950:162–164).
2   In his foundational survey of the classic neck riddle (stories in which a prisoner saves himself from execution by posing a riddle that those who have condemned him cannot answer), F. J. Norton observes that there is considerable "variation in the relative importance of tale and riddle" in the oral tradition (Norton 1942:27; see also Abrahams 1985).

3   The Scottish Travelers, so-called because of their formerly nomadic or semi-nomadic way of life, traditionally earned their living on the margins of society as metal workers (thus the pejorative term "tinker"), peddlers, beggars, horse and automobile traders, dealers in scrap, and performers. They have been justly celebrated by folklorists as superb singers and storytellers. On Traveler society and culture, see Henderson (1971), Neat (1978), and Rehfisch and Rehfisch (1975). The fullest ethnographically based and performance-oriented studies of Traveler storytelling are by Donald Braid (1993, 1997, 1998, 1999, 2002); see also Bauman and Braid (1998).

4   On the Stewart family, see Douglas (1981), Douglas (1987), MacColl and Seeger (1986), and Porter (1985).

5   AT 922 (Thompson 1961). Motifs H541.2 Riddle propounded on pain of loss of property; H561.2 King and abbot; King propounds three riddles to abbot to answer on pain of death. Herdsman disguises as abbot and answers questions; H691.1.1 How much does the moon weigh? A pound, for it has four quarters; H702.1.1 How many stars in the heavens? Two million; if you don't believe it, count them yourself; H524.1 What am I thinking?; H508.2 Bride offered to man who can find answer to question; J1116 Foolish person becomes clever; L160 Success of the unpromising hero (Thompson 1955–8).

6   AT 927 (Thompson 1961). Motifs H900 Tasks imposed; H548 Riddle contests; H792 Riddle of the unborn (Thompson 1955–8). Abrahams (1980: 28–34).

7   Friedrich Schiller recognized this potential very clearly. In his literary redaction of the Turandot story, the Princess Turandot defends the riddle test she imposes on her would-be suitors – and the execution of those who fail the test – in these ringing terms:

> I am not cruel. I want only to live free.
> I simply do not want to be possessed by another; that right,
> Innate in even the lowliest person
> In its mother's womb,
> I want to assert, a King's daughter.
> I see throughout all Asia woman
> Dominated and condemned to the slave's yoke,
> And I will avenge my wronged sex
> On these arrogant menfolk, who
> Have no other advantage over frailer women
> Than raw strength. As a weapon,
> Nature gave me inventive wit
> And sagacity, to defend my freedom.
> (Schiller 1966:29–30; my translation)

8   I have retained the spelling and format of the original sources.

Chapter 4 "What Shall We Give You?": Calibrations of Genre in a Mexican Market

1   These data were recorded on six occasions between December, 1985 and January, 1989.
2   In transcribing the calls and spiels I have set them out into lines marked primarily by significant breath pauses, though with occasional attention as well to syntactic structures and intonational patterns. My thanks to Ana Maria Ochoa for invaluable assistance in transcription and to Josefina Vasques for help in untying some knots in translation.
3   Seño is a contraction of Señora, and functions analogously to Ms. in English.
4   Graham (1981:17) defines the caso as "a relatively brief prose narrative, focusing upon a single event, supernatural or natural, in which the protagonist or observer is the narrator or someone the narrator knows and vouches for, and which is normally used as evidence or as an example to illustrate that 'this kind of thing happens.' "

Chapter 5 "Bell, You Get the Spotted Pup": First Person Narratives of a Texas Storyteller

1   For overviews of the field, see Bamberg (1997) and Ochs and Capps (1997). For representative or critically significant studies, see Crapanzano (1981), Johnstone (1990, 1996), Labov (1972), Labov and Waletzky (1967), Langness and Frank (1981), Linde (1993), Myerhoff (1982), Ochs and Capps (2001), Polanyi (1989), and Stahl (1989).
2   Motif K134 Deceptive horse sale (Baughman 1966).
3   Motif X1301.2 Remarkable length of fish (Baughman 1966).
4   Motif X1611.1 Remarkably strong wind [including tornado, cyclone] (Baughman 1966).
5   See Mullen (1978:139–45) for early exceptions.
6   For a different perspective, see Bauman (1986:18, 24, 78, 111). Stahl (1989:50–82) analyzes the tall-tale resonances of an individual personal narrative performed by one of her key sources.
7   Tale type 1960G The Great Tree; motifs H86 Inscribed name on article as token of ownership; X1116 The breathing tree; X1471 Lie about large trees; X1471.1 Two groups or gangs of men chop on opposite sides of big tree, each unaware that anyone is working on other side; X1547 Lie: river of honey (Baughman 1966). For other versions, see Bauman (1986:83–87), Mullen (1978:145–146), Sitton (1983:166–168).
8   Motifs X1402.1 Lie: the fast growing vine; X1411.1 Lie: large watermelon (Baughman 1966).
9   See motifs listed under X1651 Fog (Baughman 1966).

Chapter 6 "That I Can't Tell You": Negotiating Performance with a Nova Scotia Fisherman

1   Granger (1977:168); motifs C40l.3 Tabu: speaking while searching for treasure; N553.2 Unlucky encounter causes treasure-seekers to talk and thus lose treasure (Thompson 1955–8).
2   Motif G303.4.5.3.1 Devil detected by his hoofs (Thompson 1955–8).

Chapter 7 "Go, My Reciter, Recite My Words": Mediation, Tradition, Authority

1   This relationship of poet to performer had a wider distribution in medieval society. See, for example, Chaytor (1912:11) on the French *troubadors* and *jongleurs.*
2   On the form of medieval Irish poetry, see Williams and Ford (1992:156):

This body of poetry was composed in the syllabic metres, that is, those metres defined by a regular number and class of syllables in the stanza. The line must contain a special number of syllables and end on an accented word of a certain syllable length; the metre is determined above all by the number of syllables in the line and by the syllabic length of the final word. There is no regular stress. In addition, the following rules are characteristic of all metres of *dán direach* (strict versification) in the period 1250–1650: the last two stressed words in the stanza must alliterate; each line must end with a word bearing full accent; and the last words of a poem should echo its first words.

3   The first verse of "Neglected Merit" in Irish is as follows:

> Tríall, a reacaire, reac m'fhuighle,
>   imthigh go grod, ná gabh sgís
> gan dol d'fhéaghain chinn ar ccoimhghe:
>   fill ré sgéulaibh oirne arís.
> (Bergin 1970:55)

4   See Quain (1942:14–20) for a description of the formal structure of Fijian oral poetry and Quain's methods of translation. The principal poetic devices that characterize the epic songs include: chanted lines of relatively equal length, with syllable reduplication and the addition of a line-final extra syllable to regularize rhythm; assonant rhyme; frequent repetition of initial words; grammatical parallelism; and an esoteric, archaically tinged poetic register.

References

Abagi, Jared, Ailie Cleghorn, and Marilyn Merritt. 1988. Language Use in Standard Three Science Instruction in Urban and Rural Kenyan Schools. *Kenya Journal of Education* 4(1):118–46.

Abrahams, Roger D. 1980. *Between the Living and the Dead*. FFC 225. Helsinki: Suomalainen Tiedeakatemia.

Abrahams, Roger D. 1981. Shouting Match at the Border: The Folklore of Display Events. In *And Other Neighborly Names: Social Image and Cultural Process in Texas Folklore*. Richard Bauman and Roger D. Abrahams, eds. Pp. 303–321. Austin: University of Texas Press.

Abrahams, Roger D. 1985. A Note on Neck-Riddles in the West Indies as They Comment On Emergent Genre Theory. *Journal of American Folklore* 98:85–94.

Abrahams, Roger D. and Alan Dundes. 1972. Riddles. In *Folklore and Folklife: An Introduction*. Richard M. Dorson, ed. Pp. 129–143. Chicago: University of Chicago Press.

Allen, Graham. 2000. *Intertextuality*. New York: Routledge.

Almqvist, Bo. 1961. Um Ákvæðskáld. *Skirnir* 135:72–98.

Almqvist, Bo. 1965. *Norrön Niddiktning 1*. Stockholm: Almqvist and Wiksell.

Almqvist, Bo. 1974. *Norron Niddiktning 2*. Stockholm: Alrmqvist and Wiksell.

Andersson, Theodore M. 1966. The Textual Evidence for an Oral Family Saga. *Arkiv for Nordisk Filologi* 81:1–23.

Armstrong, Robert Plant. 1971. *The Affecting Presence: An Essay in Humanistic Anthropology*. Urbana: University of Illinois Press.

Babcock, Barbara. 1980. Reflexivity: Definitions and Discriminations. *Semiotica* 30:1–14.

Bach, Kent and Robert Harnish. 1979. *Linguistic Communication and Speech Acts*. Cambridge, MA: MIT Press.

Bakhtin, Mikhail M. 1981. *The Dialogic Imagination*. Michael Holquist, ed., Caryl Emerson and Michael Holquist, trans. Austin: University of Texas Press.

Bakhtin, Mikhail M. 1984 [1965]. *Rabelais and His World*. Hélène Iswolsky, trans. Bloomington: Indiana University Press.

Bakhtin, Mikhail M. 1986. *Speech Genres and Other Late Essays.* Caryl Emerson and Michael Holquist, eds. Vern McGee, trans. Austin: University of Texas Press.

Bamberg, Michael G. W., ed. 1997. *Oral Versions of Personal Experience: Three Decades of Narrative Analysis. Journal of Narrative and Life History,* special issue 7(1–4).

Barber, Karin. 1997. Preliminary Notes on Audiences in Africa. *Africa* 67(3):347–362.

Barber, Karin. 1999. Quotation in the Constitution of Yorùbá Oral Texts. *Research in African Literatures* 30(2):17–41.

Basso, Keith H. 1996. *Wisdom Sits in Places.* Albuquerque: University of New Mexico Press.

Baughman, Ernest W. 1966. *Type and Motif-Index of the Folktales of England and North America.* The Hague: Mouton.

Bauman, Richard. 1972. The La Have Island General Store: Sociability and Verbal Art in a Nova Scotia Community. *Journal of American Folklore* 85:330–43.

Bauman, Richard. 1977. *Verbal Art as Performance.* Prospect Heights, IL: Waveland.

Bauman, Richard. 1986. *Story, Performance, and Event: Contextual Studies of Oral Narrative.* Cambridge: Cambridge University Press.

Bauman, Richard. 1991. Contextualization, Tradition, and the Dialogue of Genres: Icelandic Legends of the Kraftaskáld. In *Rethinking Context: Language as an Interactive Phenomenon.* Charles Goodwin and Alessandro Duranti, eds. Pp. 125–145. Cambridge: Cambridge University Press.

Bauman, Richard. 1992. Performance. In *Folklore, Cultural Performances, and Popular Entertainments.* Richard Bauman, ed. Pp. 41–49. Oxford: Oxford University Press.

Bauman, Richard. 1996. Transformations of the Word in the Production of Mexican Festival Drama. In *Natural Histories of Discourse.* Michael Silverstein and Greg Urban, eds. Pp. 301–327. Chicago: University of Chicago Press.

Bauman, Richard. 2000. Genre. *Journal of Linguistic Anthropology* 9(1–2):84–87.

Bauman, Richard and Donald Braid. 1998. The Ethnography of Performance in the Study of Oral Traditions. In *Teaching Oral Tradition.* John Miles Foley, ed. Pp. 106–122. New York: Modern Language Association.

Bauman, Richard and Charles L. Briggs. 1990. Poetics and Performance as Critical Perspectives on Language and Social Life. *Annual Review of Anthropology* 19:59–88.

Bauman, Richard and Charles L. Briggs. 2000. Language Philosophy as Language Ideology: John Locke and Johann Gottfried Herder. In *Regimes of Language: Ideologies, Polities, Identities.* Paul V. Kroskrity, ed. Pp. 139–204. Santa Fe, NM: School of American Research.

Bauman, Richard and Charles L. Briggs. 2003. *Voices of Modernity: Language Ideologies and the Politics of Inequality.* Cambridge: Cambridge University Press.

Bauman, Richard and Pamela Ritch. 1994. Informing Performance: Producing the *coloquio* in Tierra Blanca. *Oral Tradition* 9(2):255–80.

Behar, Ruth. 1995. Rage and Redemption: Reading the Life Story of a Mexican Marketing Woman. In *The Dialogic Emergence of Culture*. Dennis Tedlock and Bruce Mannheim, eds. Pp. 148–178. Urbana: University of Illinois Press.

Bell, L. Michael. 1976. Oral Allusion in *Egils saga Skalla-Grímssoner*: A Computer-Aided Approach. *Arkiv for Nordisk Filologi* 81:1–23.

Bergin, Osborn. 1970. *Irish Bardic Poetry*. David Greene and Fergus Kelly, comp. and eds. Dublin: Dublin Institute for Advanced Studies.

Bødker, Laurits. 1964. *The Nordic Riddle*. Copenhagen: Rosenkilde and Bagger.

Braid, Donald. 1993. The Traveller and the Hare: Meaning, Function, and Form in the Recontextualization of Narrative. *Folklore Forum* 26:3–29.

Braid, Donald. 1997. The Construction of Identity through Narrative: Folklore and the Travelling People of Scotland. In *Romani Culture and Gypsy Identity*. Thomas Acton and Gary Mundy, eds. Pp. 38–66. Hatfield: University of Hertfordshire Press.

Braid, Donald. 1998. "Did It Happen or Did It Not?" Dream Stories, Worldview, and Narrative Knowing. *Text and Performance Quarterly* 183:319–343.

Braid, Donald. 1999. "Our Stories Are Not Just for Entertainment": Lives and Stories Among the Travelling People of Scotland. In *Traditional Storytelling Today: An International Encyclopedia*. Margaret Read MacDonald, ed. Pp. 301–309. Chicago: Fitzroy Dearborn.

Braid, Donald. 2002. *Scottish Traveller Tales: Lives Shaped Through Stories*. Jackson: University of Mississippi Press.

Breatnach, Pádraig. 1983. The Chief's Poet. *Proceedings of the Royal Irish Academy* 83C(3):37–79.

Briggs, Charles L. 1985. Treasure Tales and Pedagogical Discourse in *Mexicano* New Mexico. *Journal of American Folklore* 98:287–314.

Briggs, Charles L. 1986. *Learning How to Ask: A Sociolinguistic Appraisal of the Role of the Interview in Social Science Research*. Cambridge: Cambridge University Press.

Briggs, Charles L. 1988. *Competence in Performance: The Creativity of Tradition in Mexicano Verbal Art*. Philadelphia: University of Pennsylvania Press.

Briggs, Charles L. 1993. Generic versus Metapragmatic Dimensions of Warao Narratives: Who Regiments Performance? In *Reflexive Language: Reported Speech and Metapragmatics*. John Lucy, ed. Pp. 179–212. Cambridge: Cambridge University Press.

Briggs, Charles L. and Richard Bauman. 1992. Genre, Intertextuality, and Social Power. *Journal of Linguistic Anthropology* 2:131–172.

Briggs, Katharine. 1970. *A Dictionary of British Folktales*. Vol. 2. London: Routledge and Kegan Paul.

Burke, Kenneth. 1968 [1931]. *Counter-Statement*. Berkeley: University of California Press.

Burns, Thomas A. 1976. Riddling: Occasion to Act. *Journal of American Folklore* 89:139–165.

Chaytor, H. J. 1912. *The Troubadours*. Cambridge: Cambridge University Press.

Cleasby, Richard, Gudhrand Vigfusson, and William Craigie. 1957. *An Ice-landic–English Dictionary*. 2nd edn. Oxford: Clarendon Press.

Clifford, James. 1988. *The Predicament of Culture*. Cambridge, MA: Harvard University Press.

Cox, Philip. 1996. *Gender, Genre and the Romantic Poets*. Manchester: Manchester University Press.

Crapanzano, Vincent. 1981. Life Histories. *American Anthropologist* 86:953–60.

Crowley, Daniel J. 1966. *I Could Talk Old-Story Good: Creativity in Bahamian Folk-lore*. Berkeley: University of California Press.

Dargan, Amanda and Steven Zeitlin. 1983. American Talkers: Expressive Styles and Occupational Choice. *Journal of American Folklore* 96:3–33.

Darnell, Regna. 1989 [1974]. Correlates of Cree Narrative Performance. In *Explorations in the Ethnography of Speaking*. Richard Bauman and Joel Sherzer, eds. Pp. 315–336. Cambridge: Cambridge University Press.

Dorst, John. 1983. Neck-Riddle as a Dialogue of Genres. *Journal of American Folklore* 96:413–33.

Douglas, Sheila. 1981. John Stewart – Storyteller. *Arv* 37:19–26.

Douglas, Sheila. 1987. *The King o the Black Art*. Aberdeen: Aberdeen University Press.

Dundas, Marjorie, ed. 2002. *Riddling Tales from Around the World*. Jackson: University of Mississippi Press.

Duranti, Alessandro. 1994. *From Grammar to Politics: Linguistic Anthropology in a Western Samoan Village*. Berkeley: University of California Press.

Duranti, Alessandro and Donald Brenneis, eds. 1986. *The Audience as Co-Author*. Special issue of *Text* 6(3).

Farr, Marcia. 1994. *Echando relajo*: Verbal Art and Gender Among Mexicanas in Chicago. In *Cultural Performances: Proceedings of the Third Berkeley Women and Language Conference*. Mary Bucholtz, A. C. Liang, Laurel A. Sutton, and Caitlin Hines, eds. Pp. 168–186. Berkeley: Berkeley Women and Language Group.

Farr, Marcia. 1998. Relajo como microfiesta. In *México en Fiesta*. Herón Pérez Martínez, ed. Pp. 457–470. Zamora, Michoacán: Colegio de Michoacán.

Finnegan, Ruth. 1992 [1977]. *Oral Poetry*. Bloomington: Indiana University Press.

Firth, Raymond. 1959. Problems and Assumptions in an Anthropological Study of Religion. *Journal of the Royal Anthropological Institute* 89(2):129–48.

Flores Farfán, José Antonio. 1984. *La Interaccion Verbal de Compra-Venta en Mercados Otomies*. Mexico City: Centro de Investigaciones y Estudios Superiores en Antropologia Social.

Foley, John Miles. 1991. *Immanent Art: From Structure to Meaning in Traditional Oral Epic*. Bloomington: Indiana University Press.

Foley, John Miles. 1995. *The Singer of Tales in Performance*. Bloomington: Indiana University Press.

Foley, William. 1997. *Anthropological Linguistics: An Introduction*. Oxford: Blackwell.

Foster, Michael K. 1974. *From the Earth to Beyond the Sky: An Ethnographic Approach to Four Iroquois Longhouse Speech Events*. Canadian Ethnology Service Paper No. 20. Ottawa: National Museums of Canada.

French, David. 1958. Cultural Matrices of Chinookan Non-Casual Language. *International Journal of American Linguistics* 24(4):258–63.

Geddes, W. R. 1945. *Deuba: A Study of a Fijian Village*. Memoirs of the Polynesian Society 22. Wellington: Polynesian Society.

Genette, Gérard. 1997 [1982]. *Palimpsests: Literature in the Second Degree*. Channa Newman and Claude Doubinsky, trans. Lincoln: University of Nebraska Press.

Gerhart, Mary. 1992. *Genre Choices, Gender Questions*. Norman: University of Oklahoma Press.

Goffman, Erving. 1974. *Frame Analysis*. New York: Harper and Row.

Goffman, Erving. 1981. Footing. In *Forms of Talk*. Pp. 124–159. Philadelphia: University of Pennsylvania Press.

Goldberg, Christine. 1993. *Turandot's Sisters: A Study of the Folktale AT851*. New York: Garland Publishing.

Goldstein, Kenneth S. 1963. Riddling Traditions in Northeastern Scotland. *Journal of American Folklore* 76:330–6.

Goodman, Jane. 2002. Writing Empire, Underwriting Nation: Discursive Histories of Kabyle Berber Oral Texts. *American Ethnologist* 29(1):86–122.

Goody, Esther. 1978. Towards a Theory of Questions. In *Questions and Politeness*. Esther Goody, ed. Pp. 17–43. Cambridge: Cambridge University Press.

Gossen, Gary. 1974. *Chamulas in the World of the Sun*. Cambridge, MA: Harvard University Press.

Graham, Joe. 1981. The *Caso*: An Emic Genre of Folk Narrative. In *"And Other Neighborly Names": Social Process and Cultural Image in Texas Folklore*. Richard Bauman and Roger D. Abrahams, eds. Pp. 11–43. Austin: University of Texas Press.

Graham, Laura. 1995. *Performing Dreams: Discourses of Immortality Among the Xavante of Central Brazil*. Austin: University of Texas Press.

Granger, Byrd H. 1977. *A Motif Index for Lost Mines and Treasures*. Tucson: University of Arizona Press.

Günthner, Susanne and Hubert Knoblauch. 1995. Culturally Patterned Speaking Practices: The Analysis of Communicative Genres. *Pragmatics* 5(1):1–32.

Halpert, Herbert. 1971. Definition and Variation in Folk Legend. In *American Folk Legend: A Symposium*. Wayland D. Hand, ed. Pp. 17–54. Berkeley: University of California Press.

Hanks, William. 1987. Discourse Genres in a Theory of Practice. *American Ethnologist* 14(4):666–92.

Hanks, William. 1996a. *Language and Communicative Practices*. Boulder, CO: Westview Press.

Hanks, William. 1996b. Exorcism and the Description of Participant Roles. In *Natural Histories of Discourse*. Michael Silverstein and Greg Urban, eds. Pp. 160–200. Chicago: University of Chicago Press.

Haring, Lee. 1972. Performing for the Interviewer: A Study of the Structure of Context. *Southern Folklore Quarterly* 36:383–98.

Haring, Lee. 1988. Interperformance. *Fabula* 29(3–4):365–372.

Harris, Joseph and Karl Reichl, eds. 1997. *Prosimetrum: Cross-Cultural Perspectives on Narrative in Prose and Verse*. Cambridge, MA: D. S. Brewer.

Henderson, Hamish. 1971. Tinkers. In *Man, Myth and Magic: An Illustrated Encyclopedia of the Supernatural*. Richard Cavendish, ed. Vol. 7 (no. 102). Pp. 2853–55. London: Purnell.

Herder, Johann Gottfried. 1967 [1877–1913]. *Sämtliche Werke*, 33 vols. Bernhard Suphan, ed. Hildesheim: Georg Olms Verlagsbuchhandlung.

Herder, Johann Gottfried. 1969. *Herder on Social and Political Culture*. F. M. Barnard, ed. Cambridge: Cambridge University Press.

Hymes, Dell H. 1966. Two Types of Linguistic Relativity. In *Sociolinguistics*. William Bright, ed. Pp. 114–67. The Hague: Mouton.

Hymes, Dell H. 1975a. Folklore's Nature and the Sun's Myth. *Journal of American Folklore* 88:345–69.

Hymes, Dell H. 1975b. Breakthrough Into Performance. In *Folklore: Performance and Communication*. Dan Ben-Amos and Kenneth S. Goldstein, eds. Pp. 11–74. The Hague: Mouton.

Hymes, Dell H. 1977. Discovering Oral Performance and Measured Verse in American Indian Narrative. *New Literary History* 8:431–57.

Hymes, Dell H. 1989 [1974]. Ways of Speaking. In *Explorations in the Ethnography of Speaking*. 2nd edn. Richard Bauman and Joel Sherzer, eds. Pp. 433–451. Cambridge: Cambridge University Press.

Irvine, Judith. 1975. Wolof Speech Styles and Social Status. *Working Papers in Sociolinguistics* no. 23. Austin, TX: Southwest Educational Development Laboratory.

Irvine, Judith T. 1996. Shadow Conversations: The Indeterminacy of Participant Roles. In *Natural Histories of Discourse*. Pp. 131–159. Michael Silverstein and Greg Urban, eds. Chicago: University of Chicago Press.

Jakobson, Roman. 1960. Linguistics and Poetics. In *Style in Language*. Thomas A. Sebeok, ed. Pp. 350–377. Cambridge, MA: MIT Press.

Jakobson, Roman. 1971 [1957]. Shifters, Verbal Categories, and the Russian Verb. In *Roman Jakobson: Selected Writings*. Vol. 2. Pp. 130–147. The Hague: Mouton.

Jakobson, Roman. 1971. The Dominant. In *Readings in Russian Poetics: Formalist and Structuralist Views*. Ladislav Matejka and Krystyna Pomorska, eds. Pp. 82–87. Cambridge, MA: MIT Press.

Jasper, Patricia. 1979. *Ed Bell, Storyteller*. Videotape. Austin, TX: Austin Community Television Network.

Johnstone, Barbara. 1990. *Stories, Community, and Place: Narratives from Middle America*. Bloomington: Indiana University Press.

Johnstone, Barbara. 1996. *The Linguistic Individual: Self-Expression in Language and Linguistics*. New York: Oxford University Press.

Kabell, Aage. 1980. *Skalden und Schamanen*. FFC 227. Helsinki: Suomalainen Tiedeakatemia.

Kapchan, Deborah. 1993. Hybridization and the Marketplace: Emerging Paradigms in Folkloristics. *Western Folklore* 52:303–326.

Kapchan, Deborah. 1995. Performance. *Journal of American Folklore* 108:479–508.

Kapchan, Deborah. 1996. *Gender on the Market: Moroccan Women and the Revoicing of Tradition*. Philadelphia: University of Pennsylvania Press.

Keane, Webb. 1997. *Signs of Recognition: Powers and Hazards of Representation in an Indonesian Society*. Berkeley: University of California Press.

Keenan [Ochs], Elinor. 1973. A Sliding Sense of Obligatoriness: The Poly-Structure of Malagasy Oratory. *Language in Society* 2:225–243.

Keller-Cohen, Deborah and Judy Dyer. 1997. Intertextuality and the Narrative of Personal Experience. In *Oral Versions of Personal Experience: Three Decades of Narrative Analysis. Journal of Narrative and Life History*, special issue 7(1–4): 147–153.

Kernan, Alvin B., Peter Brooks, and J. Michael Holquist. 1973. *Man and His Fictions: An Introduction to Fiction-Making, Its Forms and Uses*. New York: Harcourt, Brace, Jovanovich.

Kirshenblatt-Gimblett, Barbara. 1990. Performance of Precepts/Precepts of Performance: Hasidic Celebrations of Purim in Brooklyn. In *By Means of Performance*. Richard Schechner and Willa Appel, eds. Pp. 109–117. Cambridge: Cambridge University Press.

Knott, Eleanor and Gerard Murphy. 1966. *Early Irish Literature*. New York: Barnes and Noble.

Kuiper, Koenraad. 1992. The Oral Tradition in Auction Speech. *American Speech* 67:279–289.

Kuiper, Koenraad and Douglas Haggo. 1984. Livestock Auctions, Oral Poetry, and Ordinary Language. *Language in Society* 13:205–234.

Kuipers, Joel. 1990. *Power in Performance: The Creation of Textual Authority in Weyewa Ritual Speech*. Philadelphia: University of Pennsylvania Press.

Labov, William. 1972. *Language in the Inner City: Studies in the Black English Vernacular*. Philadelphia: University of Pennsylvania Press.

Labov, William. 1997. Some Further Steps in Narrative Analysis. In *Oral Versions of Personal Experience: Three Decades of Narrative Analysis. Journal of Narrative and Life History*, special issue. Michael G. W. Bamberg, ed. 7(1–4):395–415.

Labov, William and Waletzky, Joshua 1967. Narrative Analysis: Oral Versons of Experience. In *Essays on the Verbal and Visual Arts: Proceedings of the 1966 Annual Spring Meeting of the American Ethnological Society*. June Helm, ed. Pp. 12–44. Seattle: University of Washington Press.

Langness, L. L. and Gelya Frank. 1981. *Lives: An Anthropological Approach to Biography*. Novato, CA: Chandler and Sharp.

Levinson, Stephen C. 1988. Putting Linguistics on a Proper Footing. In *Erving Goffman: Exploring the Interaction Order*. Paul Drew and Anthony Wootton, eds. Pp. 161–227. Cambridge: Polity Press.

Liestøl, Knut. 1974 [1930]. *The Origin of the Icelandic Family Sagas*. Westport, CT: Greenwood Press.

Linde, Charlotte. 1993. *Life Stories: The Creation of Coherence*. Oxford: Oxford University Press.

Lindenfeld, Jacqueline. 1978. Communicative Patterns at French Marketplaces. *Semiotica* 23:280–290.

Lindenfeld, Jacqueline. 1990. *Speech and Sociability at French Urban Marketplaces.* Philadelphia: John Benjamins.

Lönnröt, Elias. 1963. *The Kalevala.* Francis P. Magoun, trans. Cambridge, MA: Harvard University Press.

Luckmann, Thomas. 1995. Interaction Planning and Intersubjective Adjustment of Perspectives by Communicative Genres. In *Social Intelligence and Interaction: Expressions and Implications of the Social Bias in Human Intelligence.* Esther N. Goody, ed. Pp. 175–189. Cambridge: Cambridge University Press.

Lüthi, Max. 1976 [1970]. *Once Upon a Time: On the Nature of Fairy Tales.* Bloomington: Indiana University Press.

MacColl, Ewan and Peggy Seeger. 1986. *Till Doomsday in the Afternoon: The Folklore of a Family of Scots Travellers, The Stewarts of Blairgowrie.* Manchester: Manchester University Press.

Manhire, W. 1975–6. The Narrative Functions of Source-References in the Sagas of Icelanders. *Saga-Book of the Viking Society for Northern Research* 19(2–3): 170–190.

Mannheim, Bruce and Dennis Tedlock. 1995. Introduction. In *The Dialogic Emergence of Culture.* Pp. 1–32. Urbana: University of Illinois Press.

Maranda, Elli Köngäs. 1971. The Logic of Riddles. In *Structural Analysis of Oral Tradition.* Pierre Maranda and Elli K. Maranda, eds. Pp. 189–232. Philadelphia: University of Pennsylvania Press.

Marcus, George E. and Michael M. J. Fischer. 1986. *Anthropology as Cultural Critique.* Chicago: University of Chicago Press.

Mayhew, Henry. 1985 [1851–2]. *London Labour and the London Poor.* London: Penguin Books.

Medvedev, P. N. and Bakhtin, Mikhail M. 1978 [1928]. *The Formal Method in Literary Scholarship.* Albert J. Wehrle, trans. Baltimore, MD: Johns Hopkins University Press.

Mitchell, T. F. 1957. The Language of Buying and Selling in Cyrenaica: A Situational Statement. *Hesperis* 44:31–71.

Mullen, Patrick. 1976. The Tall Tales of a Texas Raconteur. In *Folk Narrative Research.* Juha Pentikkäinen and Tuula Juurikka, eds. Pp. 302–311. Helsinki: Finnish Literature Society.

Mullen, Patrick. 1978. *I Heard the Old Fisherman Say: Folklore of the Texas Gulf Coast.* Austin: University of Texas Press.

Mullen, Patrick. 1981. A Traditional Storyteller in Changing Contexts. In *"And Other Neighborly Names": Social Process and Cultural Image in Texas Folklore.* Richard Bauman and Roger D. Abrahams, eds. Pp. 266–279. Austin: University of Texas Press.

Myerhoff, Barbara. 1982. Life History Among the Elderly: Performance, Visibility, Remembering. In *A Crack in the Mirror: Reflexive Perspectives in Anthropology.* Jay Ruby, ed. Pp. 99–117. Philadelphia: University of Pennsylvania Press.

Neat, Timothy. 1978. The Summer Walkers. *Seer* 42:40–48.

Nicolaisen, W. F. H. 1997. The *Cante Fable* in Occidental Folk Narrative. In *Prosimetrum: Cross-Cultural Perspectives on Narrative in Prose and Verse*. Joseph Harris and Karl Reichl, eds. Pp. 183–211. Cambridge, MA: D. S. Brewer.

Norton, F. J. 1942. Prisoner Who Saved His Neck With a Riddle. *Folk-Lore* 53:27–57.

Ochs, Elinor and Lisa Capps. 1997. Narrative Authenticity. In *Oral Versions of Personal Experience: Three Decades of Narrative Analysis. Journal of Narrative and Life History*, special issue, ed. Michael G. W. Bamberg, 7(83–90).

Ochs, Elinor and Lisa Capps. 2001. *Living Narrative: Creating Lives in Everyday Storytelling*. Cambridge, MA: Harvard University Press.

Oinas, Felix J. 1978. The Balto-Finnic Epics. In *Heroic Epic and Saga*. Felix J. Oinas, ed. Pp. 286–309. Bloomington: Indiana University Press.

Olrik, Axel. 1965 [1909]. Epic Laws of Folk Narrative. In *The Study of Folklore*. Alan Dundes, ed. Pp. 129–141. Englewood Cliffs, NJ: Prentice-Hall.

Opland, Jeff. 1983. *Xhosa Oral Poetry: Aspects of a Black South African Tradition*. Cambridge: Cambridge University Press.

Paredes, Américo. 1976. *A Texas–Mexican Cancionero: Folksongs of the Lower Border*. Urbana: University of Illinois Press.

Paredes, Américo. 1993 [1977]. On Ethnographic Work Among Minority Groups: A Folklorist's Perspective. In *Folklore and Culture on the Texas–Mexican Border*. Richard Bauman, ed. Pp. 73–110. Austin, TX: CMAS Books.

Parmentier, Richard. 1985. Signs' Place *in medias res*: Peirce's Concept of Semiotic Mediation. In *Semiotic Mediation*. Elizabeth Mertz and Richard Parmentier, eds. Pp. 23–48. Orlando, FL: Academic Press.

Pepicello, William and Thomas A. Green. 1984. *The Language of Riddles*. Columbus: Ohio State University Press.

Polanyi, Livia. 1989. *Telling the American Story: A Structural and Cultural Analysis of Conversational Storytelling*. Cambridge, MA: MIT Press.

Porter, James. 1985. Parody and Satire as Mediators of Change in the Traditional Songs of Belle Stewart. In *Narrative Folksong: New Directions*. Carol Edwards and Kathleen Manley, eds. Pp. 303–338. Boulder, CO: Westview Press.

Quain, Buell H. 1942. *The Flight of the Chiefs*. New York: J. J. Augustin.

Quain, Buell H. 1948. *Fijian Village*. Chicago: University of Chicago Press.

Rehfisch, A. and F. Rehfisch. 1975. Scottish Travellers or Tinkers. In *Gypsies, Tinkers and Other Travellers*. Farnham Rehfisch, ed. Pp. 271–283. London: Academic Press.

Sahlins, Marshall D. 1962. *Moala: Nature and Culture on a Fijian Island*. Ann Arbor: University of Michigan Press.

Santamaría, Francisco J. 1983. *Diccionario de Mejicanismos*. Mexico City: Editorial Porrua.

Schechner, Richard. 1985. *Between Theater and Anthropology*. Philadelphia: University of Pennsylvania Press.

Schegloff, Emanuel and Harvey Sacks. 1973. Opening Up Closings. *Semiotica* 8:289–327.

Schieffelin, Bambi B. 1990. *The Give and Take of Everyday Life: Language Socialization of Kaluli Children*. Cambridge: Cambridge University Press.

Schieffelin, Edward. 1996. On Failure and Performance: Throwing the Medium Out of the Séance. In *The Performance of Healing*. Carol Laderman and Marina Roseman, eds. Pp. 59–89. New York: Routledge.

Schiller, Friedrich. 1966. *Turandot, Prinzessen von China: Ein Tragikomisches Märchen Nach Gozzi*. Stuttgart: Philipp Reclam Jun.

Schutz, Alfred and Thomas Luckmann. 1973. *The Structures of the Life-World*. Vol. 1. Evanston, IL: Northwestern University Press.

Scott, James C. 1985. *Weapons of the Weak: Everyday Forms of Peasant Resistance*. New Haven, CT: Yale University Press.

Sherzer, Joel. 1979. Strategies in Text and Context. *Journal of American Folklore* 92:145–163.

Sherzer, Joel. 1983. *Kuna Ways of Speaking: An Ethnographic Perspective*. Austin: University of Texas Press.

Shesgreen, Sean, ed. 1990. *The Criers and Hawkers of London: Engravings and Drawings by Marcellus Laroon*. Stanford, CA: Stanford University Press.

Sigfússon, Sigfus. 1946. *Islenzkar þój-Sögur og-Sagnir*. Vol. 8. Reykjavik: Víkingsútgafan.

Sigurðsson, Arngrimur. 1983. *Islenzk-Ensk Orþabók*. Reykjavik: Ísafoldarprentsmiðja H. F.

Silverstein, Michael. 1984. On the Pragmatic "Poetry" of Prose: Parallelism, Repetition, and Cohesive Structure in the Time Course of Dyadic Conversation. In *Meaning, Form, and Use in Context: Linguistic Applications*. GURT 1984. Deborah Schiffrin, ed. Pp. 181–199. Washington, DC: Georgetown University Press.

Silverstein, Michael. 1993. Metapragmatic Discourse and Metapragmatic Function. In *Reflexive Language: Reported Speech and Metapragmatics*. John Lucy, ed. Pp. 33–58.

Silverstein, Michael. 1996. The Secret Life of Texts. In *Natural Histories of Discourse*. Michael Silverstein and Greg Urban, eds. Pp. 81–105. Chicago: University of Chicago Press.

Silverstein, Michael and Greg Urban, eds. 1996. *Natural Histories of Discourse*. Chicago: University of Chicago Press.

Sinclair, J. M. and R. M. Coulthard. 1975. *Towards an Analysis of Discourse*. Oxford: Oxford University Press.

Sitton, Thad. 1983. *The Loblolly Book*. Austin: Texas Monthly Press.

Slyomovics, Susan. 1987. *The Merchant of Art*. Berkeley: University of California Press.

Stahl, Sandra. 1977. The Oral Personal Narrative in its Generic Context. *Fabula* 18:18–39.

Stahl, Sandra. 1989. *Literary Folkloristics and the Personal Narrative*. Bloomington: Indiana University Press.

Stoeltje, Beverly J. 2002. Performing Litigation at the Queen Mother's Court. In *Access to Justice: The Role of Court Administrators and Lay Adjudicators in the*

African and Islamic Contexts. Christina Jones-Pauly and Stefanie Elbern, eds. Pp. 1–21. The Hague: Kluwer Law International.

Szwed, John. 1970. Paul E. Hall: A Newfoundland Song-Maker and His Community of Song. In *Folksongs and Their Makers*. Henry Glassie, Edward D. Ives, and John Szwed, eds. Pp. 147–169. Bowling Green, OH: Bowling Green University Popular Press.

Taylor, Archer. 1951. *English Riddles from Oral Tradition*. Berkeley: University of California Press.

Tedlock, Dennis. 1983. *The Spoken Word and the Work of Interpretation*. Philadelphia: University of Pennsylvania Press.

Thompson, Stith. 1955–8. *Motif-Index of Folk Literature*. 6 vols. Bloomington: Indiana University Press.

Thompson, Stith. 1961. *The Types of the Folktale*. FFC 184. Helsinki: Suomalainen Tiedeakatemia.

Todorov, Tzvetan. 1973. Le Discours de la magie. *L'Homme* 13(4):38–65.

Toolan, Michael J. 1988. *Narrative: A Critical Linguistic Introduction*. London: Routledge.

Tuohy, Sue. 1999. The Social Life of Genre: The Dynamics of Folksong in China. *Asian Music* 33:39–86.

Tyler, Stephen A. 1986. Post-modern Ethnography: From Document of the Occult to Occult Document. In *Writing Culture*. James Clifford and George E. Marcus, eds. Pp. 122–140. Berkeley: University of California Press.

Urban, Greg. 1991. *A Discourse-Centered Approach to Culture*. Austin: University of Texas Press.

Urban, Greg. 1996. Entextualization, Replication, and Power. In *Natural Histories of Discourse*. Michael Silverstein and Greg Urban, eds. Pp. 21–44. Chicago: University of Chicago Press.

Voloshinov, V. N. 1973 [1930]. *Marxism and the Philosophy of Language*. Ladislav Matejka and I. R. Titunik, trans. New York: Seminar Press.

Weber, Max. 1978 [1921–2]. *Economy and Society*. 2 vols. Guenther Roth and Claus Wittich, eds. Berkeley: University of California Press.

Wells, Evelyn K. 1950. *The Ballad Tree: British and American Ballads, Their Folklore, Verse, and Music*. New York: Ronald Press.

Williams, J. E. Caerwyn. 1971. The Court Poet in Medieval Ireland. *Proceedings of the British Academy* 57:85–135.

Williams, J. E. Caerwyn and Patrick K. Ford. 1992. *The Irish Literary Tradition*. Cardiff: University of Wales Press.

Yankah, Kwesi. 1985. Risks in Verbal Art Performance. *Journal of Folklore Research* 22(2):133–153.

Yankah, Kwesi. 1991. Power and the Circuit of Formal Talk. *Journal of Folklore Research* 28(1):1–22.

Yankah, Kwesi. 1995. *Speaking for the Chief: Okyeame and the Politics of Akan Royal Oratory*. Bloomington: Indiana University Press.

Zoëga, G. T. 1910. *A Concise Dictionary of Old Icelandic*. Oxford: Clarendon Press.

Index